GROWING A JR. HIGH MINISTRY

GROWING A JR. HIGH MINISTRY

BY DAVID SHAHEEN

Group Books

Loveland, Colorado

Growing a Jr. High Ministry

Book and cover designed by Judy Atwood
Cover illustrated by Steve McInturff

Library of Congress Cataloging-in-Publication Data

Shaheen, David.
  Growing a junior high ministry.

  1. Church work with adolescents. I. Title.
BV1475.9.S48 1986   259'.23   86-19410
ISBN 0-931529-15-8 (pbk.)

Printed in the United States of America.

CONTENTS

By Wayne Rice

FOREWORD

Those of us who have worked with teenagers for a number of years have noticed a subtle but definitive change in the adolescent landscape. One way to describe this change is to say that kids today are maturing at an earlier age. As Dr. Urie Bronfenbrenner of Cornell University says, "The adolescents today are the 12-year-olds and the 11-year-olds and the 10-year-olds. That is, they are having the experiences that five years earlier, adolescents didn't have until they were 13, 14 and 15; and they, in turn, are having the experiences that adolescents used to have when they were 16, 17 and 18."

Today's junior highers are yesterday's high school students. Adolescents are being prematurely rushed into adulthood at a time when they have neither the skills necessary to handle it, nor the opportunity to take responsibility for it. They have access to more information than ever before, and suffer under more pressure and stress than ever before, yet lack the experience and adult support to cope with it all. In the words of psychologist David Elkind, modern teenagers are literally "all grown up with no place to go." They are forced to experiment more; they explore their options at an earlier age, which now comes sooner rather than later. And now we are faced with statistics like these: The United States leads the world in pregnancies among girls 14 and under; teenage suicide has increased more than 300 percent in the last decade; teenage drug addiction is increasing at a rate of more than 35,000 new cases per day; over a million teenagers run away from home each year and the percentage of those under 15 years of age continues to grow.

These statistics tell us that the time has come to turn back the tide of neglect and begin to focus on the needs of early adolescents—the 12- to 15-year-old group we call junior highers. No longer can the church afford to dismiss this group as too young, too unpredictable or too squirrelly, to warrant our time and attention. Early adolescence is a time of dramatic change in the human life span. Children become transformed into adults—physically, intellectually, socially, emotionally and spiritually—and a whole new world opens up before them. During early adolescence kids make decisions and choose values. Many surveys reveal that up to 85 percent of all Christians make decisions to follow Christ before the age of 14. Other surveys show that dropping out of church peaks at the ninth grade. It is time for the church to get serious about junior high ministry.

Only a few years ago, youth ministry was thought of strictly in terms of high school ministry. Youth workers ministered primarily with high school or college students. Parachurch organizations concerned themselves with only those older young people. Junior high school students were still considered children and those who worked with them were considered "working their way up."

But thankfully that is not the case today. Youth workers in the church and in parachurch organizations have come to realize that effective youth ministry must *begin* with effective junior high ministry. We now know the best time to reach young people for Christ and to influence their values, decisions and behavior is during those critical early adolescent years. We have learned that if we fail to take this age group seriously, we run the risk of losing the kids forever. Perhaps the most observable trend in youth ministry is the growing concern for more effective ministry to junior highers.

And to the benefit of all of us, that concern is now being translated into some outstanding resources for junior high ministry. This book is among the best of them. Pastor David Shaheen has worked with junior highers for as long as I have known him and he is truly a pioneer in the field. He was doing junior high ministry back when there were no books or resources to show him how, and he did it well. In the early '70s, his junior high ministry at St. Luke Lutheran Church in Silver Spring, Maryland caught my attention and became a model for me and for many other youth workers who know him.

Growing a Jr. High Ministry was not written by someone who theorizes about junior highers and makes pronouncements about something he doesn't know. Instead, it was written by someone who has spent most of his adult life "in the trenches," someone who has learned from experience and someone who has given that experience time to mature. That's why you will find this book so helpful and practical. It rings true from beginning to end.

As you read this book, please note that while the author has generously provided enough program material to keep you going for months, he rightly emphasizes the role of *relationships* in junior high ministry. Don't jump to the back of this book where the ideas are located before digesting the excellent guidance and affirmation he offers to you, the junior high worker, in the first part of the book. Shaheen's success with junior highers has not come merely because he has good ideas and programs. It has come because he loves junior highers, listens to them, and cares for them as a good shepherd cares for his sheep. The young people in Shaheen's church call him "Pastor Dave"—not a title, but a term of affection and appreciation.

Whether you are a professional youth minister or a volunteer, you have the privilege and opportunity to make a significant and positive difference in the lives of junior highers in your church and community. Don't get discouraged because you don't see results right away. Probably the most frustrating aspect of junior high ministry is the lack of identifiable, observable results. But if there were ever a ministry in which you did the sowing and someone else did the reaping, junior high ministry is it. Sow liberally and know that the harvest will be plentiful indeed.

INTRODUCTION

Working with junior highers is like planting a garden. By the time a child reaches the impressionable adolescent years, a great deal of soil preparation and spadework have already been done. The soil is rich, holding great promise for planting the seeds of identity, self-worth, awareness of a world beyond self and a sense of purpose. As with any garden, this one also needs to be cultivated, weeded, nourished and protected. But after all the hard work, the joys of the harvest are cause for celebration—and then the cycle begins again.

Unfortunately, junior high leaders seldom reap the harvest. This could be one reason why, in our instant-replay culture, so many junior high leaders "leave the farm." The step-by-step process of human development is often frustrating. We are programmed in our society to push a button to get results, take a pill to relieve pain, use computers to analyze information. We are impatient people. We expect teenagers to think, act, talk and believe like adults. This is not reality. A teenager is a teenager. In gardening, there is an awareness that the stalk must first grow and develop before it can bear fruit—so it is with junior high young people.

Just as there are many books on gardening, there are also many books on adolescents. Check any card catalog in a major library and you'll find innumerable titles related to the junior high years, addressing all kinds of issues, from various points of view. But this book is a bit different.

This book is meant to be practical, as well as philosophical and theological. Perhaps it could serve as a text for a course on junior high ministry as well as a handbook for volunteers. It also could serve as a reference for Sunday school teachers, parents, counselors or anyone who touches the lives of young people.

You will note that these chapters are arranged in a manner similar to a gardening manual. The first section resembles a soil analysis—it describes a junior high ministry. The second section focuses on the role of the gardener—the junior high leader. The final section discusses different ways to cultivate and nurture the seeds once they are planted—creative programming ideas.

As I wrote each chapter I tried to focus on you, the reader. What will you see beyond my words? I hope you will catch the vision of precious young people—full of energy, hope and potential, each one possessing special God-given talents waiting to be unleashed. I hope you will feel challenged to invest a part of your life to nurture these young people who are just beginning to blossom. I hope you will not feel frustrated when you don't reap the harvest, but rather that you will feel the joy that comes from planting seeds of faith, from dreaming dreams with kids about their futures, from helping them value their lives as a gift from God, from nurturing their belief in themselves. You are the people for whom this book is written.

I am deeply grateful to the many people who planted the seeds of faith throughout my life and who nurtured that faith along the way. I shall always be indebted to Martin J. Heineken and Gerhard Krodel, two of my seminary professors, who will always remain giants in my life. Others who come to mind: my first youth leaders, Charles and Lou Bettis, who have remained my friends for more than three decades, two of my associates with whom I've linked heart and mind as partners where I've been privileged to serve. There are also several special folks who have contributed to the writing of this book in ways they alone know: Robert and Helen Monroe, Michael H. Lemmons and the people of Mount Moriah A.M.E. Church, Sharon M. Spriggs, Pam Bresnahan, Fred Hopke, and Barbara Benning.

From my heart I wish to express my gratitude to Thom Schultz for his encouragement in writing this book; to Lee Sparks and Cindy Hansen who patiently edited each page; to Mike and Lydia Coburn who opened their hearts and home; to Sandy Lamb and Laurie Kaiser who offered a place to write; and to Donna Lee Perkins, my friend and secretary of 15 years, who typed the manuscript.

I am also deeply indebted to my family—Ellen, Timothy and Christopher—for the memories we share and the dreams for which we hope.

SECTION ONE

Junior High Ministry

CHAPTER 1

THE CHALLENGE TO THE CHURCH

Change occurs more rapidly now than ever before in history. Ours is no longer an agricultural society. Since the turn of the century, we have evolved from an agricultural, to an industrial, to an information society. And more change is yet to come. In the early 1900s, farmers comprised one-third of the total work force in the United States. Today, while they account for less than three percent, their numbers are still dwindling. Our high-tech society means that more than 60 percent of Americans now work in information-processing jobs. We are programmers, teachers, clerks, accountants, lawyers, politicians, managers, technicians, engineers, stockbrokers, etc. More people are employed full time in colleges and universities than in agriculture. The demand for professional workers dominates the job market. We have systematized knowledge and amplified our brain power to the point that we mass produce information like we once did cars.[1]

Today's adolescents have a particularly difficult time adapting to this fast-paced, information-filled environment. Their world is one of constant transition and frequent isolation. It identifies them by number, communicates with them via machine, teaches them with computers, and isolates them in their own homes with entertainment centers. Junior highers' parents remember when the United States was the world's industrial giant; their grandparents remember when farming was the primary industry. Parents and grandparents knew community in the neighborhood and farming areas; today's world finds us spending less time in community and more time in front of computers, VCRs and televisions.

Change occurs so rapidly, we hardly have time to react. Our reactions are not so much focused on our relationships with nature (as in an agricultural society), or with fabricated products (as in an industrial society), but on one another. We make more telephone calls, write more memos, issue more checks and send more letters than ever before.

Many people resist new technology because it's so impersonal. People need people. And that is the challenge of the church today: to balance the material wonders of technology with the spiritual demands of human nature.

The more technology is thrust into our lives, the more people will feel a need to congregate—to be with others at movies, concerts and public assemblies. For example, shopping malls are the third most frequented places in our society, following home, work or school. In *Megatrends*, John Naisbitt reports:

> In 1975, after we invented those huge screens that you could have in your living room to watch movies, Arthur D. Little issued a report suggesting that by the year 1980 there would be almost no movie theaters in the United States. What they didn't understand was high tech/high touch. You do not go to a movie just to see a movie. You go to a movie to cry or laugh with 200 other people. It is an event.[2]

Adolescents need a balance in life that puts them in touch with people. They need a ministry that values human relationships, is sensitive to their needs, and one that will personalize a seemingly uncaring and mechanical world. More than ever before the challenge to the church is to develop a ministry that reaches out, touches and nurtures these young people.

Several years ago, in a New York community, an ecumenical study was conducted to determine why people left the church. Regardless of denomination, people consistently reported the same reasons. Of all those interviewed, only one percent left because of poor preaching. Another one percent left because they believed the church was hypocritical. But the majority of people left because they did not feel cared for or close to any one person in their congregation.

From the beginning, the church has been made up of a community of believers bound together by their love of Jesus. Today the mission of the church is still to introduce people to Jesus Christ. The church is not brick and mortar, designed to hold people together. It is the love of God, and the supportive relationships between his people that spring forth out of that love, that bind us.

Adult leaders and junior high young people need to remember that our relationship with God is rooted in our relationship with Jesus. Christ modeled this relationship when he embraced *all* people, regardless of their ages, needs, sins or circumstances. Jesus' actions revealed as much as his words did regarding his heavenly Father's character. Likewise, junior high leaders' actions must reveal their love of Christ and his people.

Junior high leaders can meet the challenge to the church by modeling a Christian lifestyle and by building genuine relationships with teenagers. They must sincerely care for them, listen to them, challenge and teach them. Positive relationships with other volunteers, parents and church members also reflect the leaders' Christian attitudes. The best ministry that leaders can offer junior highers is a ministry of example.

How do you, as a junior high leader, feel about meeting this challenge to the church? What do you think about junior high ministry? How do you feel about working with junior high kids? Here's a simple exercise to help you explore your thoughts and feelings.

Junior High Ministry Inventory

Use the following inventory to rate yourself. Be honest. Put an "X" on the spot that best describes you.

Section One: What Do You Think?

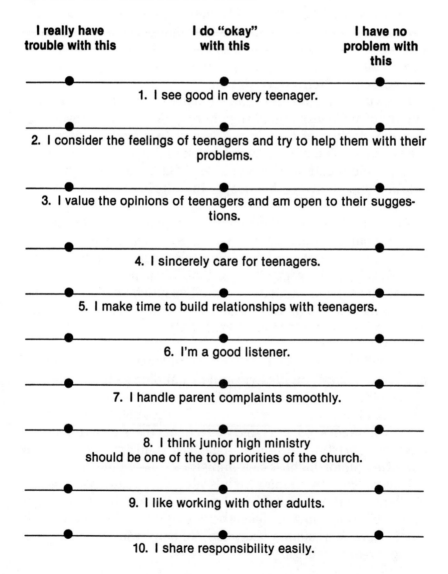

I really have trouble with this	I do "okay" with this	I have no problem with this

1. I see good in every teenager.

2. I consider the feelings of teenagers and try to help them with their problems.

3. I value the opinions of teenagers and am open to their suggestions.

4. I sincerely care for teenagers.

5. I make time to build relationships with teenagers.

6. I'm a good listener.

7. I handle parent complaints smoothly.

8. I think junior high ministry should be one of the top priorities of the church.

9. I like working with other adults.

10. I share responsibility easily.

Section Two: How Do You Feel?

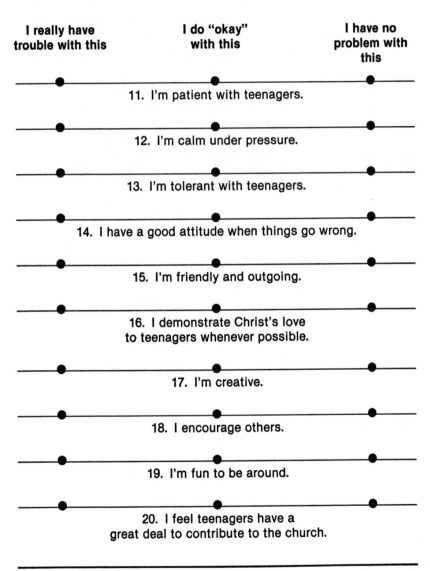

I really have trouble with this	I do "okay" with this	I have no problem with this

11. I'm patient with teenagers.

12. I'm calm under pressure.

13. I'm tolerant with teenagers.

14. I have a good attitude when things go wrong.

15. I'm friendly and outgoing.

16. I demonstrate Christ's love to teenagers whenever possible.

17. I'm creative.

18. I encourage others.

19. I'm fun to be around.

20. I feel teenagers have a great deal to contribute to the church.

Now, look at your answers. In each section, count the number you checked "okay" or "no problem." Tally your score and see how you think and feel about junior high ministry:

15-20: Hey, I'm okay! I have what it takes to work with junior high kids.

8-14: Maybe I need to reevaluate my thoughts and feelings about junior high ministry.

0-7: Help! Maybe I'm just not cut out to work with junior high kids.

Now that you have an idea of how you think and feel about junior high ministry, you're ready to move ahead and explore this book. A most important point to remember is: Above all characteristics, feelings and thoughts, a commitment to Christ must take precedence. With Christ's loving example, junior high leaders can meet the challenge facing the church today.

CHAPTER 2

JUNIOR HIGH MINISTRY MYTHS

I can still hear her voice. When we first met she was 13 . . . and very angry. Her father died several years before and her mother had remarried. Then they moved . . . hoping to begin a new life together. It didn't turn out that way. The cause of anger? Rejection! One night she ran away. Her mother called me . . . desperate. They needed help to find her. Since I knew the area, would I go look in places kids might go?

Several hours later a frail, rejected 13-year-old girl and I were sitting in a quiet room in the church. It was almost midnight. We talked for a long time. We talked about her anger at God because of the death of her father, at her mother for moving and taking her away from her friends, and at her stepfather who was "so religious he makes me want to puke"; who physically abused her and her mother "in the name of religion"; who quoted the Bible all the time and told her she was a "sinner going to hell."

Her stepfather never fully accepted her . . . and she knew it. Their relationship was based primarily on rules and regulations. He played the role of authoritarian. He was judgmental, showed no affection or compassion, and could not tolerate a point of view other than his own.

Her anger carried over to other relationships. She had trouble relating to kids and teachers at school and was considered a rebel at church. No one could crack her hard shell to reach the source of her intense feelings.

Her anger lasted a long time. More than six years. Through it all we kept in touch. Every now and then I'd see her in church or she'd sign up for a youth event. But there was always some anger in her behavior—and the need to be accepted, loved, affirmed.

One summer, while we were on a long trip together, things in her life began to fall into place. The knowledge that she was a child of God, talented, and a valuable person came to her through her interaction with others in the group. She will tell you that this experience was a turning point in her life.

But what if that church experience had never happened? What if, during her junior high years, when her immaturity prevented her from expressing anger in a constructive way, everyone in the church had turned their backs on her?

Today there are thousands of young people hurting like her. They are young adolescents trying to get a handle on life, feeling abandoned and rejected. Sadly, some of the rejection they feel comes from their church experience. Yet, we hear churches cry that the junior high years are the "last chance" to reach kids before they "run away" from religion. Some contend the church has already lost them by the time they enter the seventh grade. Other people claim that by age 15 kids dramatically decrease their participation in youth programs. Report after report indicates that ninth-graders are the teenagers most likely to drop out of church.[1]

More than one frustrated parent, pastor or youth leader has stated that the junior high age group is the most difficult to reach. Since beginning adolescence is a period of turmoil, the church is not alone in its search for effective ways to communicate with this significant segment of society. However, some institutions in our culture are successful in reaching teenagers. Astute in their understanding of the adolescents' mindset, the media attract large crowds of teenagers to rock concerts and movies, entice them to buy certain clothes and hair products, and influence their speech and behavior patterns. Yet, the church's attempts to communicate with these kids frequently results in agitated, burned-out volunteers and unsuccessful efforts to provide "good times." Far too frequently a young adolescent's assessment of the church is, "It's boring."

The good news is that not everyone in youth ministry is ready to abandon ship. The thrust of this book is: Junior high kids are *exciting* to work with; they deserve the best the church can offer. Youth leaders, committed to working with 12- to 15-year-olds, are faced with one of the greatest opportunities and challenges of the church.

Regrettably, certain myths prevail that impede the church from relating to junior highers. Leaders can easily fall prey to failure if they view the following statements as guidelines for an effective junior high ministry:

MYTH #1 Let the kids run the entire program; it's a great way for them to learn.

In many churches, junior high ministry is viewed as the "training ground" for tomorrow's leaders. "Young people are the church of the future; they need a chance to develop leadership skills." Such thinking often results in turning the leadership of the junior high program completely over to teenagers who "know what kids like." Two false assumptions are made: the kids can pull it off; and it will be a good learning experience.

Churches do a disservice to teenagers when they hold them totally responsible for the planning, promotion and execution of an activity, without providing them the necessary skills or support. Adults and junior highers must work as a team to make things happen. Adults can do certain things better than junior highers by virtue of their age and experience; by the same virtues, junior highers can contribute ideas and do certain things better.

Some adults are knowledgeable about the developmental needs of teenagers and therefore have insights into what makes an activity or event meaningful for this age group. Such wisdom can ensure appropriate activity planning, sensitivity to the kids' needs, and realistic encouragement for the task at hand. Adults can use certain methods to generate good discussions, certain techniques to create an environment where all the kids feel comfortable, and certain organizational skills to guarantee a smooth-running experience. (Ideas in all of these areas are included in this book.)

Turning the entire leadership of a junior high program over to the kids is like giving them a lighted stick of dynamite. Because they are young, still growing and in need of guidance, such responsibility can be disastrous. Without knowing the basics of why, where, when or how, the junior highers are bound to fail and feel frustrated. Kids don't like to fail any more than adults do. They also are inexperienced at handling criticism from their peers which, if not handled properly, can lead to dissension in the group. Such negative experiences discourage participation and enthusiasm, and encourage inactivity and apathy.

MYTH #2 You don't need any resources to run an effective junior high program.

Churches who care about junior highers must be willing to invest in resources to support such a ministry. Investing in a junior high ministry means providing financial support. Junior highers can help "earn their way" for a project, trip or activity, but they should not be expected to underwrite all that is necessary to feed their faith.

Investing in a junior high ministry also means: sending youth leaders to training conferences and educational seminars; supplying the necessary resources for leaders to conduct meaningful programming; providing interesting meetings; and publicizing events.

The best resource any group has is its own church membership. Our congregations are packed with people possessing a wide variety of interests and talents: Ask a bicycle enthusiast to present a lesson on bike care—then take your junior high members on a bike trip. Ask a dance instructor to teach your group how to square dance—then host a hoedown and invite other churches' junior high groups. Ask a piano player or guitar player to help lead songs prior to each meeting.

Ask junior high members to help brainstorm for ideas, teach lessons, participate in leadership teams, organize retreats, lead games, lead songs, etc. When adults and young people contribute, they both feel they have invested in the program and are needed. By investing in junior high ministry, the church shows it cares for the young people, and it appreciates those who work with the kids.

MYTH #3 The junior high program can be termed a success when all the kids in church attend.

We live in a world that places an emphasis on quantity and size . . . the bigger the better. Would you consider a worship service less meaningful if the entire congregation did not attend? It's far better to focus on those who are present than those who are absent. During any junior high activity, leaders should make certain that the kids in attendance feel their participation is necessary and valued. Spending time focusing on those who are absent only reinforces the fact some kids chose not to come.

Although it is unrealistic to think every young person should be at every activity, numbers are significant. Kids like to be with other kids—they want to be where the action is. Youth leaders should make certain those who attend an event are thanked for coming, contributing, and encouraged to come again.

Offering one program at one time to meet the needs of your junior highers may be unrealistic. An alternative could be to offer a variety of times for kids to participate. Although this alternative requires extra time and planning, it may be worth the effort!

MYTH #4 Junior high kids hate Bible study.

Young people, like adults, are not interested in a Bible study that does not meet their needs; is not challenging; lacks creativity; and is led by a humorless, dry, unprepared leader. Teenagers will thrive on Bible study if the Good News is presented in a way that makes sense, communicated in their language, and related to their life and their world.

Some people think Bible study, or all religious education, should be confined to a certain day or time such as in Sunday school. Creative Bible teachers know that some of the best Bible studies take place in a variety of settings and use a variety of techniques; for example: discussion, lecture or experiential learning conducted in a church, home, park or retreat center.

There is no end to the possibilities when it comes to searching the scriptures with kids. (See Chapter 13 and the resource section at the back of this book.) However, be cautious; searching the scriptures can lead to erroneous interpretations if sound research isn't done by the leader. Youth leaders don't have to be seminary-trained to be good Bible study teachers. They just have to "do their homework," in order to pass on the important ingredients of the Christian faith.

Meaningful Bible study doesn't have to be limited to a group of people the same age; already there is too much isolation and separation in a teenager's world. Since several generations of one family no longer live in the same house, there is much to be gained by a teenager sharing his or her scriptural insights with an elderly person, and vice versa. The Bible is full of stories where people of all ages had a profound impact on one another. Read about Simeon and Anna (Luke 2:25-38); Jesus in the temple (Luke 2:46-48); Timothy and his mother and grandmother (2 Timothy 1:5).

MYTH #5

The church is a place for religious experiences, not for discussing secular issues or having social activities.

A healthy junior high ministry relates to the young people and their world. Today's teenagers are exposed to more information and stimuli than any generation before them. Young people, active in the church, also live in the world; and the world is where their Christian lifestyle needs to be exemplified.

It is unrealistic to expect Christian teenagers to live a cloistered life. Although many of today's issues are not specifically mentioned in the Bible, Christian ethics and principles apply to them. Adolescents need a forum where they can share their feelings and formulate values on such topics. The church is the perfect place for such discussions.

Junior highers are extremely social-conscious. Relationships are a top priority in their lives. The church can provide wholesome activities where kids can build friendships, relax and have fun. Church activities are constructive alternatives to secular social functions. An effective junior high ministry provides teenagers places and times where they can be themselves, unwind with friends, and discuss their problems and concerns.

During the junior high years, kids begin to wrestle with their faith. At this stage of a young person's life, substantial disillusionment about the value of religion in daily life develops. The logic taught to them in earlier years causes teenagers to perceive some inconsistencies. For example: God loves us. The world contains many unhappy people. If God loves us, why are so many people unhappy?

Junior highers (and many adults) are troubled by such inconsistencies. In noting the contradiction, an adolescent is faced with at least five choices:

● He or she can deny the second statement and presume we are never unhappy. But a junior higher knows that's not true.

● He or she can deny that God loves us. But this possibility usually is discounted because one of God's definitional qualities is his love.

● He or she can decide that God doesn't cause unhappiness, evil does. This philosophy, at least, is consistent with the image of a loving God.

● He or she can assume that unhappiness is God's ulterior purpose for us. Although this possibility is sometimes chosen, it is not very assuring.

● Or finally, he or she can deny God exists.

The last alternative leads to profound consequences, yet it

has become a popular way to resolve faith inconsistencies. Such a conclusion denies a belief that has been regarded as true for many years. It invites the thought, "If there is no God, then all my other beliefs are questionable. What *do* I believe?" Suddenly, what was regarded as valid becomes questionable.

A 14-year-old girl was asked how her present beliefs differed from those she held several years ago. She replied, "I had a whole philosophy of how the world worked. I was very religious and I believed that there was unity and harmony and everything had its proper place. I used to imagine rocks in the right places on the right beaches. It was all very neat and God ordained it all, and I made up my own religion, but now it seems absolutely ridiculous."[2]

Every culture presents its teenagers with a set of beliefs to examine. In our society, religion is one of the major ideological tigers to be tamed. Sometimes this process leaves an adolescent temporarily without a commitment to any belief. In one interview, a 15-year-old was asked which beliefs she was most certain of: "None really. I just take things in and analyze them. Maybe it will change my opinion and maybe it won't. It depends, but I'm not really stuck to anything."[3]

Wondering produces a state of uncertainty and a need to resolve the uncertainties. A 14-year-old girl said, "I think religious attitudes change if you go to Sunday school. At the time you just accept it, but when you become older and start thinking about it and try to analyze it, that is, whether there really is a God, then it depends on what your religious beliefs are. I've asked myself this over and over again. I just started thinking about it at that time and I just can't get it off my mind; whether there really is a God. I ask myself questions. Is there a God and I have arguments inside myself. How there might not be, how there might be."[4]

Questioning their personal faith is natural and normal for junior highers. It also is normal for kids this age to be attracted to adults outside the family, and to be inquisitive about those adults' beliefs. The church is the best place for these questions to be raised and ideas exchanged. Youth leaders should listen to the kids and offer a secure setting where the kids are free to search. Leaders should not merely dispense neatly packaged answers. A church must be keenly aware of the significance of its relationship with junior highers in the development of personal faith.

The role of the church in the life of adolescents is one of nurturer. Teenagers experience growth in several areas—emotional, psychological, intellectual, social and spiritual. An effective junior high ministry keeps all these factors in mind as it reaches out to this age group.

Far too many leaders become frustrated when they don't see immediate results. We need to remember that the junior high years are a time of seed planting—a time for sowing, not for reaping. Junior highers are equally frustrated and confused because they are going through so many rapid developmental changes. Nothing is set in concrete. What was a top priority one day, won't be the next.

At this unstable stage, two things remain important for an effective junior high ministry: significant adults and significant experiences. More than anything else, these have an impact on the maturation process of the adolescent.

Young people won't remember every verse of scripture pounded in their head, the subject of every talk, or the attendance at every event. But they will remember *experiences*, and the people with whom they shared them.

Providing junior high kids with significant adults and significant experiences is not an easy task, but it deserves every ounce of energy we possess. There is no greater reward than knowing we cared enough about the kids in our youth group that we gave them our very best.

CHAPTER 3

THE DEVELOPMENT OF JUNIOR HIGHERS

Junior highers are people on the move. They are people beginning the long trek toward adulthood. As they grow and mature, junior high ministry can play a vital role in nourishing and nurturing them. What an exciting prospect! We need to adopt the perspective that we are helping these young people, that a ministry to junior highers is not an end in itself. Those who foster this posture, eagerly anticipate helping kids develop their God-given potential.

Caring adults can represent a loving God. They can affirm teenagers that their experiences are normal, that someone cares about their feelings, and that God is opening a door to guide them in their search for identity.

The concept of identity development can be traced to the writings and thinking of Erik Erickson. Although identity is important throughout a person's life, Erickson states that it reaches the crisis level shortly after the time a person enters junior high school. If adolescents do not successfully master this stage, they are described as having identity or role confusion; the ramifications will be felt for the rest of their lives. According to Erickson, an identity crisis for an adolescent is . . . "like a trapeze artist, the young person in the middle of vigorous motion must let go of his safe hold on childhood and reach out for a firm grasp on adulthood, depending for a breathless interval on a relatedness between the past and the future, and on the reliability of those he must let go of, and of those who will receive him."[1]

This suspension in midair between letting go and grabbing hold, is where junior highers suddenly find themselves. It is at this point young adolescents begin to experiment with a number of different identities, trying to find the one they feel most comfortable with. The young person who is successful in this experimental process, emerges with a sense of self that is both refreshing and acceptable.

In order to find their identity, junior highers use sensitive antennae to pick up signals about what others think of them. Kids pay close attention and assimilate the feedback they receive regarding their behavior and physical appearance. Because their bodies are a main focal point in this first step for identity, kids are extremely concerned about their attractiveness to others. This is part of the reason why junior highers spend so much time in front of a mirror.

So much is happening to junior highers that they don't understand or have any experience in dealing with. During this time, junior highers can become fearful, anxious, isolated and insecure. Imagine what goes on inside a young mind when it is bombarded with hundreds of seemingly unexplainable feelings and emotions.

The junior high years, ages 12 to 15, fall under the category of "early adolescence." This is a fairly recent category, created shortly after the 19th century due to three major social movements: compulsory education, child labor legislation, and special legal procedures for people under age 21. In earlier years, young people became adults upon completion of certain rites of passage. For example, there was a time when American teenagers were considered to be adults upon completion of the eighth grade. My own grandmother was married by age 15 and left her family to become a wife and mother. By the time she was 28, she had six children and carried the responsibility of raising them almost solely in her hands.

Today's junior highers are far from being considered fully grown adults, nor are they given adult roles. Our school system reflects our recognition of early adolescence as a stage of life. For the most part, 12- to 15-year-olds are assigned to "junior" high schools or "middle" schools—designating the fact that they have not yet reached the most mature level of public education.

Unfortunately, in the church and in the home, adolescence is not always understood. Parents who remember their junior high years probably recall them as unpleasant ones and have chosen to forget the painful parts. Churches are uncertain how to provide a ministry to people whom they perceive as "moving targets." By the time the church thinks it has answers for this age group, the kids' needs change. Out of frustration, the church throws up its hands or feels intimidated by a group it cannot control.

Who then is left to pay attention to junior highers in our society? In many ways they are left alone to struggle with growing up. Many junior highers have a negative self-image and wonder if they are of any use to the world. They get the feeling they are a bother to people, not worth caring for and a burden on society. Frequently, young people think that if they were to disappear from the face of the earth, no one would notice. Because they think the world feels this way toward them, they project these same feelings on themselves. Consequently, early adolescents are very hard on themselves, very critical and, at times, self-destructive.

We need not look too far for the source of these negative attitudes. The media have created a mind-set that says, in order to be successful, teenagers (as well as adults) need to use a certain mouthwash, or wear a certain brand of designer jeans. The sad fact is, after teenagers make the effort to improve themselves by using such products, the results are not always as promised. Vulnerable young people conclude that the lack of success or improvement is their fault.

Negative feelings also result from the news media ignoring good things teenagers do and focusing on bad things. Adolescents are labeled as being delinquent, troublemakers, drug abusers, sexually permissive, violent, generally destructive and insensitive. The occasional positive news report is done on gifted, talented, "exceptional" young people—a category not indicative of the norm.

Attention given to athletics and fitness also creates negative self-images. Those who succeed are applauded. Young people are pressured to "win at all costs." If you lose, you are removed from the team, neglected, forgotten or teased. Likewise, the current trend toward fitness is disastrous for teenagers who cannot control the growth of their bodies. Many times young people conclude that life is not worth the effort because they don't have that certain "in" look, or because they haven't achieved athletic success (few teenagers can be Olympic champions at age 14).

Society contributes in other ways to negative attitudes during adolescence. As an identity struggles to emerge, roadblocks stand in the way such as the inability to get a job. Young people seeking employment are told they "need experience." When they ask how to get experience, they are told "get a job." It's a no-win situation.

Unfortunately, the church doesn't always listen to young people's ideas about worship or service projects. When teenagers perceive, in one place after another, that they don't fit in, they feel isolated and worthless. The church must share the guilt in contributing to this attitude.

Churches can change the image of junior high ministry and young people. Rather than settling for frustrated leadership, rather than permitting an attitude of "kids are impossible," and rather than continuing to resist any change in outreach, we can see creative change well within our grasp. We can encourage opportunity thinkers in youth work to turn the present state of affairs into advantages.

We need to be patient and understanding with kids as they search for their identities. We can help junior highers understand their identity by letting them discover "Who" they belong to. We need to allow young people to risk, share and develop close friendships. We need to give kids the opportunity to make a commitment to the one who said, "I am the way." There can be no greater joy than for an adult leader to stay with a junior higher long enough to see him or her reach a turning point in his or her faith. A turning point where he or she can continue the journey of life knowing the right choice has been made.

Adults who want to make a lasting impression on junior high young people need to remember that early adolescents develop physically, socially, intellectually, emotionally, morally and spiritually. All of these aspects are pieces of a puzzle that fit together to form a junior higher's identity.

Physical Development of Junior Highers

During the junior high years young people undergo revolutionary changes in growth. After a lifetime of being smaller and weaker, they suddenly begin to catch up with adults in physical size and strength. For girls, this rapid growth spurt usually begins between the ages of 10 and 13; for boys between the ages of 12 and 15. In roughly a two-year period, girls grow 6 to 7 inches taller and boys grow 8 to 9 inches taller. Nearly all parts of the body increase in size except for the brain, which is practically adult-size by this age. Other measurable changes occur in body shape, dental maturity, basal metabolism (amount of energy used at rest) and nutritional needs.

For girls, the beginning of puberty is usually marked by breast development and the appearance of pubic hair. This happens almost simultaneously with the development of internal reproductive organs. Menarche, the first menstrual flow, occurs from ages 10 to 16.

In boys, puberty starts with the growth of the testes and the scrotum. The onset varies from ages 10 to 15. The appearance of pubic hair and the growth of the penis usually occurs at the same time as the height spurt and the development of internal reproductive organs.[2]

Just as there are variances in individual physical development, there also are differences in the growth rate of different parts of the body. The term used to describe this characteristic is asynchronism. In adolescents, an uneven growth rate means a fully developed girl may not have started menstruation; a highly intelligent girl may be socially and emotionally immature; a late-maturing boy may feel "out of place" both with his peers and with younger boys; boys may have facial hair, yet their voice has not changed; and both boys and girls may find themselves doing clumsy things or misjudging distances. Thus, it is possible for an adolescent to have several correct ages—chronological, physical, cognitive, social, etc.

These physical changes happen at different times for different individuals. It is possible for one junior high student to complete all growth and sexual changes before another adolescent even experiences the first signs of adulthood. The beginning of this developmental stage can be anywhere from ages 8 to 14—a range of six years!

We, as junior high leaders, need to realize that not all junior highers are equally grown up, physically or socially. Because of this obvious difference in maturation rate, junior highers are very sensitive to feelings of self-worth and desirability, which influences their self-image and behavior. Any divergence from the peer group, in relation to growth and development, tends to be a difficult experience. Junior highers are quick to reject or ridicule those who are different, even their peers. Therefore, late-maturing boys tend to feel rejected and inadequate, and many develop a negative self-image. We should be aware of this tendency to reject and ridicule, and constantly stress acceptance and affirmation. Use every opportunity during meetings, retreats and activities to stress the fact that we all are God's children.

Try to open and close every junior high event with affirmation activities such as giving awards. Divide the class in half and appoint a leader for each group. Tell the students that they will be making an award for each individual in the other group. The awards must focus on positive qualities and not contain offensive humor or put-downs; good examples, "Most Sparkling Eyes" or "Brightest Smile."

Distribute construction paper, glue, scissors, gold seals, ribbons and markers. Instruct each group to go to a separate room and brainstorm for ideas for an award for each individual in the other group. Have them use the art supplies to create the awards.

Reunite and present the awards one at a time. Explain how each award was selected.[3]

Another major change in early adolescents is the awakening of sexual feelings. These feelings are the beginning of a sexuality that will remain with the young people most, if not all, of their lives. Expressions of masculinity and femininity are frequently dictated by the current culture. Our sex-saturated society confuses teenagers who are trying to make decisions and develop values.

Despite the increased efforts to teach sex education in schools, young people still need to learn more. Many parents feel uncomfortable discussing the subject and make no attempt to educate their children about sex. Other parents initiate sex education, but only cover the basics. The result is that the majority of education comes from friends, magazines, books, television shows and movies. Unfortunately, this information is often incorrect or misleading.

Churches that don't include sex education from the Christian perspective are deleting a critical ministry to this age group. From a theological point of view, sex is created by God, is intended to be good and should be expressed in a responsible manner. By not recognizing this human aspect, churches send the message that sex is wrong and miss the opportunity to help young people integrate a healthy sexuality into their total personality. As a consequence, young people's sexuality becomes distorted and can lead to years of maladjustment and abuse. Time Magazine reports:.

There are 11 million teenagers in America today who have had sexual intercourse from time to time. No more than 20 percent of them use contraceptives regularly. Each year more than a million American teenagers will become pregnant, four out of five of them unmarried. . . . Many become pregnant in their early or mid-teens, some 30,000 of them under age 15. If present trends continue, *researchers estimate, fully 40 percent of today's 14-year-old girls will be pregnant at least once before the age of 20. . . . Teen pregnancy imposes lasting hardships on two generations: parent and child. Teen mothers are, for instance, many times as likely as other women with young children to live below the poverty level. According to one study, only half of those who give birth before age 18 complete high school. On average, they earn half as much money and are far more likely to be dependent on welfare: 71 percent of females under 30 who receive Aid to Families with Dependent Children had their first child as a teenager. Infants of teen mothers have high rates of illness and mortality. Later in life they often experience educational and emotional problems. . . . According to one study, 82 percent of girls who give birth at age 15 or younger were daughters of teenage mothers.[4]*

Sex education is one of the greatest ministries the church can offer to parents and teenagers, and will be appreciated beyond measure. It's time for the church to talk freely and frankly in positive, affirming ways about sexuality. Sadly, to ignore this aspect of adolescent development is to contribute to the increasing sexual activity of our teenagers. (Chapter 13 includes a retreat on sexuality to use in your junior high ministry.)

Two other areas frequently overlooked in early adolescent development are the important role of nutrition and the impact physical development has on self-image.

Adolescents are particularly vulnerable to eating disorders and nutritional disturbances. This is true even for those who practiced excellent nutritional habits prior to puberty. Research shows that adolescent boys have greater nutritional needs than girls, and that adolescent girls have the poorest nutritional habits.

An adolescent's appetite is subject to mood as well as hunger. However, there is no fixed association between mood and appetite—the same state of mind will lead one adolescent to raid the refrigerator and another to skip dinner.

Normal adjustment problems during adolescence can lead

to serious nutrition disorders such as anorexia nervosa (self-starvation) and diabetes mellitus (a chronic form of diabetes involving hunger, thirst and gradual weight loss). The majority of adolescents do not have serious eating disturbances of this magnitude. Obesity is the major problem facing junior highers. Research shows a steady increase in obesity from childhood through middle age. Other studies indicate 10 to 30 percent of all high school students are obese.

Helping junior highers develop good nutritional habits is just as important a ministry as helping them develop a solid understanding of their sexuality. Effective junior high leaders express a concern for the total person—this is another area in which we can show how much we care. It is important to know that "the pattern of diet permits the individual to achieve maximum genetic potential for physical and mental development. Second, food habits are conducive to delaying or preventing the onset of degenerative diseases that are so prevalent in our society. Third, food habits are part of the satisfying human relationship and contribute to social and personal enjoyment."[5]

Anyone who has worked with teenagers knows how important food is to them. Any caring adult should develop an awareness of this important aspect of their growth, especially as it reflects on kids' self-esteem.

Generally speaking, early adolescence is a time of good physical health. Accidents are the leading cause of physical disability and death. Acne is the most common medical problem. Yet, their good health record is partially tainted by self-inflicted and socially-inflicted problems such as venereal diseases, drug and alcohol addiction. Common diseases include mononucleosis, juvenile diabetes, and allergies, especially hay fever, which is the most common allergy disorder, and asthma, which accounts for about 25 percent of all school absenteeism.[6]

The most precious part of the human psyche is the self-image. It is essential that kids' self-images be developed in healthy, positive ways because the self-image will gradually extend outward, assuming the major responsibility for perception of self in relation to others and the world. Leaders should be sensitive to how painful it is for some teenagers to think about the way they appear to others. Girls may hate to be looked at. They may adopt a hunched or cringing posture to minimize their height or breasts; they may wear voluminous or bizarre clothing to conceal their bodies; they may cry for no apparent reason. Girls may react to menstruation with quiet satisfaction, or with feelings of uncleanliness, or with a sense of panic. Boys, who are traditionally less modest about their bodies, may find all kinds of excuses to keep from exposing their bodies in school locker rooms, at the swimming pool, or in a cabin on an overnight retreat. They fear they look grossly different from their peers.

I remember so well the seventh-grade boys showing up at summer camp for the first time and being afraid to change their clothes in the cabin—even to the point of sleeping in their jeans, changing clothes in their sleeping bags or in the bathroom. Taking group showers at camp can be a real threat to boys who are not as "mature" or "grown up" as the others. They fear ridicule—and sometimes their fears are realized.

Special care also should be taken to help junior highers cope with any major body defect or disability. Handicapped teenagers may be extremely self-conscious. Physical deformities, whether real or imagined, can devastate a self-image and impact social acceptance by causing isolation. Worry over such deformities can drain necessary energy needed for learning, and can affect emotional stability through the projection of frustration and depression.

Caring adults will help junior highers deal with their physical changes and needs. Kids need to be assured that the changes happening to their bodies are normal, that God created them, and what God created is good. Caring for adolescents means helping them through the painful, awkward moments by supporting and affirming them. After all, we survived adolescence; the kids need to know they will too.

Social Development of Junior Highers

Nothing is more important to junior highers than relationships. The way they relate to others is part of their identity development and is intricately connected to their second psychological birth. During the search of self in early adolescence, kids gradually break away from parents and, at times, from friends. This can be a very frightening process. More than anything, teenagers need time, support and guidance as they search their pasts in order to plot their futures. How the kids "fit in" with others is of critical importance.

All social changes occurring in this stage of life are the beginning steps of "identity formation": acquiring an acceptable philosophy of life, defining a role in society, formulating political points of view, exploring a variety of lifestyles, developing special interests, and seeking moral models. This stage in a teenager's life marks the beginning of accepting more and more responsibility for one's behavior and future life.

As junior highers become increasingly aware of the world around them, they search for true friends—people they can trust, who will listen and understand. Because junior highers have a strong desire to belong to someone, and since they are gradually withdrawing from family, loneliness becomes a new fear. In fact, fear of being rejected by peers can cause such anxiety that young people will often conform to a group's behavior in order to be accepted.

Parents and peers are the two strongest influences on teenagers. Although there is some disagreement on which of the two is stronger, peer pressure seems to be increasing in importance as families become more separated. Adolescence is the time when kids become critical of parents and begin questioning the things they've been taught. They don't want to be seen in public with parents or family for fear of damaging their "image." Parents don't always know when to "let go" and, as a result, highly emotional clashes disrupt family ties.

The conflict with parents stems from the powerful influence the home has on shaping attitudes, values, political and religious beliefs. In struggling to become their own person, adolescents want the conclusions that result from their questioning to be their own. They need to feel they own their beliefs, feelings and conduct.

During this autonomy struggle, challenges arise that add to the tension. For the first time, junior highers begin to verbalize their viewpoints about the future, the occupations they wish to pursue and their feelings about the world. It is a healthy sign that they are beginning to think analytically and critically, and it is a necessary step in achieving self-determination. Erik Erickson says that the process of thinking analytically and critically has a profound impact on ego identity (a coherent sense of self).[7]

At the end of junior highers' struggle to form an identity, their experiences are integrated into their personalities and will determine the way they act as adults. Junior highers become confused when their way of relating to the world fails to meet the expectations of significant adults or society. A quote from *Children With Learning Problems* states that feelings of failure, frustration and bewilderment cause bizarre behavior, different from any behavior in other stages of life:

> *. . . should a child feel that the environment tries to deprive him too radically of all forms of expression which permit him to develop and to integrate the next step of his ego identity, he will resist with the astonishing strength encountered in animals who are suddenly forced to defend their lives. Indeed, in the social jungle of human existence, there is no feeling of being alive without a sense of ego identity. To understand this would be to understand the troubles of adolescents better—especially those desperately seeking for a satisfaction of belonging, be it in cliques, gangs or in inspiring mass movements.[8]*

An unsettling factor for adolescents is that they are unable to reach their goal of independence. The desire is there but not the means. As a result, junior highers find a great deal of security and support among people their own age. Ironically, in their search to be on their own, they first become a part of a crowd, getting caught up in fads, cliques, and conforming to the culture of which they are a part.

Since school is the place where junior highers spend much of their time, they live in a world surrounded by their peers. Their determination to survive in this environment impacts the way they act, talk, dress and believe. Peers play a significant role in whether or not a teenager will be "accepted."

Selective groups of peers or "cliques" play a big part in a junior higher's world. They are tightly knit groups that rarely permit others to join. Although they provide a social insurance policy for members against feelings of isolation and loneliness, those on the outside experience the very thing cliques exist to prevent. Cliques are very selective as to whom is allowed in. They set their own standards of popularity. Cliques can be vicious and threatening to outsiders. Although the behavior of cliques is regarded as unfair and even cruel by those on the outside, it is almost impossible for junior highers to avoid them.

I remember a beautiful young girl feeling crushed and rejected by her classmates during the year of "designer jeans." They no longer accepted her at the lunch table or included her in after-school activities because she did not have the right label on her jeans.

Rejection is a most traumatic, devastating experience—especially during adolescence when rejection is based upon things beyond the kids' control or experience: looks, personality, home, family, ability or skill, behavior, language, religion, or simply being new in the neighborhood. Adolescents can be very hard on each other; rejecting their peers is one way to make themselves feel superior and important.

Saying "no" to negative pressures from a group takes a lot of courage on the part of an early adolescent, just as it does for adults. Thus, it is difficult for kids to make principles a priority over friends. Junior highers are not ready to sacrifice their friends for a belief. They lack the confidence to risk ridicule or rejection. All of us, at one time or another, have done things because of group pressure and not because we wanted to.

Junior highers are the people most vulnerable to such pressure—and at times, it can have undesirable effects. In their quest for recognition and acceptance, they may choose friends who do not meet with their parents' approval; they may participate in risky or unhealthy activities; or they may take on an attitude of pseudosophistication to cover up their worries, fears, doubts, and insecurities. Traumatic moments occur when the kids realize they've made some bad decisions; it is especially important for caring adults to help kids through these trying times.

It is difficult for junior highers to think beyond themselves. They live in an egocentric world and find it difficult to empathize. They think everyone is watching them, that people are far more interested in their behavior and what they are wearing than who they are. This is one reason why the advertising media are so successful in appealing to kids' insecurities.

The church can play a major role in helping young people develop socially. The church can communicate a unique message to the kids: "You are special. You are made in the image of God. He loves you." An effective junior high ministry helps kids feel special as individuals; it encourages young people to be themselves without risking rejection. The worst thing that can happen to a junior high ministry is for it to become a place where all the kids look alike, think alike and act alike.

With the help of caring leadership, a junior high group can be the ideal setting where kids can feel secure about themselves and free to talk about their friendships. When friendships go through times of strain or tension, the church is where such experiences can be discussed openly and honestly. Friendships are complex and demanding, but there is no better place than the church to explore them.

It is sad when teenagers feel excluded or alone in a group. Unfortunately, many groups do not know how to handle a loner; they are inexperienced in dealing with kids who act strangely in order to gain attention. With the help of skilled adult leaders, these awkward situations can be overcome.

Adult leaders can teach openness, acceptance and hospitality by modeling these traits. Adults can warmly and enthusiastically welcome new people; they can mix and mingle with all members of the group and show the kids that they are loved and cared for. Leaders can design group experiences that focus the kids' attention on things they have in common, rather than on things they don't. For example, instead of forming small groups according to schools, form small groups according to birthday months, eye color, hair color, favorite foods or favorite television shows.

We can focus discussions on topics such as "Comments and actions that hurt people" or "Affirming things friends have done for me."

We can deliberately mix people in a group. If kids had a choice of whom to sit next to, or whom they wanted in their small group, it would always be their friends. We sometimes need to deliberately break up friends in order to create situations where kids who don't know each other spend time together. This works best when their attention is focused on something they have in common, like a work project. Such common ground relieves pressures and helps the kids feel relaxed with one another. From that point, conversation will bridge the gap to building new friendships.

The need to belong is inherent to everyone. We gravitate toward people we feel most secure and comfortable with. The greatest thing leaders can teach impressionable junior highers is the true meaning of what a friend we have in Jesus.

Intellectual Development of Junior Highers

Much of our knowledge of intellectual development has stemmed from the comprehensive research and theories of the Swiss psychologist Jean Piaget. His work on this subject has informed and guided the efforts of nearly a generation of researchers. Although some current scholars question his methods, his work still dominantly influences what is known about the way the mind works.

Piaget believed that we pass through a series of stages in developing our ability to think. These stages represent increasingly comprehensive ways of thinking. During adolescence, a young person acquires several new intellectual capabilities at a level called "formal operations." Basically, this means junior highers begin to think in terms of the purely abstract and hypothetical. The capacity for abstract reasoning can be illustrated in their response to questions such as: "If Joe is shorter than Bob, and Joe is taller than Alex, who is the tallest?" In contrast to children who can only solve the problem by actually placing people in order to find the answer, on the level of formal operations, adolescents can order their thoughts in their minds alone.[9]

During formal operational thinking, adolescents think about

their future and the kind of society in which they want to live. They can grasp abstract principles and ideals such as liberty, justice and love, and they begin to picture in their minds the "perfect world." In short, the adolescent discovers the joy of being a dreamer.

Piaget said that such thinking creates a new kind of egocentrism. Adolescents get caught up in the unlimited power of their thoughts, yet they don't attempt to test their dreams with reality. As kids gradually assume adult responsibilities, they learn the limits and meet resistance to their ways of thinking.

David Elkind has taken Piaget's cognitive stages and applied them to education. His work has profound implications for the learning experiences we design for junior highers. According to Elkind, here are some characteristics of junior highers:

Junior highers have the capacity to deal with combinational logic—to consider a wide range of possibilities in problem solving. This is one of the reasons why teenagers begin to rebel against parents or others in authority. They want to know not only where an adult figure stands, but why, and are ready to debate the adult's point of view . . .

Another characteristic is junior highers' ability to introspect—to evaluate themselves from the perspective of others as to their intelligence, personality and appearance. A new sense of self-consciousness or a preoccupation with self emerges. This introspection makes junior highers secretive. They recognize now that their thoughts are private . . .

Junior highers can now construct ideals and reason out contrary-to-fact propositions—they can conceive ideal families, religions and societies. Naturally, when they compare these with their own, they find them defective.[10]

Adult leaders can help kids grow by patiently helping them assess their own limitations, and by providing interesting and challenging experiences where teenagers can learn firsthand. Junior high leaders should offer plenty of chances for the kids to mix and mingle, to reach out to others and to become aware of the realities of their community and world. We should encourage teenagers to relate to one another without the threat of being "watched." The more comfortable kids feel at church with their peers, the more they will want to be there. A domineering, authoritative, strict, "we-have-all-the-right-answers" atmosphere will create a greater barrier between leaders and kids than if the church doors were padlocked.

We, as junior high leaders, should affirm, support and encourage junior highers' ideals and dreams, especially when dreams become mixed with reality. This means helping them realize that their dream of traveling to Hawaii to surf isn't as simple as it sounds, but it's not impossible. We can help kids explore realistic ways they can achieve their goals, and support them in their efforts to reach them.

The same holds true when it comes to dealing with issues such as the church. What the church is "supposed to be" may not always jell with reality. Instead of allowing the kids to complain about inconsistencies, we can help them think of contributions they could make to help the church be true to its mission—the place where Jesus' love is shared and declared. Kids might think of service projects, or realize their presence on Sunday positively affects other worshipers. The process of discussing the "ideal church" can be a real eye-opener for kids. They discover that things don't just happen, and if they want their church to be special, they must share in that responsibility. The spirit of enthusiastic young people can transform the spirit of an entire congregation—it's catching!

Emotional Development of Junior Highers

Determining where junior highers are in their emotional development can be a very frustrating experience. Emotional development is more difficult to determine than physical, social, intellectual or spiritual development. This is true, partly, because young adolescents' moods change radically. Kids struggle to understand their feelings as much as adults struggle to understand the kids' feelings.

Emotions exert a powerful force in all of our lives. For early adolescents, this is compounded because the kids are just beginning to understand what their feelings mean, and how to control them in a socially acceptable manner.

Junior highers are definitely emotional. Their preoccupation with self can cause several mood changes within a short period of time. There is no predictable pattern to the way they feel. The same person can be loud and rowdy, or quiet and shy, in a matter of minutes. They have mood swings, from low to high, as if they were two different people. This emotional swing also can be observed in group behavior. The emotional state of a group determines whether a planned activity will succeed or fail. For example, if the group's emotional level is too high or too low, holding a serious discussion will be difficult.

Junior highers also are vulnerable to emotional appeals. Leaders soon discover that they can get junior high young people to do almost anything if they appeal to their emotions. Shrewd adults have become adroit manipulators of adolescents' feelings in order to sell cosmetics, clothes, jewelry, stereos, toothpaste, etc. Soft drink commercials distort reality by sending physical, action-oriented, covertly sexual messages that heavily impact feelings to create a response.

Like so much of what they see on television, adolescents can have a distorted view of the world and themselves. A great deal of their time is spent on self-reflection, an activity that is an inescapable part of the search for identity. To the outside world a junior high young person may seem full of excitement, but deep inside he or she may be experiencing excruciating pangs of fear. Adults tend to forget what it was like to be an adolescent. Some adults assume that because they survived adolescence, they are in the position to correctly appraise the emotions of teenagers and channel them in appropriate directions. Assumptions like these can lead to potential disasters. We cannot predict junior highers' emotions. Kids will not react the same way to the same thing. Psychologists tell us no set emotional pattern is determined until kids reach the senior high years. In the meantime, junior highers are likely to translate their emotions into various forms of behavior. And, since young people respond to things differently, all kinds of behavior will simultaneously occur.

Rather than feeling overwhelmed at junior highers' variety of emotions and behaviors, we should rejoice that they are alive! They are maturing into fully integrated adults. Emotions are the mirror of one's maturity. Because this is the age when a young person begins the search to find his or her place in the world, it is only natural to expect experimentation and mood swings. Depression can be the result of harsh self-criticism; anxiety can be linked to the first step toward autonomy; dramatic behavior can be associated with a need for attention; a brutal disregard for others' feelings may be a mask for sensitivity and insecurity.

Emotions sometimes become so strong that they overtake a young person. Intense feelings of joy, sorrow, remorse, or separation can even immobilize a young person. Kids cannot move away from self-concern unless someone significant offers them comfort or is willing to listen. Kids need consistent, mature adult models when their young feelings are on a roller coaster ride. Patience certainly is a virtue at this point. Adults will need to condition themselves emotionally to "tough it out."

However, not all emotional mood swings and behaviors are acceptable. Certain predetermined codes of conduct and what is acceptable behavior need to be stated. At the beginning of your junior high program, both the leader and the kids should set standards they feel are appropriate. Kids and adults should share their opinions, and then arrive at a compromise. Together, set consequences for unacceptable behavior. Such prearrangements can mean there will be no need to embarrass someone in front of the group. Consequences are set well in advance and therefore are expected.

If a disciplinary problem occurs, it is best to address the person privately rather than in front of the group. This type of sensitivity has a positive effect on a group's attitude and often encourages the group to speak to each other about behavior concerns. It's the attitude or atmosphere we create as leaders, rather than a list of rules, that will affect the need for discipline.

Studies indicate that parents who use authoritarian, decision-making methods have children who show little independence. The kids' decision-making abilities are severely hampered by fear. Likewise, if adult youth leaders use authoritarian methods, the group will continue to act immaturely. It is unrealistic to expect there won't be times when emotions dictate behavior that will need correction or guidance. Caring enough to see such experiences as opportunities for learning and growth, will result in stronger individuals and a stronger group.

A distinction needs to be made between "normal" behavior for this age group and that which is considered deviant. Although the majority of junior highers are not experiencing deep emotional problems that manifest themselves in antisocial behavior, many 12- to 15-year-olds do have serious disturbances. In fact, it is at this age that some disorders such as schizophrenia and depression appear for the first time. Most of the socially unacceptable behavior exhibited by junior highers stems from conflicts with parents, school relationships or their self-concept.

Many adolescents deal with conflicts through the abuse of drugs such as alcohol and marijuana. It is now estimated that one in 25 12- to 13-year-olds, and about one in seven 14- to 15-year-olds smoke marijuana once a month. Junior high boys are twice as likely as girls to smoke marijuana once a month. Junior high boys are twice as likely as girls to smoke marijuana on a regular basis.[11] Most research indicates smoking marijuana interferes with short-term memory, intellectual performance, reading comprehension, problem-solving, and other tasks that require concentration and coordination.

To what extent do parents and friends influence the use of marijuana? Relying on my own experience, it seems that associations with peers who smoke marijuana are more likely to influence a junior higher to smoke than anything else.

Many adults do not consider alcohol as a drug. This is unfortunate since more and more teenagers engage in social drinking. Statistics indicate alcohol is the most commonly used and abused psychoactive substance among teenagers in the United States.[12] Alcohol is a depressant that primarily affects the central nervous system. Many teenagers mistakenly assume that alcohol is a stimulant when in reality, it slows down many of the brain's functions. When alcohol use becomes a problem, it is usually determined by a complex set of factors. A report issued by the National Institute on Alcohol Abuse and Alcoholism concluded that among groups of people who use alcohol extensively, the lowest rate of alcoholism is linked with the following factors:

- Young people are exposed to alcohol at a young age within a strong family or religious group. The alcohol is served in quantities and often diluted.
- The beverage served is usually thought of as a food and served at meals.
- Parents set an example of moderate, rather than excessive drinking.
- No moral significance is placed on drinking—it is considered neither right nor wrong.
- Drinking is not viewed as proof of adulthood or virility.
- Abstinence is viewed as socially acceptable.
- Excessive drinking or being intoxicated is not approved of.[13]

Suicide is another way some adolescents deal with conflict. Since 1955, suicide attempts have tripled for junior highers. In 15- to 19-year-olds, suicide ranks as the fifth major cause of death, outranked only by accidents, cancer, heart disease and homicide.[14] The increase in suicide for this age group is a symptom of the stress that many experience as they grow from dependent children to independent adults.

We can't predict that a young person will attempt suicide, but there are some warning signs: a previous attempt at suicide, severe family problems, loss of a loved one, other stressful events, or any mention of the subject.

It is important for junior high leaders to be aware of suicide, of alcohol and marijuana abuse, and other negative means of dealing with conflict. We need to help kids cope with stress, tension and depression by loving them and accepting their feelings. We need to forgive their outbursts and be patient as they search for reasons behind their emotions. We need to provide positive avenues of expression in activities such as singing, playing games, dancing and serving others. These activities help kids release tension, and at the same time create community and acceptance. There is absolutely no substitute for feelings of belonging.

Moral Development of Junior Highers

Lawrence Kohlberg, Harvard educator and psychologist, has developed theories that help us understand junior highers' value development. According to Kohlberg, moral development takes place in sequential stages, each stage building on the previous one. People pass through the stages at various speeds and may stop at any point. Only a few reach the highest level of moral thinking.[15] Following is a summary of Kohlberg's stages.

Level One: Preconventional Morality

At middle childhood this level becomes evident. Children make moral judgments solely on the basis of anticipated punishment and reward.

Stage 1 - the focus here is on the power of authority figures and what one must do to avoid displeasing those who have power over you.

Stage 2 - the focus here is on the pleasure motive. A person does what they have to do in order to get what they want from others. There is a sense of fair exchange based on pragmatic concerns.

Level Two: Conventional Morality

During late childhood (ages 10-11), right behavior is viewed as that which is accepted, approved and praised by those who are authority figures. A person seeks to avoid guilt by behaving in ways approved by the social conventions of the culture.

Stage 3 - the focus is on gaining approval of those closest at hand in judging behavior. The desire is for good interpersonal relations.

Stage 4 - the focus is on maintaining the social order. At this stage, one obeys rules because they exist.

Level Three: Postconventional Morality

Beginning with early adolescence, an individual is capable of determining right and wrong on the basis of personal decisions rather than on society's standards.

Stage 5 - the focus is on what is just in terms of an individual's rights and freedom. Here laws are upheld, but if they need to be changed are done so using the democratic process.

Stage 6 - the focus is on determining right or wrong based on one's conscience. These are viewed as universal principles by which justice is achieved. This level is not attained by many people.

At stage three, the junior higher is ready to leave behind the egocentric and hedonistic ways of thinking, and becomes concerned with moral decisions in relationship to his or her family, peers and religion. Adolescents base their moral decisions on what family, peers and the church believe to be right, and on what will help and please those belonging to these groups. Behavior at this stage is determined by intention.

At this stage, junior highers think God is concerned with the way they behave and is ready to forgive them in a fair and impartial way. For kids, the church should be a loving, caring community where they can feel a special loyalty. Junior highers will go along with what the church says is right and, in essence, accept the church's value system.

However, conflicts emerge when what pleases the church differs from what the peer group feels is acceptable. As a result, peer judgments greatly influence the kids' moral decisions. When they become aware of these differing points of view, the kids experience personal turmoil.

Pressure to conform can be so intense, it can prevent the individual from forming his or her own moral values. Although it's sad to report, few adults know how to handle this kind of peer pressure. Why is it youth leaders shy away from counteracting the immature value system of peer groups? Could it be adults feel they have nothing better to offer? Do they want to avoid conflict? When conflicting morality issues arise, adults should take the opportunity to talk with the kids. Such experiences are invaluable in helping young people fully develop.

At stage four, authority is defined in a broader sense. The young person now recognizes that if society is to survive, order is important. Rules for conduct are understood as having been established to maintain this order.

The mind-set of a person on this level is to think that God's chief concern is for people to keep his commandments and that they will be judged accordingly. The Bible and the teachings of the church also require unquestioning obedience.

Again, there can be a real moral dilemma when young people become aware of corruption in the church, and when morality seems to be absent from church behavior. Kids may be shocked to discover that a general set of standards is not adequate to deal with every situation. With this comes a recognition and acceptance of certain inadequacies in the moral structure upon which they've developed a value system.

At stage five, the individual has matured to the point where he or she can look objectively at society and think independently. There is an earnest attempt to discover universal principles and to adopt them in order to make decisions and take action. It is important to think in terms of the greatest good for the greatest number. Here, laws are viewed as being made for a smooth-functioning society and for the mutual benefit of the majority. If it becomes prudent to change a law, it is done by using accepted methods.

The implications of this level mean that a young person discovers the freedom God gives us to act and the responsibility we have for making our own decisions. Since an individual is a responsible agent in God's creation, he or she will accept or reject what he or she has been taught. This is the moment when young people decide their own religious and moral references for life. In Kohlberg's view, this cannot happen without healthy peer interaction. It is only as kids enter into discussions with others that they find their views questioned and challenged, and where they are motivated to think of new, more comprehensive positions. This is difficult for adults to do, let alone a young teenager. Nonetheless, changes do occur if opportunities are provided for considering another's point of view.

Leaders can do a lot to foster moral development by creating a secure environment where honest, genuine discussions, grappling with moral issues, can take place. We can do this by encouraging everyone to express his or her point of view, even when we are unsure of our own viewpoint. We help kids by letting them know there are no "right" or "wrong" answers.

We do junior highers a disservice if we give them "the answers" in the midst of their struggle. Often adults rationalize doing this if they are running out of discussion time or if they fear the kids will reach conclusions contrary to their own. Let's not rob inquisitive minds of the chance to formulate their own ideas and opinions. We must also allow them the freedom to change their minds; at 15 they may not reach the same conclusions they did at 14. And, we must also keep in mind, most moral issues have existed for centuries—even the test of time hasn't resolved them.

We can help kids develop morals by teaching them to empathize. Although making moral decisions is a reasoning process, empathy expands a person's perspective and allows him or her to consider other viewpoints. Some other practical guidelines for helping kids to develop morally include:

• Probe the effects of kids' moral decisions.

• Help them consider the feelings of others who are affected by their decisions.

• Help them clarify their feelings about others' decisions that affect them.

• Affirm them when they are a source of joy, comfort or courage to others.

• Listen carefully to the reasons they give for their decisions.

• Provide opportunities for discussions on what they believe to be fair courses of action.

• Focus on reasons for their decisions rather than on their behavior.

• Be realistic in our expectations as to what young people at this stage are capable of comprehending.

Spiritual Development of Junior Highers

Having considered the physical, social, intellectual, emotional and moral development that takes place during the junior high years, we come to the last piece in the puzzle which touches every aspect of our lives: spiritual development.

The older generation always has been concerned with what young people think and believe. Nonetheless, only recently has there been any effort to understand the workings of a young mind—how it constructs ideas, concepts and beliefs.

James Fowler is considered a pioneer in constructing a theory of faith development that closely parallels Piaget's and Kohlberg's theories on intellectual and moral development respectively. He has suggested that faith has sequential characteristics—we begin with a simple faith and move to more complex levels. Individuals vary as to the level they attain; a person rarely reaches the highest level. Fowler firmly believes that the images, values, beliefs, symbols and rituals of an individual's faith are critical factors in shaping his or her personality and behavior. In the struggle to find meaning in life, faith is the cornerstone.

Following is a summary of Fowler's six stages of faith development; junior highers could be anywhere from stage two to stage four in their development.

Stage 1: Intuitive-Projective Faith

This is an imitative, fantasy-filled phase of early childhood when the examples, moods, actions and language of primary adults are a powerful influence.

Stage 2: Mythic-Literal Faith

Children at about 6½ to 8 years of age begin to adopt for themselves the stories, beliefs and customs that indicate they belong to a specific faith community.

With this level of maturity comes the ability to solve problems using information close at hand. Kids can separate real from make believe, especially when reading stories. They can grasp some insight into cause-and-effect relationships. Parents, teachers and peers are the primary sources of their religious beliefs. Ritual, symbolism and music also greatly influence them. God is still thought of in human form, and the world is considered an orderly place, highly predictable. Codes of conduct, church teachings and religious attitudes are understood literally and expressed without question.

Stage 3: Synthetic-Conventional Faith

At the onset of adolescence, an awareness exists of a larger world beyond self and of various areas in which life takes place (family, peers, school, church, etc.). Faith plays a meaningful role in forming a coherent picture of how the individual relates to a more complex spectrum of individuals.

Stage 4: Individuating-Reflexive Faith

Near the end of adolescence a transition takes place in which a person takes seriously the responsibility for his or her commitments, life style, beliefs and attitudes.

Stage 5: Paradoxical-Consolidative Faith

This stage usually is not attained until adulthood, at about age 30, when a person recognizes the integrity and truth in others' faith commitments. Without compromising what he or she believes, a person can confidently respect truth in the lives of others, yet remain true to what he or she values, to the point of taking risks and paying a price.

Stage 6: Universalizing Faith

This kind of faith is rare. At this stage a person dwells in the world as a transforming presence, but is not of the world. There is a sense of universal community and fellowship with people from any faith tradition—a true sense of oneness with all people.[16]

Junior high leaders can benefit a great deal from studies about faith development and human development. For example, if readiness for learning unfolds in stages of increased intellectual capacities and wider social experiences, it follows that readiness is also needed for the learning of religion. We do not try to teach an abstract idea like the Trinity to 3-year-olds, nor do we expect them to have well-developed moral values.

The study of human development provides keen insights into our spiritual development. Faith is an act of the whole person and involves psychological functions for, ". . . faith comes from what is heard" (Romans 10:17), meaning interpretation and understanding must take place. The trust we place in God is not much different from the trust we practice in our relationships to others. The way we come to know God through hearing the Gospel is no different from the ways we come to know anything else in the world. In *Faith Passages and Patterns*, Thomas Droege says:

> *What we learn to know and trust can, of course, be very different, and therein lies the limit to what psychology tells us. So for a knowledge of God we look to the Scriptures as the source of the revelation of God and his will and ways. But for an understanding of how human beings come to know and grow in faith in that God, we can look to psychology for considerable help.*[17]

This may be a new way of thinking for many people. Some separate religion from the rest of life and place it in a box all its own—not connecting faith with any of the struggles that must be faced each day. Others maintain that faith is a gift, that salvation comes by grace alone, and adamantly oppose any notion that the individual plays any part in faith development. Nonetheless, an awareness of how our mind develops faith need not deny the work of the Holy Spirit. The ability to perceive God's work in our life can lead to an even greater openness to his presence.

Through the years, we wrestle with our faith, and we form images, concepts, and principles to express what we believe. Think of the ways your image of God has changed since you were a child. As we mature, our beliefs take different shapes. This growth in faith is related to the way we share and pass on to others our beliefs as we worship together.

Working with junior highers allows us to relate to a group of kids who are just beginning to understand the meaning of being responsible for their own decisions. This is the time in their lives when they comprehend that if the Christian faith is to be one's own, a personal decision to develop it must be made. No one—parent, pastor or peer—can decide for them. Adolescents' commitment to Christ may not occur like a flash of lightning or in a highly dramatic moment; it may evolve silently, without much awareness of it at all. Yet a decision about faith, either for or against, is crucial in this time of transition.

Being in a state of transition means putting an end to what was, and entering into something new. Confusion, doubt, uncertainty, and what may appear to be a loss of faith, are usually experienced at such times. Junior highers are not at the point of making a personal decision for which they accept total responsibility but they are on their way to that crossroad. Although we probably won't be with them when they do make the decision, it is our task to help them pack for the journey.

Fowler maintains that many people remain in stage three the rest of their lives. This is due in part to the many institutions in our society, including the church, that reinforce stage-three thinking in their members.

For example, many churches offer membership or confirmation classes for junior highers. The classes are made up of questions and answers which are meant to explain the faith. Young people are not expected to generate questions of their own, and certainly are not expected to have already formulated their own conclusions.

At stage three there is little or no resistance to this type of faith nurturing, as long as the authority figures (the church) are supported by significant people in the young adolescent's life (parents and friends). In earlier generations, many young people assumed the same faith as their parents. Roles were clearly defined; a person could go through stage three without any difficulty. In today's pluralistic society, it is not that simple for junior highers. They are likely to be surrounded by people whose judgments and expectations differ.

For an early adolescent, differing expectations are a source of much tension. One way to relieve this tension is for junior highers to act one way with friends and another way with parents. They think this is a great solution, until they find themselves in a situation where both are present. Perhaps this is one reason why kids feel uncomfortable having parents act as group leaders; it puts them in an awkward position with their peers.

Another way to cope with people whose judgments differ is to rank the people in an order of importance. Usually friends get the top spot and all others become subordinates.

During stage three, junior highers have the ability to see themselves as they think they appear to others—or they compose pictures of themselves the way they'd like to be. Fowler wrote a couplet that expresses this way of thinking: "I see you seeing me; I see the one I think you see."[18] Naturally, kids want to be viewed as "okay" by everyone.

Junior highers hunger to be accepted by others, as well as by God. They want to believe in a God who knows them the way they are, and who likes them anyway—despite their inadequacies, faults, limitations and failures. A person at this level of faith development is strongly attracted to an image of a God who is deeply personal and affirming. Talks and stories about God being a friend, companion, counselor or guide mean a lot to them. Since this is the age when significant people in kids' lives are terribly important to the formation of self, a personal God—one who loves and affirms—is potentially the most significant influence.

Although junior highers feel very strongly about religion, their faith is basically an unexamined one. They may be able to talk about their images and values, yet they are unable to think critically. Junior highers rely a great deal on authority figures to form and sustain their beliefs. Such reliance makes it an awesome responsibility for pastors, youth leaders and parents since this ultimately means they are the ones who create the teenagers' images of God. You can imagine what it does to kids' self-esteem to be constantly bombarded with an image of God as judge, who punishes the wicked, and condemns to hell those who break his laws.

It is highly probable that within a group of junior highers there will be differences in terms of their spiritual maturation, just as there are differences in terms of their physical and emotional development. Some kids may be in stage two, and a few may be ready to advance to stage four. This does not mean that one kid's faith is better than another's. Kids might be sensitive to this issue. They may feel that someone in the group is more religious than they are. Adults need to remind junior highers that God doesn't rank us according to the achievement level of our faith. Every person is loved unconditionally by God, regardless of accomplishment. Some in the group may be more spiritually mature, but it is not for us to judge the quality of that faith.

All that we do and say will be measured against whether the kids trust and believe us. We are probably providing them their first experience in deciding on their own whom they trust in the church.

We have a wonderful opportunity to help kids understand that God can be trusted and that his promises are true. What an awesome responsibility when we realize we represent these promises. We can assure young people that God has power and has an orderly plan for the universe. The world of an adolescent can quickly fall apart. From their point of view, the world can be a very confusing place. They leave their childhood with both an eagerness and sense of fear. Much of their day-to-day concerns can be threatening—losing friends, achieving at school or pleasing parents. Every decision has the potential of turning into a traumatic experience.

Like adults, young people seek things that make them feel secure. When we face adversity, we all reach for stability or safety. Sensitive adults want to be dependable because they know that teenagers need stability. Kids need to know that adult leaders are always available to care for and support them. Dependable and caring adults reflect a dependable and caring God. Kids use their experiences to translate the concepts they are taught.

As junior high leaders, we are privileged to communicate that everything is under control, that love and life are secure, and that God works for good in all things. We can create a caring atmosphere by helping young people develop friendship skills and by letting the junior highers talk about their feelings. Feelings need to be responded to with empathy. Hugging young people when they feel lonely, crying with them when they are deeply hurt, sharing in their struggle to relate to the opposite sex, laughing with them on joyous occasions, or being excited at times of celebration, all strengthen the bond of love between leader and young people. When the kids are sure of our genuine concern, they can understand and accept a God who weeps, a God who suffers, a God who reaches out. God's promise is not that life will be without problems or pain, but rather that he will keep us secure in his everlasting, loving arms. He will keep a light burning somewhere so we are not completely overwhelmed by the darkness. Adults can help teenagers understand that we all have to work through temporary setbacks in order to live a full, healthy and normal life. We can help kids through these tough times and afterward, reflect on how struggles help us to grow—God does not abandon us in our times of need.

Another critical factor in religious development is acceptance. The kind of acceptance kids find with adults or within a youth group impacts their understanding of an accepting God. It is senseless to say "God loves you" to someone who feels rejected, harshly or cruelly judged or ridiculed.

Teenagers can be very hard on each other. The labels they use to identify their own peer group often project negative images. Titles such as nerd, jock, freak, space-head, etc., are not necessarily used in complimentary conversation. Yet, kids may be given these titles even if a group is made up of only four people! As adults, we can foster an accepting environment by helping the kids establish ground rules; for example, no one is to be judged right or wrong, and no one is to be laughed at.

Faith is experienced before it is understood, it grows as knowledge is gained, and it finally shapes behavior. Bible stories alone cannot be the source of teenagers' beliefs. Only as they experience the meaning of the scriptures in their relationships with others will the truth of Christian faith be understood. Anytime we have the opportunity to open the Bible with a group of kids, we should ask ourselves:

● What is the promise of God in this story?

● How can I help the kids experience this truth?

Fowler says that faith is communicated most effectively through the telling of stories. However, far too often adults assume that everyone gets the same meaning from stories he or she hears. We know now that this is not the case. We need to anticipate young people's understanding of what is being said. One very simple method to ensure they have understood what was said is to ask the kids to repeat what they have heard. Naturally, we'll get a variety of responses. We must be careful not to impose "corrections to the story" based on our own interpretations.

The limits of a person's understanding within a certain stage of faith development must be respected. We need to encourage each young person within our care to use his or her abilities and talents to the fullest. By doing so, we offer kids the best possible situation through which their faith can move from one stage to another.

During our opportunities to nurture the kids' faith, it is natural that teenagers will have doubts and questions. Honest doubting has its place in faith development. Doubts may arise as the result of being at a transition point in their lives—as a result of letting go of what they believed as children. Troubling questions need to be discussed in order for kids to grow. As we encourage each young person to grow in his or her faith, we need to be prepared for the fact that some may actually outdistance us!

Throughout this chapter, junior high ministry has been identified in relational terms: The stages of development are related to each other; junior highers are related to others and their world. Faith also is rooted in relationships—a trusting relationship with God that finds its initial expression in people. The church, working as a nurturing community, is an optimal environment for faith to grow. Nurturing churches surround teenagers with a sense of security and support, give them experiences appropriate for their level of development, guide them through the time of transition, encourage them in making decisions, and constantly assure them of God's love and care.

CHAPTER 4

BASIC INGREDIENTS FOR AN EFFECTIVE JUNIOR HIGH MINISTRY

A church was looking for a new pastor. When the search committee members met with the denomination officials, they requested a minister who could preach well-prepared and inspiring sermons; visit the sick, elderly and shut-ins every day; be a dynamic stewardship motivator; have skills in counseling and teaching; pump new enthusiasm into the Sunday school; belong to several community groups; conduct stimulating Bible studies; be able to play the piano and direct the choir in times of emergency; and spend much of his or her time relating and meeting with young people! More than one denomination official has told me that churches want someone who can preach well and who works well with youth.

Just as search committees and congregations have pictured their ideal pastor, people also envision the ideal junior high program. Just what is it every youth leader, every church, every parent wants?

In recent years a number of studies have been conducted on what makes youth programs effective and successful. Certain characteristics consistently appear in results taken from churches across the country. One thing is clear—families with teenagers gravitate toward ministries that have effective, exciting programs in place for this age group. Growing churches have strong youth programs.

During 1982, the Center for Early Adolescence published a report titled *Early Adolescence and Religion: A Status Study*, a compilation of extensive data gathered by Anita M. Farel. Much of the study's information came from on-site visits by the author to a variety of youth programs and through subsequent interviews with young people, youth leaders and parents. She discovered some common threads, even though the ministries were quite diversified. One of those threads was the churches' responsiveness to the total developmental needs of junior highers. A conscientious effort was made to provide a wholistic ministry for this age group.

Farel's report concurs with my experiences. Combining my observations with Anita Farel's research, let's explore the ingredients for an effective junior high ministry.

1. An effective junior high ministry is relational. Relational youth ministry means *meeting kids on their turf.* Kids like youth leaders who take the time to visit them at home, or who attend school activities such as basketball games, plays, concerts, science fairs, dances, parties, etc. By visiting junior highers at home or school, we express an interest in the kids as individuals; we validate that their lives are important to us outside the church. Such a time investment will prompt junior highers to introduce us to their friends. The extra effort could even lead their friends to Christ. This kind of interest and evangelism makes an impact, not just on youth group members, but on their friends, parents and community leaders as well.

A relational youth ministry requires leaders to *love junior highers unconditionally.* Just as God's love is unconditional, leaders unconditionally should accept the kids for who they are, not for what they do. Kids need to see the mistakes adult leaders make, the struggles they have in living the Christian faith, and the importance of forgiveness. Junior highers need to be around people who understand their struggles, who affirm them in their journey toward maturity, and who do not judge or condemn them.

Relational junior high ministry means *not giving up on the kids*. Junior highers need to be challenged to develop their talents, taught responsibility and encouraged to grow spiritually. Kids need leaders who are patient, reassuring and who believe only the best of them. Our faith, regardless of our age, grows only as it is nurtured. Especially with this age group, adult leaders play a vital role in encouraging kids to develop their God-given talents.

A relational ministry to junior highers means *not being afraid to touch*. Junior highers need hugs, touches and warmth—personal components in a high-tech world. We need to learn how to use our bodies to demonstrate warmth. Loving people rarely hug and grab everyone in sight, but they use a delicately developed sense of touch every time they are with someone. They listen with their eyes and draw close to the person during conversation. At appropriate moments, they touch to keep the interaction warm.

Many parents stop touching their children about the time they enter first grade. Soon afterward, children often stop touching one another. While other societies accept touching as part of even casual relationships, our culture considers it normal for people *not* to touch one another. We find it appropriate to be touched only by people who are licensed to do so: doctors, hairdressers, therapists. Yet, even these professionals are careful to remain cold and aloof for fear their touches will be misinterpreted.

In many churches, people find it difficult to accept the "kiss of peace" or the extension of the hand of fellowship during worship because it is so contrary to what we experience everywhere else. It just doesn't seem natural to embrace, hug or touch total strangers, even within the family of God. One of the distinguishing features of Jesus' ministry was the way he touched people—lepers and children alike. We need to follow Jesus' example and touch each other more often.

Recently an old friend recalled a visit in my office when she poured out her heart. She couldn't remember the problem or visit exactly, but she recalled one thing . . . I had hugged her on the way out.

I believe it is important to hug junior highers, pat them on the back, or put a hand on their shoulder during a conversation. Just as we choose words carefully in our conversations with one another, we also need to develop our body language.

There are many times when touching someone is not only appropriate, it is more eloquent than anything we possibly could say. Grieving people often wish others would hug them, hold their hands, or just "be there," rather than search for the right words to say. A troubled teenager may be comforted more with a hug and our presence than with words. The Bible often relates touch with the healing process, or restoration of relationships. We can do more than is imaginable by simply reaching out with our touch.

2. An effective junior high ministry provides a comfortable setting in which young people can explore their Christian faith. Teenagers respond to places that make them feel welcome. Providing a comfortable setting means more than allotting space on the bulletin board for youth activities, including youth group announcements in the Sunday bulletin, or setting aside a certain area for the "youth room." A comfortable setting is one in which junior highers are *accepted and affirmed.*

Affirming junior highers means treating each of them as a whole person. The congregation should encourage them to gather for social events, participate in service projects, receive instruction, and feel free to be both active and quiet. In such an environment, there are times when junior highers are very much a part of church activities, and there are times when junior highers take part in their own activities.

We need to recognize that junior highers are a part of the church; they too belong to the family of God. Kids don't want to wait until they are "adults" to be a part of the faith community. If God places no age restrictions on us, why should we? When adolescents know that their contributions are welcomed, their energy appreciated, their presence affirmed, they will eagerly participate in activities.

3. An effective junior high ministry connects religious traditions with a variety of self-discovery opportunities. The traditional methods used by the church to nurture faith can be very effective if appropriately geared to the kids' readiness. Retreats, discussions, singing and special outdoor activities all contribute significantly to a sense of belonging to a faith family. It's not just doing these things that nurture faith, but the opportunity to discuss what is learned, that makes these experiences so meaningful.

Junior highers' faith can be nurtured through *worship* with the adult community of faith. The kids can identify with the larger family of God by attending worship, hosting a fellowship period, singing in a choir, or serving as ushers and greeters. A church that accepts young people as full members, will engender an eagerness on the kids' part to participate.

Junior highers can create and conduct worship that is their own. It can be a tremendous learning experience for them to talk about the purpose of worship, the structure of their liturgy, Christian vocabulary, and the patterns followed in the church year. Planning a worship experience provides an opportunity for individuals to talk about parts of worship that mean the most to them, including what they find helpful in sermons, hymns and prayers.

Junior highers' faith can be nurtured through *study groups*. These studies can focus on topics such as "What Jesus means to me," "Why I find it difficult to talk with God," "Things that make me wonder if God exists," "Why I feel the way I do," or "Our God-given abilities and talents."

Junior highers' faith can be nurtured during *service or outreach*. Opportunities to help others in need contribute significantly to a person's self-esteem. Junior highers discover they can pass on their God-given gifts to others. The young people can sing to nursing home residents, read to shut-ins, repair elderly members' homes, visit with new members, teach lessons to nursery school kids, etc. Once the teenagers know what service means, they'll never be the same again.

In Washington, D.C., a remarkable blind woman began a radio station to serve the visually handicapped. Called "The Washington Ear," this station daily airs such services as reading the Washington Post each morning, reading current best sellers, etc. In order to inform subscribers of the station's programming and services, a monthly newsletter is produced. One local youth worker enlisted a small group of junior highers to meet monthly at the station and address the newsletters and prepare them for mailing. Although a simple task, it involved the group members in service, and gave them an awareness of the needs of the visually handicapped.

4. An effective junior high ministry fosters mutual understanding by involving both young people and their parents. Junior highers are very dependent people. Parental approval has a heavy impact on a young person's ability to participate.

An effective youth program involves the *help of parents* in many, many ways. This is so important that we'll devote an entire chapter to involving parents (see Chapter 7). Parents' devotion to driving kids from place to place, chaperoning, helping as coaches or counselors, and fixing meals are significant signs of their support and involvement in the church's ministry. Parents also play a major role in cultivating their children's faith and may welcome leaders' advice and help.

In effective junior high ministry, leaders *listen to parents' concerns,* acknowledge their importance, and keep them informed about junior high youth group activities. The ministry should provide a support network for parents, offering opportunities for them to talk about mutual concerns. Parents appreciate and need seminars, films, or discussion groups that affirm them in their God-given responsibilities. It is a special cause for celebration when the young people themselves plan an event to affirm the positive role parents play in their lives. For example, kids could plan, and pay for, a parents' night out to dinner. Or kids could plan a parents appreciation night and bestow awards such as "Most Patient Parent," "Best Listener" or "Most Giving."

Although there are times when teenagers do not welcome parental involvement, there are ways to bring the two groups together for their mutual benefit. Frequently this happens when parents and kids work side by side on a service project, or when they laugh, sing or play together in a relaxed setting. Overnight retreats or fun-in-the-sun days in the park are settings conducive to sharing and growth. Parents and junior highers will remember and cherish the special times spent together; the church should be one place where such experiences happen.

5. An effective junior high ministry provides for separate groups and activities from senior highers. Many youth leaders ask, "Is it possible to combine my senior high group with my junior high group?" The answer is, "It's possible, but it's best to keep them separate." The reason is junior highers are so different from senior highers in a variety of ways.

Physically junior highers are changing due to puberty; most senior highers are through the major changes and are becoming more comfortable with their bodies. *Intellectually* junior highers have a limited understanding of others; senior highers have a greater ability to see another's point of view. *Emotionally* junior highers experience wide mood swings; senior highers have more of an understanding of why they feel as they do. *Socially* junior highers are extremely sensitive to how others view them; senior highers are more self-assured in their self-identity.

In light of all these different needs and abilities, it's difficult for leaders to program for junior and senior highers together. One church offered a meeting on sexuality for both junior and senior highers. Kids were afraid to participate; nobody said a word. The junior highers were embarrassed to ask questions for fear of appearing "dumb" to the older kids; the older kids were hesitant to speak of feelings and experiences they felt the younger ones knew nothing about.

By having separate groups, leaders can plan more effective programs that focus on kids' specific needs. There is much more potential for growth because leaders can concentrate on individual kids and their individual concerns. Veteran youth worker Dub Ambrose says, "If junior and senior highers are grouped together, particularly when dealing with teenagers' major concerns, both age groups will suffer." Kids will be bored and won't receive the encouragement and support they need to grow.

Some churches and leaders feel they have no alternative but to join junior high with senior high. For example, the church may have few young people in the congregation, or the youth leader chooses to give only one night a week for the program.

Parents with both senior and junior highers might wish to make only one trip to the church. Whatever the reasons, following are some guidelines for combined junior and senior high groups:

● Allow junior highers as well as senior highers to be leaders. It may seem easier to allow the older kids to lead, but younger kids also have much to offer. Everyone's input is important.

● After a topic is presented, form discussion groups according to age level. Ask adult volunteers to help facilitate discussion within each group.

● Make sure volunteers know the difference between junior and senior highers so they won't have unrealistic expectations.

● Play games where everyone wins; where no one is the "laughed-at loser."

● Plan special events for each age group. For example, take the junior highers on a one-day hike and picnic; take senior highers on an afternoon bike trip across the city, stopping at various points of interest.

● Combine kids for other special events. Plan a dance, host a concert, invite a guest speaker, etc. You could plan these events with other churches. This allows for a larger attendance and helps kids meet others in the area.

If at all possible, separate junior highers from senior highers for a more effective ministry that is focused on kids' needs.

6. An effective junior high ministry articulates rules that kids appreciate and respect. Early adolescents, like all of us, need a sense of protection and security. Our society is based on certain codes of conduct designed for everyone's welfare. We feel threatened when such rules are violated, especially by people we trust.

Youth groups function much better when each participant understands what is expected of him or her. Kids interpret a lack of discipline as a sign that no one cares. Naturally, in any junior high group, certain kids will test the limits to see if the rules are enforced. Adult leaders need to be consistent. Knowing that some things will not be tolerated contributes to a sense of security. The failure of adults to carry out discipline communicates a message of inconsistency and apathy that is not conducive to a smooth-running program.

Often it is the way rules are presented that influences kids. All too often kids hear rules such as "Don't stand in the doorway," or "Don't decorate the fellowship room." A natural response to such directives is to do the opposite. State rules positively. Rather than saying, "Don't be rude to others" say, "Treat others the way you would like to be treated."

Junior high leaders should include the kids in setting standards of behavior and determining consequences for broken rules. When the young people help in the decision-making process, they feel better about the rules and they develop more self-discipline.

Letting the kids set clearly defined rules says a lot about your confidence in them to assume responsibility. This process may take a little longer, but the young people will grow closer as they struggle with issues such as what's important in the way they treat each other, how they feel about their group's reputation, their care and concern about safety matters, etc. Groups that care about each other are groups that others want to be part of.

7. An effective junior high ministry is guided by mature adults who are comfortable with young people and who are willing to explore sensitive issues with them. The primary task of adolescence is to gain independence (see Chapter 3). Adult leaders can help junior highers take their first steps toward independence from home by bridging the gap as a trusted friend.

The most effective adults in this role feel secure and comfortable with young people, are genuine, have a healthy self-esteem, and don't feel threatened by teenagers or feel the need to act like them. Junior highers can quickly spot someone who is not sincere. Open, honest, caring adults are the ones kids relate to and consider their friends.

Mature adults are excellent models for the maturing teenager. Mature adults realize teenagers need to talk about problems they face, no matter how small they seem. Sometimes kids test adults to see what their reaction will be before they will reveal the real problem. When kids know leaders will listen and respond honestly, they feel safe in discussing more sensitive issues.

Mature leaders recognize their limitations and know when to refer a problem to someone else. This means keeping a referral file and becoming knowledgeable about community-help organizations. Leaders can spot problems such as suicidal tendencies, alcoholism or drug abuse, then encourage and direct the young people to seek the proper professional help.

Knowing what is important to young people, how to communicate and how to earn their respect, makes adults an important part of their lives. Respect has to be earned; and that comes as leaders invest themselves in the group.

8. An effective junior high ministry includes time for laughter, joy and physical activity, as well as time for contemplation and opportunities to be alone. Junior high youth groups need a healthy balance between quiet times of self-reflection and fun activities. If a group only focuses on serious thinking and meditation, kids will become restless and bored. If a group only focuses on fun and games, kids will only develop surface relationships and experience little growth. Careful planning allows time for kids to seriously consider a topic or project, as well as time for the kids to relax and unwind.

Alert youth leaders also recognize the need for flexibility. We must constantly try to read the feelings of our group and respond accordingly. For example, a leader may plan 10 minutes for games, 20 minutes for lecture, 20 minutes for discussion, 10 minutes for refreshments. The kids may finish discussing the topic in 5 minutes. Rather than sticking to the schedule and struggling through 15 more minutes of discussion, the leader could gather everyone for a rowdy relay. Flexibility often makes a difference in the success of an event.

Junior highers become bored with programs and leaders who do not recognize the joy in life. Leaders who make mistakes need to laugh at themselves and tell jokes with the kids from time to time. Humor can be an effective teaching tool. A quick wit used in a positive way will make your times together much more enjoyable. Unfortunately, moments of joy, wholesome humor and excitement are much too rare in our Christian experience. Junior highers need to know that laughter is a significant part of our lives. Balance is the key when mixing all of these ingredients for a successful junior high program.

9. An effective junior high ministry encourages mutual acceptance and friendship among young people. Relationships play a powerful role in a young person's life, but they become exclusive when cliques are formed. Unlike a school setting, the church should be a haven where kids can test their behavior with others, and hopefully "be themselves." The church youth group contains a variety of kids the leader is expected to work with: athletic, non-athletic; musical, non-musical; outgoing, shy; etc. A variety of methods can be used to get the kids to think about relationships with people who are different from themselves. For example, discussions can focus on questions such as:

● What qualities do you look for in a friend?

● How do you want others to treat you?

● How do you feel when you are rejected?

● What does it mean to be accepted and loved unconditionally by God?

After such discussions, kids could write down the qualities of good friendships and review them from time to time as a self-evaluation.

A youth group that works hard on mutual acceptance and friendship will grow. Kids who feel welcome invite others to be a part of the group. This requires a basic trust among members, based on acceptance of the individual and a group's recognition that even though people are different in many ways, they have a lot in common. Junior highers especially identify with needs stemming from loneliness, poor self-image, and the need for acceptance. Caring adults help create a comfortable environment by their own acceptance and patience with everyone.

SECTION TWO

Effective Leadership

CHAPTER 5

CHARACTERISTICS OF AN EFFECTIVE LEADER

Effective junior high leaders all share some of the same characteristics. With desire, commitment and hard work, these characteristics can be developed—practical skills can be learned. By incorporating the following qualities into their leadership style, adults can be secure, confident and effective in their work with junior highers.

Effective Leaders Are Pastoral

Frequently we overlook a key factor when staffing our junior high ministry: the importance of basing relationships on biblical principles. Churches shouldn't assume that just because they have hired a staff person or have recruited a volunteer, that they automatically have strong, biblical-based leadership. Because junior highers are so impressionable, it is extremely important to fill the position with the right person.

There is more to filling this position than writing a job description or filling an empty office. We must develop and abide by a basic Christian leadership philosophy: Effective leaders are *pastoral.*

Both the Old and New Testaments use the shepherd to portray God's steadfast love for his people. The word "pastor" comes from the Latin, meaning shepherd. Its metaphor is applied to the kind of responsibility given to all who are a part of the Christian community (1 Peter 5:2-3).

I once was a member of a church staff which strongly emphasized that all people, including office secretaries, building custodians, clergy and program directors, were to think of their relationship with others from a pastoral perspective. Each person viewed his or her task as an opportunity to care for people, just as a shepherd cares for his or her sheep. There was no concern for rank or status when it came to ministering. An envelope was addressed with as much care and concern as a prayer was offered by a hospital bed. The church custodian made it a point to know the names of the church nursery school children and followed their lives once the school year was over. As the kids grew older, they continued to enjoy visiting with the custodian. It was something very special to observe.

The shepherd image has great meaning for adult leaders. From biblical times to the present, the shepherd's role has been to meet the needs of those placed in his or her care. The Bible contrasts the characteristics of good and bad shepherds. Ezekiel compares the good shepherd who was concerned for his flock's welfare to the shepherd whose only concern was personal gain (Ezekiel 34). In John, Jesus contrasts the characteristics of a shepherd who loved his sheep to a hireling who cared nothing for the sheep (John 10). Pastoral leadership is modeled after Jesus, the Good Shepherd. Following are three characteristics, distinctive of pastoral leadership:

1. Shepherds know their sheep by name. Because shepherds spend a great deal of time with their flocks, a special intimacy develops between them. There are times when the two are inseparable.

To the casual observer, the sheep may all look alike, but

shepherds know each sheep by name and distinguishing marks and characteristics; they can identify one sheep in an entire flock. Likewise, the sheep will only respond to their shepherd's voice. Others may try to lead the sheep away from the pack, but they will not follow.

Knowing junior highers by name is the first step in building close, personal relationships. Once we call someone by name, we acknowledge his or her existence. We feel like we matter when someone calls us by name.

Let kids discuss the importance of names and personal relationships by asking these questions:

● What does a name tell you about a person?
● Is your name part of your identity?
● Are you known by any other name? Explain.
● Do you know why your parents chose your name? If so, explain.
● How do you feel about your name?
● Do you know what your name means? Explain.
● What do your friends call you?
● How do you feel about the nicknames your friends have given you?
● Would you change your legal name if you could? If so, to what, and why?
● How does a person make his or her name important to others? Does it have anything to do with character?

Discussing such questions reveals many concerns junior highers have about themselves. Careful listeners will detect how the kids perceive themselves, how they project their image to others, how they feel their peers and adults picture them, what they hope for, and the importance their faith plays in shaping self-concept.

Intimate relationships take time. Leaders who develop a level of trust do so by investing time in young people. A pastoral concern means spending time at school events, learning about each teenager's home life, what kind of things the kids do in the community, talking to them about spiritual questions, sharing in their dreams, having an awareness of their social and physical needs. Pastoral concern comes from expressing empathy, being honest, unconditionally loving the kids, being available when they have a need (never too busy to talk), being respectful (even during disagreements), trying to be understanding by looking for the motives behind their behavior, and trying to learn about their world (listening to their music, watching their movies and television shows, reading their magazines and books).

Young people open up when they know they are respected and taken seriously. Leaders who communicate this respect and interest find themselves on the receiving end of raw emotions and endless questions. Such sharing will never take place outside an environment of trust. Most of us wait to reveal deep needs or hurts until we have confidence in the person with whom we are sharing such feelings with. We must trust that he or she will handle our feelings with care.

2. Shepherds lead their sheep. A shepherd is the strong and courageous figure at the head of the flock whose main concern is for those entrusted to his or her care. A shepherd pays attention to each individual within the fold, and feels a sense of responsibility for the whole group. A shepherd instinctively knows when something is wrong and takes the necessary precautions to provide protection. Much of what a shepherd knows has been learned on the job. He or she is knowledgeable of the grazing areas and, when water and shelter are needed, the shepherd finds it. If the task is more than the shepherd can handle, he or she asks for help. As an old Scottish preacher once depicted the shepherd in a sermon based on Psalm 23, "The Lord is my shepherd . . . aye, and more than that, he has two fine collie dogs, goodness and mercy." A shepherd is not hesitant to use the tools of his or her trade, the rod and staff, to guide the sheep or assist them along the way.

Leaders need to know where they are going and need to develop a plan for where they want to go with their group. (A shepherd can only go as far as his or her sheep can walk.) Goals must be realistic and attainable. Leaders cannot expect to accomplish something their group is incapable of doing.

Experienced junior high leaders have learned that certain leadership methods are effective, depending on the abilities of those in the group. A working knowledge of different techniques is important. The leader is then able to determine which method is appropriate for which circumstance. There are times when he or she may need to exercise a lot of control, while on other occasions a "wait-and-see" approach would be more effective.

Following are some examples of leadership methods:

● *Total Control*—Leader takes complete charge of the youth group, makes all decisions, and sets the rules. Young people have no say in any matters related to their welfare. Leader plans all programs and comes up with the solutions to all problems.

● *Chief Planner*—Leader determines the direction the group will take and suggests a number of possibilities. The group is permitted to discuss things, but the leader ultimately controls what will happen.

● *Consultant*—Leader determines the guidelines within which the group functions. The group is allowed to make decisions, except when the adult knows best. The leader consults with the group to get reactions to ideas before making decisions.

● *One voice, one vote*—Leader permits young people to practice the democratic process to determine the program or activities. Leader helps the group members examine courses of action and consequences; and, without influencing their thinking, permits rule by consensus in all matters.

● *Wait and see*—Leader takes a wait-and-see stance, letting junior high members make all decisions and do whatever they choose. No direction is provided, which ultimately results in the group members selecting their own leaders.

Although it is unlikely that we would adopt only one of these styles and use it to handle every situation, it is helpful for us to know these styles and use them in the appropriate situations.

Being a leader entails physical involvement. That means developing the stamina to work alongside the group and to battle against discouragement. Being theologically knowledgeable helps, but a strong faith that is nurtured through prayer and community will provide the inner strength to survive the tough times. Persistence in staying with the group through difficult times affirms to the kids the leader's depth of commitment.

Pastoral leaders are compassionate, sensitive and tender,

yet tough. They recognize when a member of their flock is vulnerable or needs help to heal a hurt. Junior highers feel secure in such a leader's care.

Pastoral leaders do not let their group scatter. They notice when someone is missing, and make a determined effort to keep close. They nurture interpersonal relationships in order to create a sense of community. When done with a sincere heart, young people will feel warmth, acceptance and understanding that makes them want to belong to such a group.

3. Shepherds nourish their sheep by moving them to new pastures. Nothing lasts forever. A good grazing pasture, once it has been worked over, holds little nourishment. It is the shepherd's task to find a fresh supply of food and water, keeping the flock on the move. It's moving on to new places, in search of the basic necessities, that sustains growth.

Leaders find themselves trapped from time to time copying other groups' programs. They read of a junior high group that successfully held an unusual event and immediately they imagine how fun it would be to do the same thing with their group. Chances are, expectations such as these will lead to disappointment if the group isn't ready or able to handle such a program. What is good for one group may not be good for another.

Leaders can get in a programming rut by constantly duplicating what others have done, or by continuing to do the same old thing that's been done for years, rather than looking at the specific needs of their group. Tailoring events to meet the specific needs of a junior high group will greatly improve the ministry.

Pastoral care of a junior high group requires constant evaluation and feedback from the kids. Perhaps the kids will sit down with the leader and talk about an event, or a written assessment might be more appropriate. It is always good to evaluate an activity with the group, asking such questions as:

● What did you like about the activity?
● How could we have improved it?
● What should the group plan to do next as a result of what we've learned?

Evaluation should be a natural part of any leader's work with young people. Evaluation works best as an ongoing process of group dynamics, especially if there are predetermined areas of concern. When kids are asked to share their feelings about an activity, they know their opinions are respected and that the leader has a strong desire to make the group's time together meaningful. (See Chapter 8 for more details on evaluations.)

Evaluations help you know when your group is ready to move on to greener pastures. Evaluations indicate when your group is ready to try something a bit more challenging, something that takes more effort. Leaders see these opportunities as healthy learning experiences. Like a shepherd who leads the flock to new grazing land, there is an element of risk involved. It takes courage to venture into unfamiliar territory.

Moving ahead also means the leader is committed to staying with the group. It is a sign he or she cares and is willing to stick with the group. Junior highers will be eager to try new ideas if they feel comfortable and secure with their leader. They will not be afraid of failure, because effective leaders can turn failures into positive learning experiences. For a leader to be able to express God's steadfast love, he or she must possess integrity; a strong faith and trust in God; and a constant, invincible love for young people.

Effective Leaders Are Good Listeners

It is essential that junior high leaders know how to listen. Listening is an important aspect in building quality relationships with young people. A good listener begins with a healthy attitude that says, "These young people are important. The kids each have something important to say and I can learn from them if I listen. I may need to concentrate and must try not to overreact if I disagree with what they say. What's important is to understand what each person is saying and feeling."

There is a vast difference between listening and hearing. Listening is not merely hearing the words and being able to repeat, verbatim, what's been spoken. Listening takes concentration. It is the ability to relate to the other person, to try to experience what he or she is feeling, to be conscious of the emphasis he or she puts on certain words or ideas, to help the person interpret what he or she is trying to communicate, to make certain there has been no misunderstanding in what's been said. Listening requires a *desire* to listen. It involves putting aside our own concerns and anxieties and giving others our full attention.

We all value good listeners. Our self-esteem grows when we know someone cares enough to listen to our feelings or opinions. Young people often define a good leader as someone who lets them express what they think and feel, without putting them down. Somehow, we must open the doors of expression. Much of getting young people to talk depends on the questions asked.

There are four kinds of questions: closed, open, informational and feeling. *Closed questions* are the kind that can be answered with a simple yes or no. (Do you like to swim? Did you start swimming this year?) *Open questions* ask for an opinion or explanation, which encourage the person to talk. (Why do you like to swim? What was the funniest thing that ever happened to you in a swimming pool?) *Informational questions* lead to specific answers, but have a limited response. (When did you start swimming?) *Feeling questions* focus on emotional reactions or ideas that stimulate further conversation. (How do you feel about going to swimming practice before school while all your friends are home in bed sleeping?) A good listener asks good questions. There are six words Rudyard Kipling wrote about in the following poem that help us ask good questions:

> *I keep six honest serving men,*
> *(They taught me all I knew)*
> *Their names are What and Why and When*
> *And How and Where and Who.*

Informational and closed questions are effective when beginning a conversation with a shy or withdrawn person. Once the climate has "warmed up," open-ended questions can be asked. Many adults don't like to ask feeling or open-ended questions for fear of prying. The truth of the matter is, early adolescents are anxious to have someone show an interest in them. Unfortunately, most of us are programmed to ask only informational or closed questions, which don't tell us much about how others are feeling. Knowing how to ask these four types of questions is a skill leaders should acquire that will facilitate conversations expressing care and warmth. Following are open-ended questions that encourage people to talk:

- How do you feel about . . .
- What do you think about . . .
- How would you change . . .
- What do you like most about . . .
- What kinds of . . .
- What was your experience like . . .

Frequently, a person offers unsolicited information when answering a question. Good listeners pick up on this. Being alert can lead to discussing problems that are really bothering someone or uncovering a need that requires special attention.

What kinds of questions do you feel most comfortable with? Look over the following list. Some of the questions are good, some are poor. Put a check next to the ones you consider good.

```
_____  1. Did you have a good day?
_____  2. How do you feel about this?
_____  3. Do you like your work?
_____  4. Do you have any ideas on the subject?
_____  5. Oh, really?
_____  6. Would you explain this to me?
_____  7. Will you accept the new offer?
_____  8. What is your reaction to this situation?
_____  9. Do you love me?
_____ 10. What is your opinion on the subject?
```

Questions 1, 3, 5, 7 and 9 are poor because they can be answered with a yes or no. Questions 2, 4, 6, 8 and 10 are better because they will stimulate further conversation.[1]

Harry Emerson Fosdick, celebrated pastor of Riverside Church in New York City during the 1930s and 1940s, was asked the secret of posing a good question. His reply was, "I suppose the secret . . . is to realize that questioning and listening are inseparable. The asking of good questions represents listening at its highest level and that, of course, can never be faked or turned on—it must come from within. I believe it's the quality of attention that makes all the difference."[2]

John Drakeford, in *The Awesome Power of the Listening Heart*, says that listening involves more than just our ears. It is a multisensory experience, focusing on the whole person who is talking. Leaders who want to listen effectively to junior highers will do so using all of their senses.

1. Good listeners use their eyes. We can learn many things by watching people as they talk. People reveal a great deal about themselves by the way they dress (neat, sloppy, expensive, modest, flashy), by the way they act (confident, insecure, belligerent, courteous), by their posture (tense, slouched, erect, fidgety), and by their eyes (shifty, worried, intense, sad, narrow, wide, sparkling, dazed).

Eye contact tells people we are paying attention. A deliberate wink silently confirms that we understand what others are saying.

2. Good listeners use their ears. Noise pollution has taken a toll on our delicate hearing systems. For example, many specialists report that years of listening to electronically amplified rock music may result in an early hearing loss. A very real possibility exists that when we say something, kids won't hear us, either because of the irritating sounds of traffic outside the window, or the music blaring through their Walkmans.

There are several other elements that distort our hearing: not communicating accurately, using the wrong words to describe feelings, placing emphasis on the wrong things, interference of background noise, and the inability of the listener to grasp what is being said.

Ear-listening requires that a person ask questions such as:

● Can I summarize in one sentence what someone is trying to tell me?

● Do I understand the words the person is using? What do the words being used mean to the person talking? (Interrupting to ask, "What do you mean?" isn't rude, but shows your genuine desire to understand what someone is saying.)

● What things keep me from concentrating on the other person? Could it be I have a hearing impairment?

● How hard do I try to understand what the person is expressing?

3. Good listeners use their heads. Sitting like a motionless lump while someone is trying to talk to you, does little to motivate that person to tell you more. The way we move and hold our heads conveys how involved we are in what is being said.

Studies show that the angle at which we hold our head indicates how closely we are listening. The head held in a slightly tilted position is often the sign of a good listener. Nodding the head indicates attention is being paid; it signals that the listener is alert, involved and caring.

The way we touch our head with our hands also can reveal whether or not we're listening. For example, listeners who close or roll their eyes and place their head in their palm, give the impression of extreme boredom. Stroking the chin can send a positive message of reflective listening.

4. Good listeners use their hands. The rapidly moving fingers of someone signing to the deaf demonstrate how hands can be used to communicate nonverbal messages. Not so obvious is our informal system of gestures. In our society, applause is used as a means to communicate approval and appreciation. In India, people put their hands together in a prayer position to express a warm greeting. Nonverbal messages are delivered by the way people straighten their ties, play with their glasses, adjust their belts, or bite their fingernails.

John Drakeford relates the story of a woman who poured out her story to him. He never said a word as she told about her experiences. Finally she stopped and asked, "What do you think of that?" He looked at her for a moment, then pinched his nose between his thumb and index finger. That gesture communicated precisely and simply what any number of words could not.

The use of hands in listening leads us to consider the often neglected and misunderstood use of *touch*. Touching is a sign of acceptance. Holding a person's hand while he or she talks can reassure and indicate to the person he or she is not alone.

Once someone has shared his or her struggle or pain, a hug, a hand on his or her shoulder, or an arm around him or her during prayer will clearly signal interest and concern.

Using our hands often can communicate more than words. Junior highers who feel rejected, unlovable, awkward, misunderstood or ugly, particularly need to be touched while they pour out their troubles. Telling people we care for them seems shallow; we also must show them.

5. Good listeners use their bodies. Our efforts to convince someone we are listening will be fruitless if our *body language* tells them we are not. Leaning toward the speaker is a good example of body language. It tells the speaker we are genuinely interested. Leaders who lean back in a chair, with legs crossed and both hands clasped behind their head, convey an attitude of superiority or authority. The leader who smiles and conveys warmth is the kind of person junior highers want to get to know. If kids perceive an adult to be sullen or somber, they won't open up.

More than anything else, the kind of listeners we are will determine the kind of confidence or trust junior highers place in our hands. Our listening skills will determine the degree of influence we have on the kids. Their overall perception of us stems from how well they feel we listen to them.

It's not impossible to be a good listener. With patience and determination, the skill can be mastered. One of the difficulties youth workers experience at first is what to do in those awkward moments of silence. Silence calls for special listening techniques. Don't force it. If there are moments of silence in a conversation with someone, listen! Silence sends messages, too. For example, there is the sulking person's *silence of withdrawal*. It's used as an emotional curtain to separate two people. The silence of withdrawal says, "I'll wear you down by refusing to talk."

Defiant silence comes from people who dare you to relate to them in any way. The defiant, silent person is determined to sidestep any effort you make; reaching out to them is like trying to hit a moving target. These people usually are so angry they will do anything to prove they don't need you.

The *silence of rebuke* is used to get someone's attention by making him or her feel uncomfortable. A teenager who does not appreciate the way he or she is being treated may decide to show displeasure by refusing to communicate.

Creative silence is used to think and reflect. Like any creative activity, this kind of silence requires self-control and a lot of practice. For many of us, 10 seconds of silence can seem like an eternity. But a good listener allows silence to run its course because the other person needs time to think before responding. Waiting patiently during such silence communicates, "Because of my interest in you, I'm willing to sit in silence as you wrestle with deep thoughts. I care." Anxious adults who feel uncomfortable with silence often interfere with the reflective thought process, or unwittingly impede the young person building up the courage to express himself or herself. A person needs quiet time in which to think.[3]

Believe it or not, junior highers can tell if we're genuinely listening and concentrating on what they are saying. In order to master the skill of listening, we must learn that there are certain deterrents to conversation, for example:

● Fixation on detail—We gain a better understanding of a situation if we are given some background information, but we do kids a disservice if we are picky and insist on precise details. Asking for every minute detail not only is annoying, but so frustrating that conversations usually end quickly.

● Assuming what a junior higher is going to say before it is said—Some people don't let others complete a sentence. Whether it's motivated by an eagerness to show how much they want to help, or whether it's a subtle way of stating they know what the person is talking about, it's rude. As soon as the conversation begins, no matter what the subject, the "assumer" interrupts. It is impolite to interrupt a person to begin with, let alone trying to outguess what he or she is trying to say. None of us appreciates being around people who put words in our mouth, especially the wrong words. Constantly cutting someone off eventually does just that.

● Persistent questioning—The "fact finder" slows down any conversation. Imagine how a junior higher, eager to share his or her excitement after winning a prize at the science fair, feels when the conversation is bogged down with rapid-fire questions: "Where was the fair? How many entries were there? Did they have refreshments? Were parents invited? Who were the judges? Was the room nicely decorated? Who announced the winners—the principal?" Etc., etc. Kids seldom want to tell about something special in their lives if someone relentlessly quizzes them.

● *Daydreams*—A good listener doesn't make side trips or allow his or her mind to wander while someone else is talking. Have you ever been talking to someone on the phone and you just *know* that person was going through mail, sorting through things, or paying attention to someone else in the room? Even without seeing someone, you can sense if he or she is really listening to you or is mentally wandering. Junior highers also can sense such signals.

How many times have you asked yourself, "What kind of a listener am I?" Periodically checking on how you come across as a listener can be a helpful exercise to improve your ability to relate to young people. For example, do you ever ask people if they know you are genuinely interested in them? Do you try to put yourself in the other person's shoes when he or she talks? Do you try to pick up hidden feelings? Do you find your own emotions interfering with what someone else is expressing? Do you find yourself making prejudgments? Do you make an effort to summarize what someone is telling you? Can you avoid the impulse to interrupt and complete another's sentences? Do you listen to others the way you'd like them to listen to you?[4]

Here's a case study from an article in GROUP Magazine that is helpful in determining the kind of listener you are. Which response best fits the way you would handle this situation?

> Lori has a problem and seeks you out when you're alone. She says, "You wouldn't believe what a rotten day I had at school. Everything seemed to go wrong—that place stinks. I studied hard for the test today and this teacher switched the rules and tested us on stuff he must have covered last Wednesday, the only day of school I've missed all year. I'm so fed up I'd just as soon drop out of school."

Now think for a moment. What is it Lori needs to hear from someone? Which response is that of an effective listener, the kind of person kids relate to?

ADULT #1

"I don't blame you for being upset, but that's the way it is in real life. I know just how you feel. Last month I thought everything was falling apart in my office. Just when I had my final report ready for my boss, he switched the rules on me. Here's what happened to me . . ."

ADULT #2

"Come on, don't let it get you down. Your grades have been decent enough in the past to pull you through. If not, you can take charge of the situation the rest of the year and get your grades up. Don't let situations like that get the best of you. Remember, every one of those teachers has your best interests at heart."

ADULT #3

"How come you signed up for that math course anyway? I remember once before you told me how hard math was for you." (Pause—adult walks over to the small stack of mail.) *"I'm looking for the tickets to tomorrow night's ball game. My friend and I are going—should be a good game. Oh, what did this teacher do that bugged you so much?"*

ADULT #4

"Sounds like you really had a rough day. Care to tell me more about it?"

If you were this young person, with a need to talk about your problem, which response would be most helpful to you? Which would be least helpful? Rank them from best to worst: 1 = best, 2 = next best, etc.

Here's what happens in each response:

Adult #1: Shifts the focus to self rather than recognizing Lori's needs. Seems sympathetic, but detracts from what Lori wants to talk about. Adult #1 is an ineffective listener—blowing it when given a chance to listen. This listening style says, "I can top that!"

Adult #2: Like Adult #1, Adult #2's intentions are good, but he or she is doing a poor job of listening. Talks a lot and likes to tell others what to do. Is an expert at giving advice Lori hasn't even asked for. A great moralizer, usually a judgmental person, often interrupts the person talking with, "Yes, but . . ."

Adult #3: Is disinterested and apparently ignoring the fact that Lori has a deep concern. Steps away from Lori and loses eye contact. Thinks he or she is listening, but Lori is convinced otherwise. This person comes across as non-caring by "listening with half an ear" (maybe less).

Adult #4: Immediately focuses on Lori and tunes in to her feelings. Has begun a listening process, demonstrating an interest in what Lori is saying and feeling. This adult is a listener who recognizes Lori's need to talk and provides that opportunity for her. This adult will continue to focus on Lori, putting aside his or her own needs in order to listen to Lori and try to understand what she is experiencing. This is "listening with the heart." Adult #4 is opening communication with Lori by drawing her out and inviting her to talk—and then by being a sensitive and interested listener. He or she will do this by:
- Focusing on what Lori is saying
- Responding to Lori's feelings
- Having eye-to-eye contact (but not a staring contest)
- Not dominating the conversation
- Not judging or moralizing with little lectures
- Giving little or no advice (unless asked for; and then, cautiously)
- Showing acceptance and understanding
- Responding with an occasional nod, smile, etc.
- Watching and listening for nonverbal communication—tone of voice, increase in volume, facial expression and body language (80 to 90 percent of the message is

nonverbal).[5]

Effective listeners can be *trusted*. This means not only is the person someone who listens, but someone who can discern what needs to be kept confidential. An awareness of what is privileged communication between two people and respecting the trust it implies, spells the difference between an honest relationship and a superficial one.

Junior highers, like adults, proceed cautiously in revealing things about themselves. Kids often will begin discussing a subject different from the true issue to test the listener. If they receive a warm, genuine response, chances are they'll feel secure enough to talk about sensitive or troubling concerns. They will openly discuss things they are experiencing, thinking, feeling and questioning. The same pattern holds true in group conversations. Whatever the topic of discussion, the members may begin with socially accepted responses, or what they perceive to be expected, before divulging what they really think. In this way they test the water.

Personal, sometimes embarrassing, information that is shared or learned in group discussions should be kept confidential by all members. If kids find out their peers or adult leaders are gossiping about them, they are less likely to be open and trusting. Honoring an individual's or group's confidence is an awesome responsibility. You'll never have to worry about your relationship with junior highers if they know you can be trusted.

It's natural for us to talk about the exciting activities of the group, how pleased we are with the way a certain project or program went, or how happy we are about the way people are relating to each other. However, this is when we are most prone to break a confidence. What the group is doing, learning, or celebrating can be shared, but private conversations should be kept confidential.

Keeping a confidence is not to imply that an exchange of ideas or points of view never takes place. Quite the contrary. As an active listener, the leader is deeply involved in the experiences and feelings of individuals in the youth group. But, effective listeners realize that some things are not to be repeated. It is better to err by saying too little rather than by saying too much. Once a confidence is broken, it can never be restored.

The first and foremost way of letting junior highers know we care about them is to listen. The more we listen, the more the kids will want to be around us.

Effective Leaders
Have an Enthusiastic, Positive Attitude

Junior high young people are full of energy; they like people who are exciting and who respond to action-packed events. They will get as excited about the program as the adults who lead it. If the leader is dull, tired and indifferent, the junior highers will spot it in a minute. We truly get back from kids what we give them. Enthusiasm breeds enthusiasm.

One of the highest compliments a leader can receive is "He believes in what he does." Or, "She gives the ministry 100 percent!" Kids like to be around leaders who are alive, energetic, enthusiastic, and who zealously include everyone in the activities. The leader's mood definitely impacts a group. If a leader does not enjoy the activities, the kids won't either. A positive attitude means being eager to move forward and committed to making the most of every situation.

One very real problem in many churches is the lack of resources, facilities and support. Many leaders use such conditions as excuses to fail. Junior high leaders who want to succeed in junior high ministry overcome adversities. Problems are only those things we allow to be problems. Overcome a lack of resources by relying on church members to lead meetings. Overcome a lack of facilities by rotating meetings to different members' homes. Have the hosts be in charge of refreshments. Overcome a lack of support by involving church members and parents. Publicize junior high activities, and have the junior highers sponsor all-church events such as a summer picnic or a winter carnival. Thinking positively means not using the word impossible, but dreaming of things to accomplish with the group, and then making them happen.

Wanting to make the most of every situation is the mind-set

of an effective leader. A positive attitude enables leaders to look at the good in every situation and see the chance to work constructively through every problem.

Effective Leaders Have Integrity, Courage and Dedication

Sometimes a junior high leader is faced with a situation where he or she must take a stand. By nature, young people put adults to the test, but there are times when a leader must draw the line because of what he or she believes is ethical or truthful. Such stances may not be popular to take with the young people. For example, young people have a way of attacking their peers' weaknesses. They will pick on someone because of a handicap, personal appearance or social standing. The leader may be tempted to ignore it, but when he or she takes a stand and displays integrity by explaining why such treatment of others is wrong, respect for the leader will be gained.

Junior high leaders who possess integrity and courage are considerate of the needs of others, don't feel the need to play favorites, are not afraid of a challenge, and take a positive approach to pursue their goals. Integrity means people are the same, no matter who they are with. Such consistency is a key to achieving open, trusting, relationships with this age group.

One thing that turns off young people faster than anything is someone who is a phoney. They can spot an impostor a mile away. Effective leaders don't dress differently to impress the kids or use language that is not part of their normal vocabulary.

Effective, dedicated leaders are an inspiration to be around. These leaders have a strong faith, a sense of commitment to the church, a deep relationship with Jesus Christ, and a genuine love for young people. They can guide and influence others to commit their lives to a higher purpose. Dedicated leaders are committed to the principle that each young person possesses a potential that needs to be nurtured. They take a personal interest in each individual as a child of God.

Dedicated leaders see themselves set apart for a special

purpose and look upon their relationship with teenagers as something to treasure. They treat those with whom they work with respect and affection, and eagerly anticipate each occasion they have to be together.

Effective Leaders Are Cooperative and Organized

One of the secrets to getting along with others is learning to be flexible. There is no room in junior high ministry for people who insist that things always be done their way. Nothing can kill a group quicker than a lack of tolerance for ideas, suggestions or offers of help.

The ability to adjust to the needs of others is an indication the leader is listening and is perceptive to the feelings of the group. Leaders who have a sense of cooperation soon find themselves surrounded by people who want to work with them toward a common goal. Young people love to feel they are a part of what is going on; and having a leader who is flexible and receptive to their input creates an atmosphere of community.

An effective leader capitalizes on cooperation and involves others in the ministry. One persistent complaint of youth leaders is their lack of enough time to get everything done. Allowing others to help is half the battle; deciding what it is you want to do and setting up a plan to accomplish your goal is the other half. (See Chapter 8 for more details of a master plan and goals.) An organized leader keeps the total picture in mind while systematically establishing a pattern by which a task is to be completed.

Successful business managers' motto is "Plan your work and work your plan." They have learned that their work environment is more pleasant when they know what they are going to do and how they are going to do it. Included in such time management is allotting time for adjustments, changes and emergencies so discouragement and frustration are done away with.

An organized junior high leader knows how to design and implement a project. If that means working with others, the plan includes doing things in a harmonious and united way that is orderly and effective. Such a climate is preferable to one in which the leader is painfully trying to do it all alone.

Effective Leaders
Love Kids and Show Their Appreciation

When people feel needed and appreciated, they willingly help; when people feel taken for granted, their enthusiasm dwindles and their involvement disintegrates.

Saying thank you is a simple thing to do and it reflects good manners. Such gestures may ensure additional help and support from people whose gifts and skills add a great deal to our ministry.

Being a grateful leader is being a good role model for young people. Teenagers need to see others being shown appreciation, as well as themselves.

Junior high young people crave affirmation. Affirmation is a vital link to their self-worth. There are occasions when it is appropriate to applaud someone for his or her efforts, but to express approval to an adolescent at a time he or she leasts expects it, makes a lasting impression.

Many adolescents feel inferior, unattractive, inadequate, worthless or unloved. Such a self-image often makes a person turn inward and become angry. Distress over personal faults, lack of self-confidence, anxiety over relating to the opposite sex, poor relationships with significant adults (especially parents), and anxiety about faith, can have a devastating effect on a young person's ability to function. Junior highers who lack self-confidence will not attempt any activity which they might fail. Adolescents with low self-esteem have difficulty perceiving God as a loving and accepting person.[6]

Leaders who are loving, caring and accepting model a God who is loving, caring and accepting. Youth leaders who develop the habit of regularly expressing approval and love soon discover a positive atmosphere permeating the youth group. Messages of love and acceptance not only develop self-esteem, but also make reprimanding messages more meaningful. Individuals who know they are loved can accept discipline without feeling threatened or the need to exhibit more negative, attention-getting behavior.

Youth leaders can improve kids' self-images by complimenting their appearance, applauding a kind gesture, encouraging a courageous stand, or praising the sharing of a talent or of time.

I remember one weekend when we were discussing love and sex with senior highers. The members were asked to talk about body image and how they viewed themselves. One of the more attractive girls described herself as fat and ugly. "You mean you used to be fat and ugly?" one of the other kids asked.

"No, that's how I see myself," she replied.

If anything, the young girl was underweight and had a beautiful complexion. Why then, did she perceive herself that way?

It turned out that when she was in seventh grade she was unattractive. Her friends, parents, brothers and sisters made fun of her physical appearance. That experience was planted in her memory and no one had ever bothered to change the way she felt about herself. Unnecessary, low self-images, such as this girl had, are very common in young people.

We can bring out the best in others by affirming them and by letting them know we believe in them. We can make a difference by believing in their potential. Most of us, at one point in our lives, have been fortunate enough to have someone who took a special interest in who we were—often overlooking the stupid or foolish things we did, and found in us what no one else had made the effort to see. Our young people may not remember every youth group meeting or every serious talk, but they will remember our affirmation and belief in them for years to come.

CHAPTER 6

DEVELOPING VOLUNTEERS

There is no such thing as a solo act in junior high ministry; a variety of adults is needed to ensure quality and quantity. Although none of us possess all the qualities that constitute the ultimate leadership model, each of us has qualities to contribute. Put us all together, and we make a great team!

Most of us find we work better as a team. Many aspects of youth ministry cannot be accomplished without help. Several adults working together can not only be fun, but beneficial to teenagers. Junior highers should be exposed to a variety of personalities, to people who are committed to one harmonious relationship—blending the best of their talents. This is what being part of the body of Christ is all about.

Many people believe that effective youth leaders have to be in their early twenties or younger, single (or married to an attractive mate), a super guitar player or musician, and have the most fashionable material possessions (nice home, fancy car,

VCR, elaborate stereo system, stylish clothing, etc.). Although this type of person appeals to junior highers, and presumedly understands their culture and struggles, these stereotype qualities should not be the basis for recruitment. Young people need to relate to adults for reasons other than good looks, personality or wealth.

In my own experience, I've found that young people feel most secure with someone over 35 years of age when they need help. Similar conclusions have been reached from research done in areas of faith development. These studies show that a number of years need to pass between youth and adulthood to gain a perspective of life and develop faith. This is not to say that a junior high leader must be over 35 to be effective. What it does say is that there is no perfect age or type of person for junior high ministry. There may be certain characteristics that make a ministry more meaningful, but the optimal situation is one that balances ages and styles of leadership.

Ultimately, those responsible for working with junior highers will recognize the need for helping hands. In 99 percent of the cases, this means recruiting volunteers. The more people involved in making junior high ministry happen, the more kids who will be affected. Each of us knows our limitations in terms of time and ability to personally reach the kids in our ministry. Our efforts increase only as we link heart and hand in a spirit of mutual ministry.

Obstacles to Recruiting Volunteers

Working with a team of volunteers makes youth work much more enjoyable, yet many full-time leaders fail to seek help. Following are some recruiting obstacles that need to be overcome:

1. Insecurity. Many youth leaders feel good about themselves only if they are busy. Their self-esteem is founded on their performance. Sharing the spotlight can be a threat. Leaders who lack self-confidence fear that people will think they aren't doing their job if they ask for help. Lack of self-confidence makes it difficult for such people to trust volunteers. Some leaders worry they won't be able to dominate volunteers the way they do the kids. Such concerns stem from a fear of exposing weaknesses and of being observed by others. When such attitudes prevail, it is difficult to build a team with any sense of togetherness or trust. Yet the fact remains: Teamwork enhances a junior high ministry. Youth leaders are more effective when they have the help of volunteers.

2. Fear of imposing on others. Many leaders fail to ask for help because they don't want to impose on others. This assumption can result in many willing adults feeling unwanted. We should never conclude that someone is too busy to be involved unless we ask. How many times have you experienced sitting in a group when a name is mentioned and someone automatically says, "She's too busy." Often we don't ask for help because we fear rejection. Remember: The person we'd like to work with might have a valid reason for not being available; we'll never know until we ask.

3. Pride. Junior high ministry is especially frustrating because little recognition is given to its leaders. This is due in part to the nature of early adolescents, but also in part to our need for affirmation. In order to keep good volunteers, we need to affirm efforts.

Recently, I talked with a young woman who had always dreamed of entering youth ministry full time. After a year of full-time youth work, she couldn't wait to quit because of her relationship with the youth director. He assigned her menial tasks, set project deadlines, and then signed his name and took credit for all of her work. You can imagine her frustration from lack of recognition. Full-time youth leaders' egos often keep them from recruiting and using great volunteers. They feel threatened working with someone the kids really like. In this situation, helpers are frequently restricted to mechanical tasks because their gifts threaten the youth leaders. Until leaders feel positive about themselves, little harmony will exist between leader and volunteers.

An unhealthy pride also can cause leaders to think that they are indispensable. They find it difficult to admit someone else has a great idea (maybe even a better one); someone else can organize an event; someone else can think, create and produce exciting experiences on their own. Therefore, some full-time youth leaders are reluctant to allow volunteers to be creative, make decisions or function without supervision.

4. Lack of vision. Many junior high leaders lack vision; they focus only on the present. Little attention is given to long-range goals or master plans. Getting the job done and maintaining the daily or weekly routine occupy all the leader's time to the point they say they don't have time to enlist additional help. Without a sense of vision, of expanding opportunities to meet the needs of young people, little is accomplished. Leaders must dream of exciting possibilities, open the door to others, and involve them in making those dreams happen.

5. Inability to plan. Volunteers quickly sense if their talents are needed and their contributions significant. Youth leaders need clearly defined objectives and reasons why helping hands are needed. Likewise, they need a written plan stating how volunteers are to function and how they will be recognized, encouraged and evaluated. This is especially important in working with junior highers since visible results and affirmation from the kids are rare.

6. Lack of time and energy. Time and energy are necessary to train and develop an effective ministry team. Many leaders do not know how to train volunteers; as a result, they are reluctant to recruit anyone. Knowing help is needed is one thing, but knowing how to recruit, train and keep volunteers is another. Feelings of inadequacy or time constraints can only cripple a youth leader's effectiveness in the recruiting process.

Successfully Recruiting Volunteers

Even though the traditional pool of volunteers is not what it once was (with both parents working), people will still make time to do the things they feel are important. A basic human need is to feel wanted and feel we can make a difference. People volunteer when they feel needed. People volunteer when they see an opportunity to learn new skills or to use the ones they already possess. Volunteers seek places where a spirit of caring community exists and where they feel accepted. This environment contributes to their self-esteem and their need for affirmation. Sometimes people volunteer to help with a youth group: out of a desire to grow spiritually; to share their God-given gifts with others; because they like to be involved in a cause they believe in; and to overcome feelings of loneliness. Presently in our society a strong desire exists to feel committed, connected and creative.

> *If using our gifts and sensing fulfillment and peace is associated with our work, we can thank God. Many people find the best use of gifts does not coincide with how they earn their paycheck. The sense of unfulfillment, caused by that creative being inside us, needs attention, and perhaps it is after the nine-to-five routine that the unrest is quieted. It may be in our leisure hours that we engage in the kind of mystery where we feel free to express our gifts.*[1]

Recruiting volunteers for junior high ministry means more than selecting warm bodies to fill empty spaces. Recruitment of effective volunteers requires the following steps:

1. Decide what kind of help you need. Because it's important to match the right person with the right job, needs should be determined in the initial recruitment stages such as:

- What kind of person is best suited for the task?
- Where can we find such a person?
- How will we ask the person to volunteer?
- How will we support the volunteer?
- What criteria will be used to evaluate the volunteer?
- How will the volunteer be recognized?

Recruitment does not mean taking the first hand raised, it means inviting people to serve. In seeking volunteers, leaders need to make time to get to know what gifts people possess. Only then can good matches be determined.

It takes time and effort to get to know people individually. Standards need to be set for the tasks at hand; don't just enlist any warm body. If the right person can't be found for an activity, don't offer it. It's better not to offer an activity rather than risk that a bad match will disappoint parents, the kids or the congregation. Let's look at several ways to recruit volunteers:

● *One-on-one*—Go directly to the people you feel can do the job. Tell them why they are being asked, why you feel they are right for the job, what their role would involve, what your expectations are, how much time would be required, and the length of the commitment. Then challenge them to accept the opportunity to serve. During the conversation, allow time for questions. This is not the time or place to twist arms or make people feel guilty. They have the right to say no and should be allowed to do so gracefully. (Don't forget, circumstances change. Just because people say no once, doesn't mean they won't be available or willing another time.) Ask them to think about your request and suggest a time when you'll contact them for an answer. A follow-up letter to your visit, indicating you're keeping them in your prayers while they decide, is another sign of your genuine desire for them to become part of your team.

● *Take some kids with you*—It means a great deal to potential volunteers to have the young people tell them directly why they want their help. Imagine what it would be like to have an entire youth group go to someone's home and ask him or her to get involved. Not only do the kids learn from the experience, it will inspire the potential volunteer; he or she can see the kids' desire for additional leadership.

● *Invite prospective volunteers to an activity*—Adults often are reluctant to work with junior highers because of their fear of adolescents and their fear they have nothing to contribute. They may have heard all kinds of myths about adolescents, or just not feel comfortable with this age group. Inviting them to come and observe an activity or meeting can eliminate a lot of uneasiness. Prospective volunteers need to see other enthusiastic adult helpers, the way they relate to the kids, and the tasks that need to be done. When adults visit, involve them in the activities. Potential volunteers gain a better understanding of junior high ministry when they play a game or join in a group discussion, rather than observe from the sidelines.

● *Let volunteers recruit volunteers*—Happy volunteers find it difficult to contain their joy. When a need is made known, volunteers can do more to enlist the help of others than the pastor or paid staff with all their powerful arguments. There is something contagious about adults sharing their enthusiasm and talking about the rewards that come from working as a team with young people. Most likely, they'll express personal growth and satisfaction as well as other reasons why they feel investing time and love with this age group is so important to the church.

● *Make a public appeal*—Make general announcements in the church newsletter, hang posters, attend new member and congregational meetings to explain the need, or ask junior highers for names of potential volunteers. Once a list of names is compiled, make appointments, either by phone or letter.

Use one of the following involvement questionnaires when making a public appeal.[2] Ask adults to fill out the forms and return them to you. Remember, once you establish where people's interests are, get to know them before you make a commitment.

Involvement Card

Name _____

Address _____

City_____State_____ZIP_____

Phone (business) _____ (home) _____

Age (circle one):

18-25   26-35   36-45   46-55   56-older

Rank the following (1 is the activity you most enjoy; 7 is the activity you least enjoy):

( ) leading groups (teaching, organizing)   ( ) hosting meetings
( ) providing support needs   ( ) furnishing transportation
( ) record-keeping   ( ) driving the church bus
                                              ( ) visiting and telephoning

Special skills you have (musical; mechanical; financial; cooking; with computers; with children, youth, young adults, adults, etc.):

1. _____   2. _____

3. _____   4. _____

( ) I would like someone to call on me **right away** concerning how I can become involved in junior high ministry.

Work experiences in the church:
Please list some previous churches you've attended, tasks undertaken and dates of your involvement.

_____

_____

_____

To keep ahead of the need for volunteers, have adults in your congregation fill out the following Adult Involvement sheet once a year.

Adult Involvement

Teach:
_____ Sunday school
_____ Sailing
_____ Canoeing
_____ Swimming
_____ Cardiopulmonary resuscitation (CPR)
_____ Lifesaving
_____ Guitar
_____ Dance
_____ Karate
_____ Tennis
_____ Bowling
_____ Calligraphy
_____ Other _____

Lead:
_____ Exercise/aerobic class
_____ Singing
_____ Recreation
_____ Bible study
_____ Share group
_____ Hike
_____ Telephone committee
_____ Other _____

Coach:
_____ Basketball
_____ Football
_____ Softball
_____ Volleyball
_____ Other _____

Loan my:
_____ Darkroom
_____ Boat (type) _____
_____ Home (for get-togethers)
_____ Cabin/tent
_____ Pickup truck
_____ Computer
_____ Videocassette recorder
_____ Video camera
_____ Slide projector
_____ Film projector
_____ Motor home
_____ Swimming pool for parties
_____ Ice cream freezer
_____ Copy machine
_____ Graphic arts supplies

Assist with:
_____ Bicycle team
_____ Drama presentations
_____ Child care
_____ Host/hostessing
_____ Choir or music
_____ Paper staff
_____ Ushering
_____ Video/media
_____ Creative movement/mime
_____ Outdoor activities
_____ Clown ministry
_____ Puppet shows
_____ Substitute (fill in where needed in emergency)

Other:
_____ Prepare snack supper
_____ Prepare refreshments for parties
_____ Help prepare meals for retreats
_____ Make homemade ice cream
_____ Provide decorations for special occasions

_____ Drive for carpool
_____ Conduct survey
_____ Help with workcamp project
_____ Photography
_____ Work on social concerns project

_____ Play instrument _____

_____ Plan/design treasure hunt

_____ Public relations: write articles for local newspaper, make posters, radio or television announcements

_____ Help with fund raising

_____ Serve on parent/teen relationship panel

_____ Work on retreat

_____ Operate _____ videocassette recorder

                    _____ film projector

                    _____ slide projector

_____ Use my influence with public, government and school officials

_____ Provide fish for fish fry

_____ Supervise light construction

_____ Provide child care for youth workers

_____ Assist in program planning

_____ Youth sponsor

_____ Bus committee _____ driver

                    _____ maintenance

_____ Counselor

_____ Youth newsletter

_____ Answer telephone _____ hours from_____

                    _____ day(s) week   M   T   W   TH   F

                              (circle one)

_____ Telephone committee

_____ Volunteer _____ typist

                  _____ receptionist

_____ Donate money for youth who cannot afford retreats/trips (circle one):
$25 $50 $75 $100 $ _____

_____ Lifeguard for swim parties

_____ Chaperon parties

_____ Adopt a youth for discipleship

_____ Help with school study night (once a week)

A combination of all the above recruiting methods may work best. Keep in mind, the object is to recruit people to a cause as well as to a specific task. While it may be true you need a basketball coach, the person who fills that role needs to see his or her ability and interest being matched with a ministry need. A coach's relationship with the team members may be the only contact some of the kids have with the church. Coaches can nurture friendships among players that will lead to a greater involvement in other junior high church events. A person recruited to do a specific task is helping the youth ministry team accomplish its goal by involving kids in the total ministry of the church.

2. Training a team of volunteers that works well together.
The second recruitment step is implementing a comprehensive training program. The length of a training period depends on the program that is offered and what the volunteers will be doing. Part of the volunteers' job descriptions should include a requirement for them to participate in such training. Junior high ministry is so important, that a training or orientation session should be conducted with staff before every major program.

In designing a training session for volunteers, both the leader's and the volunteers' expectations need to be addressed. It is only fair that volunteers know what needs to be done, what the objectives are for the year, how much time will be required, and how the volunteers fit together as a team. Not all approaches to junior high ministry are alike. Each situation is unique; what works in one place may not work in another. However, the one constant, regardless of where the ministry takes place, is the need of junior highers. Training sessions make volunteers aware of the kids' needs and teach them how to meet those needs. Following are some additional training session elements:

● Familiarize each volunteer with his or her responsibilities.

● Overview the developmental characteristics of junior highers (see Chapter 4).

● Relate the importance of being a role model.

● Discuss your basic philosophy of junior high ministry.

● Give insights into the present youth culture.

● Relate certain statistics and characteristics about your junior high group to help volunteers get "a feel" for the kids.

● Give an overview of techniques for teaching, listening and conducting discussions (see Chapter 5).

● Examine the master calendar for the year.

● Offer a training session during a three-week period. Use this agenda:

Week 1 Review Section One of this book, "Junior High Ministry"
Week 2 Review Section Two, "Effective Leadership"
Week 3 Review Section Three, "Creative Programming"

● Sponsor a training session during a retreat. Use this agenda:

Friday	6:00 p.m.	Registration and check-in
	7:30 p.m.	Session 1: "Overview and purpose of retreat"
	9:00 p.m.	Refreshments and free time
Saturday	9:00 a.m.	Session 2: "Junior High Ministry" (use Chapters 1-4)
	10:30 a.m.	Break
	11:00 a.m.	Session 3: "Leadership" (use Chapters 5-7)
	12:30 p.m.	Lunch
	2:00 p.m.	Session 4: "Planning" (use Chapters 8-9)
	4:00 p.m.	Free time
	5:00 p.m.	Dinner and free time
	7:00 p.m.	Session 5: "Programming" (use Chapters 10-15)
	9:30 p.m.	Refreshments and free time
Sunday	10:00 a.m.	Service of commitment to junior high ministry
	11:30 a.m.	Communion
	Noon	Lunch

Volunteers need to see where they fit into the overall picture and to realize the importance of their relationship to the group. The way they carry out their assignments, express concern for each individual's growth, and act as responsible, mature adults can make or break a junior high ministry.

If several people work with the junior highers in your church—in choir, Sunday school and youth ministry—an all-day seminar on junior highers would be very helpful. Seminars provide mutual support of the various roles and people working with the same young people; they provide opportunities to share experiences and see how ministries complement each other. The more junior high volunteers are in touch with one another, the better the program will meet the needs of the kids.

3. Relax and have fun together. We become so task-oriented in our church programs that we don't take time to stop and catch our breath, or just plain relax. Even God set aside time to rest. It's important to spend time together with no set agenda, time to have fun, relax and enjoy each other.

Volunteers need to feel the support of being in community. The New Testament contains many instances of Christians fellowshipping with one another. We are baptized into the community of faith, we worship in community, our spiritual life is nurtured in community. So, if we attempt to relate to junior highers without a community of support, we'll soon find it difficult to sustain meaningful relationships. The time together needs to include opportunities for spiritual growth. Those who continuously minister to junior highers, also need to be ministered to; their cups need to be refilled.

In some churches, volunteers go out together for pizza after each program. In other churches, volunteers plan a biannual weekend retreat just for themselves. Bible study, singing, prayer, plus good food for thought, challenge volunteers to grow and help them appreciate the fellowship they receive being part of the junior high team.

4. Help volunteers feel a part of the junior high team. Volunteers should be on the junior high mailing list to ensure they receive everything the kids do. This keeps volunteers informed of all scheduled events.

In addition to an initial training session, adults should meet regularly to make decisions regarding their responsibilities, to talk about what is happening in the ministry that is good or needs improvement, to evaluate the program, to brainstorm for new ideas, and to wrestle with concerns regarding the entire group. Being involved in such meetings helps volunteers see that they are truly part of the junior high ministry.

5. Recognize volunteers. Anyone who has ever been a volunteer knows the satisfaction gained from a job well done. However, if no one recognizes the volunteers for their efforts, they soon wonder if it was even necessary to show up. Youth leaders who value their volunteer staff make certain the volunteers know they are appreciated. During regularly scheduled volunteer meetings, take time to thank them for carrying out specific responsibilities, recognize specific things that happened as a result of their help, remember special events or anniversaries in their life. Host a volunteer-appreciation banquet and invite spouses and family members—the silent partners in their volunteer efforts. Talk about their life outside junior high ministry; write notes of appreciation and put them in the volunteers' church mailboxes. So often, acts of kindness like these take so little time, yet mean so much. Neglecting to say thank you, or show your appreciation is contrary to a Christian's lifestyle and is just plain inconsiderate.

6. Offer new programs and responsibilities. Constantly evaluate existing activities; decide which to keep and which to delete. Don't bore or stagnate volunteers by repeating the same old program or withholding them from new or different responsibilities. Constantly repeating certain activities can make volunteers feel complacent, dull and listless. Challenge your volunteers to think of new and creative ways to accomplish certain objectives, new projects, new songs, new ways to involve more kids.

7. Allow volunteers to fail. No one likes to fail, but there are times when things don't go as planned. With the youth leader's approval, volunteers need to feel free to try new ideas. They also need to know they are trusted to accomplish some things on their own. Leaders need to encourage new ideas and help volunteers evaluate what works, what doesn't, and why. Volunteers will not always succeed, but failures can be turned into learning opportunities that usually lead to a stronger program. People make mistakes all the time; it's what they do as a result of their mistakes that makes a difference.

8. Hold volunteers accountable. This is one of the most positive parts of our relationship with volunteers. Giving them certain responsibilities not only communicates our trust, but also how much they are needed. It is also important that volunteers know their work will be reviewed and evaluated periodically. This means we maintain standards and we are interested in the ways volunteers use their special gifts and skills. By holding volunteers accountable, we tell them they matter, that what they're doing is important, and that we care.

9. Confront problems honestly. Occasionally, even the most conscientious volunteer will do something that creates a problem. When a conflict or an issue needs to be addressed, take steps to correct the situation. For example:

● Always maintain open communication and stay on top of the situation.

● Review the volunteer's specific responsibilities and see if he or she clearly understands them.

● Make certain you understand the problem.

● Examine alternate ways to handle the situation in order to prevent a similar occurrence.

● Close your discussion in firm agreement that you want to continue working together.

If our attempts to work through problems with a volunteer are unsuccessful, we may be forced to realize that the volunteer's talents do not match the group's needs. We may have to dismiss the volunteer. In *Volunteer Youth Workers*, the authors list several questions for leaders to ask themselves prior to dismissing a volunteer:

> *Dismissing a volunteer is not easy; however, occasionally you may make a mistake and recruit the wrong person for a job. What do you do? In the first place, remember the volunteer is a child of God—dismissing him or her should be the last resort. Pray for guidance in the issue and thoroughly think through the situation. Did you clearly communicate the job description? Have you given the volunteer enough guidance and direction? Have you faced up to your role in the failure?*[3]

If we have explored every avenue and we still feel the best thing would be to dismiss the volunteer, there are several ways to do so. The obvious way is simply to ask the person to resign. A more positive approach is to recognize the person's time, talents and desire to serve. Then discuss other areas where the person might better be able to contribute. This approach requires that prior to the interview we explore alternative ways to use the volunteer. It is essential to find a good match; the volunteer's skills with the church's needs.

Ending a relationship that we had great hopes for is not pleasant; emotions and self-worth are involved. Yet, with prayer and care, we can bring dignity to the process by dealing with the issue face to face.

In summary, getting people involved in providing a ministry to junior highers leads to great opportunities and programs. If your junior high group has genuine, specific needs; if the volunteer's responsibilities are clearly stated; if the volunteer successfully meets the group's needs; and if the volunteer is praised and appreciated—he or she will be back to do more. And, the volunteer who gladly returns might even bring along a friend who also wants to experience the joy of serving.

CHAPTER 7

WORKING WITH PARENTS

Parental support and involvement are essential for an effective junior high ministry. Working with parents can be a source of great satisfaction for a junior high leader; it also can be a cause of tremendous stress. In junior high ministry, youth leaders can get caught in a tug of war between what parents expect and what the church actually offers.

Parents usually feel one of three ways about junior high ministry: indifferent, that it is a specialty for qualified professionals, or that it is a cooperative venture. The first attitude opposes the church. An indifferent position maintains that parents alone are responsible for guiding and nurturing their children, including their spiritual development. Parents refuse to acknowledge a need or reason for outside help.

The second attitude is opposite the first. In this case, parents feel they have a full-time job just providing the basic necessities of life, and that spiritual matters should be placed totally in the hands of the pros. These parents look to church leaders to train and educate their children. Their teenagers' spiritual development is turned over to the institution that is considered by society the best equipped for this specialized task.

The preferable attitude, and fortunately the most common, is one of cooperative sharing. This attitude recognizes that junior high ministry is important, and that it requires teamwork. Parents who feel this way recognize the importance of relationships—that junior highers and their parents need the help of many people throughout their spiritual journey.

Parents who believe in cooperative sharing appreciate junior high ministry and encourage their teenagers to participate. Churches that believe in cooperative sharing strive to meet the needs of junior highers and offer support to parents in their God-given responsibility. Both parents and church view each other with respect and are committed to a mutual ministry. Both family and church look upon their relationship as a privilege and an exciting time to be linked together through worship, educational experiences, social events, and activities that meet the needs of parents as well as adolescents.

We, as junior high leaders, should create and nurture cooperative sharing. A partnership with parents means we listen to parents' concerns, attempt to interpret what is happening in young people's lives and why, and find a place in our ministry for parental involvement. These three factors can lead to a happy and productive relationship of mutual encouragement and support.

Just as leaders work hard to build rapport with junior highers, parents also should be given special attention. All aspects of ministering should be applied to parents as well: listening, affirming, building trust, responding to needs, developing a pastoral relationship, and involving them in programming.

A partnership in junior high ministry means involving parents. Whether it's better to involve them as leaders or as "behind-the-scenes" supporters, is debatable. Many junior highers prefer their parents not act as sponsors. They feel inhibited in discussions or in activities if their parents are leading. Likewise, many parents feel uncomfortable in this situation. Experience indicates that everyone benefits if parents are involved "in the background" rather than in direct leadership positions. If it is necessary for parents to be directly involved with the junior high group, talk with the teenagers first to find out how they feel about it. Parents may say, "No problem," while their junior higher says, "No way!" Even in ideal parent-child relationships, it is my opinion that it's best to ask other church members to be leaders and ask parents to fill supportive positions. For example, parents could host a junior high event in their homes, prepare meals or provide refreshments, provide transportation, coach, lead special interest groups, make costumes for drama productions, help build sets, work with makeup or lighting, make telephone calls, help with mailings, gather materials, type, file, drive the church bus, play a musical instrument for group singing, or work with audio-visual equipment. Parents can be involved in many ways and feel they are a valued partner in the junior high ministry.

To develop and maintain a meaningful partnership, the lines of communication need to be open and frequently used. The most common parental complaint is a lack of information and communication with the junior high ministry. Not feeling informed leads to confusion, conflict and criticism.

A meaningful partnership also requires support. Junior high leaders are in a unique position in that they can help parents understand their young adolescents and the world in which the kids live. The rest of this chapter suggests ways to support parents in this important partnership.

Parents Night

One of the best ways to fully inform parents about the junior high program is to conduct Parents Night every year. Since most youth groups base their schedule around the school year, the most logical time to hold a Parents Night is in September. In 90 minutes or less, leaders can accomplish several objectives:

● Introduce the church's philosophy or approach to working with junior highers.

● Explain the goals for the year.

● Provide information and a calendar listing dates, times and places of planned events.

● Give parents the opportunity to meet the leadership team and hear their hopes, dreams and motivations for working with junior highers.

● Explain the opportunities available for parental involvement and enlist their help with specific tasks.

● Explain the support system available to the parents.

● Nurture parents' enthusiasm by having an inspirational, fun time together.

Hosting Parents Night communicates to parents that you want them to feel a part of the exciting things planned for their kids. Although such a meeting requires a comprehensive plan and a lot of advance work, it will create a firm foundation on which to build the entire year's program. Parents appreciate receiving information about scheduled events, meeting those who work with their teenagers, hearing the leadership's enthusiasm, and understanding their important role as part of the junior high ministry team. Parents also appreciate meeting with other parents and learning of the support system available to help them when they have a need, problem or concern.

Following are some guidelines for preparing a Parents Night, examples of items to include in the meeting, and several meeting tips.

1. Before Parents Night. Complete the first four steps at least two weeks prior to the meeting. The last two can be done closer to the event.

● *Publicize*—Utilize posters, bulletin boards, newsletters and announcements on Sunday morning. Send parents a special post card announcing the date, time, place and purpose of Parents Night.

● *Decide on the theme*—Invite those who work with junior highers (the youth director, choir director, Christian education director, etc.) to help create a theme for Parents Night. The theme should capture in a few words the upcoming year's emphasis; for example, "Building Forever Friendships" or "Spread Around a Little Love."

● *Delegate responsibilities*—Meet with junior high leaders and interested teenagers and make specific assignments. For example, ask the Sunday school superintendent to explain the junior high curriculum and introduce the teachers. Ask the choir director to explain the choir activities, rehearsal times, performances and special events planned for the year. Ask a piano player or guitar player to lead singing. (Be sure to supply song books or sheet music at the meeting.) Ask a teenager, parent or leader to prepare a devotion relating to the theme. Have him or her present the devotion when the meeting opens.

Discuss the time allotted for each presentation, what each presentation should include, and who will introduce each speaker. Print an agenda to ensure a smooth-running meeting.

●*Prepare a booklet of junior high ministry information*— Include a calendar of the year's activities, a brief description of each program and special event, beginning and ending dates, etc. Ask the leaders to help write descriptions of the programs. Make copies to distribute to the parents.

●*Decorate the meeting room*—Use banners, posters, streamers and balloons to emphasize the theme. Create displays of recent junior high activities. For example, to illustrate last year's canoe trip: Cut posterboard in the shape of a canoe. Post pictures on the posterboard and add captions. Cover a table with a blue sheet and prop up the makeshift canoe. Place a canoe paddle and a life preserver nearby. These ideas help create a colorful, festive atmosphere for the meeting.

●*Gather "Help Wanted" forms and miscellaneous items*— Collect paper and pencils for taking notes, brochures, newspaper articles, sample magazines of helpful information. Gather volunteer information through the use of Help Wanted forms. Adapt this form to fit your own needs, then make a copy for each parent.

Help Wanted

Child's Name _____

           First   Middle   Last

____ _____ _____ _____

Age   Birthdate   Grade   School

Child's Name _____

      First   Middle   Last

_____ _____ _____ _____

 Age   Birthdate   Grade   School

Child's Name _____

      First   Middle   Last

_____ _____ _____ _____

 Age   Birthdate   Grade   School

Address _____

      Street   Apt #   City   State and ZIP

Phone _____

Mother's Name _____   Occupation_____
Place of   Work
Employment _____   Phone _____

Father's Name _____   Occupation_____
Place of   Work
Employment _____   Phone _____

I (we) am (are) available to help on Tuesdays with the following . . .

_____ provide transportation   _____ help in the kitchen
_____ provide office help   _____ substitute teach
_____ chaperon   _____ other

---

2. At Parents Night. Here are some examples of what to include in Parents Night.

● *Provide a welcoming atmosphere*—As parents arrive, have Christian music playing in the background. Ask several leaders to greet parents and hand out name tags. Keep in mind that some parents may never have attended a meeting like this before. A cordial welcome gets the meeting off to a good start: "Hi, I'm Jeanne and I teach 7th grade Sunday school. We've been expecting you and we're so glad you're here." If you don't know the parents' names, ask them and then introduce them to other parents. Invite them to look at the displays around the room.

● *Sing songs*—Group singing is a good way to begin a meeting. Introduce each song by briefly explaining when and how it is used with the young people. Say something like, "Picture yourself sitting around a campfire at the end of the day. The stars are bright, the air is brisk, and the fire feels warm. The guitarist strums a chord and leads a beautiful song of thanksgiving . . ."

● *Present the devotion*—Scripture and prayer should be related to the theme. For example, if the theme is friendship, the devotion could center around verses such as Proverbs 17:17, "A friend loves at all times" or John 15:13, "Greater love has no man than this, that a man lay down his life for his friends."

● *Follow the agenda*—The leader responsible for the entire junior high program should give a five- to seven-minute presentation on the goals, objectives and philosophy of the junior high ministry. Examples can be given about how goals or objectives are achieved and evaluated.

Distribute the activities booklet and let each junior high leader enthusiastically describe his or her program. Keep it short, vital and exciting.

● *Request support from parents*—List the activities where parent volunteers are needed, then encourage their participation. Distribute the Help Wanted forms. Collect them after the parents have completed them.

● *Conclude the meeting*—Indicate that a ministry to junior highers includes a ministry to parents. Tell how the leadership team will support the parents, and describe the programs that will be offered specifically for parents.

Briefly review the meeting, offer a word of appreciation for the parents' interest and support, and ask that they pray for the junior high ministry. Encourage parents to stay a few minutes, enjoy refreshments and mingle with the others.

3. Tips for Parents Night. Parents Night is probably the most important part of communicating the partnership that exists between home and church. Therefore, it is vital to follow these important tips.

● *Present accurate information*—Be precise on dates, and starting and ending times. Because junior highers still depend on their parents for transportation, parents need to know when to have kids at the church and when to pick them up.

● *Be positive and enthusiastic*—How the leadership team projects itself will be reflected in the parents. If the team presents an unorganized, boring meeting, the parents will feel bored and frustrated. Parents will then share these negative feelings with their teenagers, which will cause the kids to be less enthusiastic. On the other hand, if a junior higher is uncertain he or she wants to participate, an enthusiastic parent will encourage him or her to at least try some activities. Enthusiasm is catching among parents. One parent, who speaks of the vitality of the junior high program to other parents, will perk interest in the ministry.

It is not necessary to tell parents about activities the leadership planned, but that fell through. Parents will begin to distrust a leadership that conveys weakness or disorganization.

● *Dress professionally*—Remember, this is a meeting for parents. During many junior high activities it may be appropriate to wear jeans and a T-shirt, but Parents Night is the time to look like a professional. Appearance makes a lasting impression.

● *Employ humor*—Parents enjoy a good story, especially if it relates to raising a teenager; but be sure to avoid any embarrassing or hurtful jokes. Tastefully sprinkle enjoyable, humorous stories throughout the presentation.

Parents Night starts the year off with *communication* by: giving parents an overview of the program and the upcoming year, asking parents for their assistance, and introducing parents to the junior high leaders. However, communication should not begin and end at Parents Night. Immediately following the meeting, communication can continue with a letter or phone call thanking the parents for attending. Throughout the year, informational meetings can be scheduled prior to special events, specifically for those involved.

Another way to keep parents informed is to produce a bimonthly newsletter. Include details about events such as dates, places, times, costs, registration procedures, requests for additional help, etc. The newsletter also should include material specifically for adults such as newspaper clippings, book or movie reviews related to current trends in the youth culture, etc. Parents appreciate information that helps them better understand their teenagers.

Confidentiality

Parents need to understand that although the leader is not a substitute parent, the kids may seek out the leader to share personal concerns. There are times when leaders are trusted with a confidence they cannot share with parents. Most of the time these concerns will be minor and not life-or-death matters. Nonetheless, our integrity with kids will rest on what we know and what we tell.

Youth leaders can be put in a precarious position with parents. What do we do when an adolescent shares something about his or her parents that the parents surely wouldn't want anyone to know? Is it best to keep the parents sheltered from secrets their child has shared with us? Should we advise parents if their son or daughter is involved in an illegal activity? What should a leader do if a teenager's behavior on a weekend retreat or group trip requires confrontation and accountability?

Because junior highers trust us with certain information, we are in a dilemma whether to discuss the situation with their parents. Next to parents, kids seek out youth leaders for advice, guidance, information or counsel. Kids turn to leaders they feel they can trust. (See Chapter 5.) Parents need to understand that we would never abuse this privilege, yet there are times when we absolutely must keep information confidential. The opposite also is true. There will be times parents speak to us about concerns, fears, hopes or problems that must be kept confidential.

We can avoid being "caught" between parents and teenagers by refusing to promise confidentiality. If parents or kids refuse to talk until we promise never to divulge a word, we can respond by saying, "I care about both parent and child. I hope you'll trust me to act responsibly on your behalf." The person may decide not to talk, but it's important for the leader to provide that choice and not commit to secrecy before being made aware of the problem. Caring leaders will follow up and remind the person that they are willing to listen when the time is right.

Anyone who has close relationships with junior highers will

inevitably possess information about intense struggles. Wrestling with such sensitive information can cause sleepless nights for a youth leader. Following are some questions leaders must ask when determining who should be made privy to certain knowledge:

● Is what I've been told correct? Are there ways to check the validity of what I've learned?

● Why have I been selected to receive this information? Why weren't parents told?

● Where is the junior higher headed if he or she continues this behavior or does not resolve the problem?

● What difference would it make if parents were informed? Should they be told?

● If I go to parents and tell them what I know, what effect will it have on my relationship with them? on my relationship with their son or daughter?

● What approach would be best for all involved?

● Is the situation endangering someone's life?

Involving parents can have negative as well as positive consequences. It might be wise to explore how teenagers feel their parents would react to the concern. Would the parents fall apart? react with inappropriate discipline? accuse or place blame? respond sensitively and constructively in the best interest of their child?

If a decision is made to talk to parents, following are three ways to inform them.

1. The junior high young person speaks to parents alone. In this instance, the leader does not discuss the matter with parents. This takes a lot of courage on the part of the teenager, especially if he or she does not know how the parents might react. It is a strong step by the young person to communicate directly with his or her parents.

2. The youth leader talks to the parents. In a situation where trust has been established between the young person and the youth leader, this approach is workable. The leader not only should share the reason why it seems advisable to talk to parents, but ask the young person for permission to do so. Discussing concerns such as, "Would my involvement be welcomed by your parents?" or, "Would my talking to your parents help open the channels of communication between the two of you?'' indicates a sensitivity and a desire to do the right thing. If the teenager says no to the offer to help, be prepared to respect his or her wishes.

3. The junior high young person and leader together go to the parents. In this setting the leader accompanies the teenager to provide support and encouragement. Where necessary, the leader's presence can provide a bridge to bring the two together on a sensitive matter. Before the meeting, it is essential that the leader and young person understand what is to happen, the reason the youth leader is to be there and that neither party will place blame on the parents. Clarify the leader's role. Will you be there to listen? to explain the problem or concern? to suggest ways in which it can be resolved?

Needless to say, if the issue is a delicate one, a great deal of thought needs to be done before talking with parents. Trust demands confidentiality—any broken promise of confidentiality can lead to disaster.

Ministering to Parents

Parental involvement in junior high ministry requires ministering to parents as well as to kids. Like their offspring, parents often feel frustrated, alienated, and unequipped to raise a teenager in a time so different from their own adolescence. They look to professionals or institutions to do for their sons and daughters what they feel they cannot do—or what they feel the professionals could do better. Parents need to be nurtured and encouraged too.

As many differences exist among parents as do among teenagers. This may be the first experience some parents have had with an adolescent; for other parents, this junior higher is the last of their children to grow up. Methods or styles of parenting vary greatly. Although parents' rules, patterns of discipline, strictness or permissiveness differ, they have one thing in common—they want to be the best parents they possibly can. So, while their teenager is entering adolescence, parents are stepping into uncharted territory. The good news is, in order to be effective, parents don't have to have a degree in adolescent psychology or live perfect lives. They simply need to be honest in their struggles and to invest themselves in their teenager's life.

An excellent resource for leaders and parents is Merton and Irene Strommen's book *Five Cries of Parents*. Based on solid research with more than 10,000 families and their experiences, they have identified five needs of parents: understanding themselves and their kids; understanding the qualities of a close, caring family; understanding moral beliefs; sharing personal faith; and accepting outside help in crises.

Despite the emphasis in recent decades on the deterioration of the family, the rising divorce rate, and the burden of single parenting, our culture is resurrecting a new awareness of parenting skills and family relationships. Having children is now seen as something that brings happiness and fulfillment, as well as responsibility and stress. Churches that care about young people understand the importance of encouraging and affirming parents.

The vast majority of parents are hungry for knowledge about appropriate methods of discipline, communication skills and their teenagers' puzzling behavior. When there is uncertainty at home, confusion results. Parents' confusing behavior and lack of self-esteem have a profound impact on their adolescents' behavior (and vice versa). The results are powerful interpersonal needs that should be addressed by the church. Parenting courses, seminars and workshops are well received, as long as they touch on relevant issues. Following are some parental needs that the Strommens address:

1. Fear of failure. Although every mother and father feels, at one time or another, they could be doing a better job, more than half of the 10,467 people surveyed indicated, "I am not as good a parent as I should be." The greatest concern of most parents is that they will fail.[1]

●*Anger*—A significant factor that affects a parent's feeling of failure is regret over the way he or she handles anger. Dealing with anger is a skill few adults possess. Situations that cause anger need to be worked through with their children.

Effective leaders recognize the importance of dealing with anger. We can help parents by offering classes or seminars that focus on this topic. We can ask a psychiatrist or family counselor to speak to parents and teenagers about potentially explosive situations, and how to deal with anger in a positive, constructive manner.

● *Divorce or separation*—Losing a spouse through divorce or separation also leads to feelings of failure. Parents who lose a spouse can feel pressure, grief, shock, fear of the future, resentment, self-pity, frustration and even rage. Often their fear of talking about their feelings with their children adds to the trauma adolescents experience. Junior highers usually blame one of the parents or themselves in a divorce.

No church or youth group is immune from the rising divorce rate. Single parents are a part of every community. The church is slowly becoming aware of its subtle ways of excluding people; people who desperately need the church during their valiant effort to be both mother and father. Sometimes this exclusion is due to insensitivity or to the traditional emphasis the church places on family.

One of the most helpful ministries a congregation can provide single parents is a forum, or support group, that offers insights on how to deal with their feelings, how to communicate with their teenagers, and how to instill healthy concepts of right and wrong. Later, if the divorced parents remarry, we must try to understand the stress parents and teenagers experience in stepfamilies—a growing phenomenon in our society. Stepparents are struggling to understand and assume their new roles and will need the church's support.

Churches can ease parents' fear of failure by acknowledging that parents fight some of the same battles and feel some of the same feelings as their teenagers. We can support parents by helping them understand what life is like for a junior higher. Many parents have suppressed memories of the painful periods of their own adolescence or have failed to recognize that times have changed. In our mobile society, parents who grew up in a rural area may be raising children in an urban environment. While the basic needs of adolescents have remained the same throughout the years, the way those needs are met is greatly influenced by the world in which they live.

Following are some suggested events to hold for parents to

help them overcome their fear of failure:

—Plan an evening for parents, designed to serve as a "refresher course" on what it's like to be a junior higher.

—Review the five areas of development covered in Chapter 4 to give parents an idea of what to expect during the adolescent years.

—Conduct a three-week series on listening skills. Use some of the ideas in Chapter 5. Include a presentation on listening skills and provide opportunities for parents to practice them.

2. Close family life. Parents and teenagers need a close family life. Family closeness fortifies children with a resistance to life's toxins. The Strommens show that:

> *Adolescents in a close family unit are the ones most likely to say "no" to drug use, pre-marital sexual activity, and other antisocial and alienating behaviors. They are also the ones most likely to adopt high moral standards, develop the ability to make and keep friends, embrace a religious faith, and involve themselves in helping activities. All of these characteristics pertaining to adolescents from close families are significant—which means that the evidence cannot be attributed to mere chance.[2]*

● *Open communication*—Open communication contributes to close families. Junior high leaders can provide learning experiences that deal with the essentials of communication. Focus discussions on topics that weigh heavily on an adolescent's mind. Parents and teenagers are concerned about many of the same issues; for example, nuclear arms, world peace, world hunger, self-image, self-assurance, relationships with friends and family, etc.

● *Discipline*—Another factor that contributes to close families is discipline. Based on the analysis of discipline styles, Strommens' research suggests the following guidelines for parents:

—An adolescent needs clear, firmly established rules.

—A flexible stance, blended with good judgment, is important.

—Consistency in defining and applying discipline is essential.

—Disciplining must be a private affair.

—The use of sarcasm or "rubbing it in" brings negative results.

—Conflict can be handled in a positive way.[3]

● Trust—Trust is also important to close families. Parents should respect their teenager's need for privacy. Parents who listen in on phone conversations, read their child's mail, clean out rooms and throw away items without asking, or go through desks and dresser drawers, basically distrust their child. Without trust, relationships deteriorate. Family trust is reflected in the trust husband and wife have in one another.

3. Moral and faith development of teenagers. An adolescent's values are communicated primarily through the parent. The influence of peers takes over only when a loving and caring relationship with parents is absent.

Parents need to resolve, in their own minds, what is right or wrong before attempting to explain their position to their teenagers. Parents cannot dictate what their child will think. Only as parents honestly communicate their struggle with moral issues can they hope to influence their maturing child's decisions.

Religion greatly influences the lives of junior highers and their parents, yet the subject seldom, if ever, is discussed in the home. There are a number of different theories as to why this is. One reason may be that today's parents received little biblical training and feel inadequate to teach religion at home. Another explanation given by parents is their belief that only clergy and trained leaders are qualified to teach. Still another reason might be that parents do not agree on matters of faith. Some parents also find it difficult to communicate their faith because it is not meaningful in their own life.

Unfortunately, religion and faith development are largely ignored in most books about parenting or adolescent development. Youth leaders need to encourage parents to break the silence about spiritual matters. We can help parents understand that junior highers are beginning to have doubts about religion. These doubts should not be feared, but seen as opportunities to talk, to probe, to learn what different faiths teach, and to study the scripture in formal and informal settings.

Parents also must understand that junior highers are vulnerable to powerful media messages that teach contrasting values. We can lead parents through an examination of the music their teenagers listen to, the movies they see, the television they watch, and the printed media to which they are exposed. The church could conduct a seminar or mini-series for parents in which the influences of today's culture are examined and guidelines given to help parents discuss the content of media's messages.

The church can offer parents some practical clues on how faith can be shared at home. Faith needs to be understood as a natural part of daily activity in the home. Parents need to be encouraged to create an environment where junior highers feel free to ask questions without feeling stupid, getting hurt or being ridiculed. Debates can lead to an awareness of what people believe and why, without anyone being declared a winner. When young people learn that their parents are committed to open discussion, carried on in a spirit of humility, they will grow in their ability to share personal experiences and ideas. This kind of atmosphere also strengthens a parent's faith, especially in a time of crisis.[4]

Faith also can be shared during structured times. Family devotions, attending worship together, praying before meals or on special family occasions, are all part of the faith heritage parents can pass on. Finally, faith can be taught by doing. Bible stories can be read, songs can be memorized, and prayer offered, but in the final analysis, when we "practice what we preach," teenagers experience an unequaled concern for others. We do a great service to parents by providing opportunities for families to help others. By reaching out to people in need, a family will develop a special bond, a sensitivity to the struggles of others, and experience the joy of giving.

4. Seeking help from other sources. As hard as it may be for some parents to accept, there will be times when they can't go it alone. Parents are reluctant to ask for assistance for fear of embarrassment, or fear others see it as a sign of failure. On the other hand, there may be parents who desperately need help in coping with problems they feel unequipped to handle or understand. As mentioned before, youth leaders can provide valuable assistance to parents by supporting them in their concerns and being knowledgeable of available resources to meet their needs.

Parents need to be affirmed and put in touch with sources of strength. Parents frequently find themselves going through changes at the same time their children enter adolescence. So often, during periods of transition, people need support and stability—not ambiguity—in their lives. People respond to churches that meet their needs, and one thing is certain: Parents of teenagers want a church that meets their needs as well as those of their teenagers.

SECTION THREE

Creative Programming— Tips and Ideas

CHAPTER 8

CREATING A MASTER PLAN

Good leaders and good junior high programs go hand in hand; and the key to making that marriage work is a solid biblical foundation. Part of our responsibility in working with early adolescents is the initial laying of that foundation.

A biblical foundation affirms junior highers as children of God—they are important in the life of the church.

A biblical foundation places Christ at the center of everything. All that we do or say should be to the glory of God.

A biblical foundation confirms leaders as models of Christianity. More than exposing young people to the Christian faith, adults provide experiences which help teenagers make the right decisions that will impact their daily lives. Adult leaders promote situations with teenagers that affirm the Christian principles of love of self, love of neighbor and love of God.

Once a solid biblical foundation is established, we must begin planning effective programs. Upon examination of any junior high ministry that is successfully reaching young people, we discover a master plan—goals and objectives, plans for carrying them out, and ongoing evaluation. We discover adult leaders who possess a realistic awareness of who they are, and leaders who are aware of the kids' needs.

How do we develop such a master plan? How do we determine the needs of our young people? How do we provide nurturing experiences? How do we establish objectives? How do we evaluate our progress? Developing a master plan that meets the kids' needs takes several steps.

STEP #1 Learn as much as you can about your kids.

Leaders need to learn all they can about the kids before they can expect to accurately read the kids' needs. Although several methods can be used to gather information, it's important to give each junior higher the opportunity to provide his or her input.

Brainstorming is one method of gathering information. Ask the group members to suggest what they think would make the ministry exciting. Discuss activities they've enjoyed in the past and ones they'd like to experience in the future. Discuss concerns such as divorce, death, suicide, friendships, plans for the future, support and acceptance from family and church members, etc. Listen carefully to the kids and the underlying needs their comments reveal.

Another method of gathering information is to *survey* the group. Have adult leaders complete the surveys first to see how closely their answers match the kids'. Following are sample surveys that focus on issues concerning junior highers. Adapt them to fit the needs of your group.

Survey One

Rank your concerns in order of importance; 1 is what you are most concerned about, 10 is what you are least concerned about.

Relationships with parents ____   Making & keeping friends ____
Questions about sex _____   Personal appearance _____

Cheating in school_____
Racism _____
Relationships with peers _____
Questions about God _____
Finding a purpose in life _____
Your future _____
Other _____

Survey Two

Mark each continuum to indicate the degree of your feelings about each issue.

Abortion   Strong Feelings   No Feelings

Death penalty   Strong Feelings   No Feelings

Violence in school   Strong Feelings   No Feelings

Drug abuse   Strong Feelings   No Feelings

Drunken driving   Strong Feelings   No Feelings

Survey Three

Answer the following questions:

1. What activities do you participate in when you're not in school?

2. To whom do you go for emotional support? advice?

3. What do you enjoy reading?

4. What do you enjoy watching on television?

5. What are your greatest worries?

6. What type of music appeals to you? What does it say to you?

7. What values are important to you?

8. How do you feel about the future?

9. What do you want most in life?

Survey Four

Complete these statements:

1. When I pray, I ask God for ...

2. The thing that bothers me most about myself is ...

3. If I had one wish for this youth group, it would be ...

4. Someday I'd like to talk to my parents about ...

5. The one thing that really makes me angry is ...

6. The one thing that really makes me happy is ...

The two easiest ways to gather information about kids are to *listen* to them and to *observe* them. Thoughtfully listen to the junior highers during meetings and special events. What do they talk about with one another? Watch kids during church or when you see them around town. What does their behavior reveal? Visit with kids at home and get to know them personally.

STEP #2 Analyze the Information.

Once information has been gathered from the kids by written surveys, brainstorming, observing and listening, we need to analyze it. Only through pondering the facts and implications can we apply what we've learned to programs. Analyzing information should provide answers to these questions:

1. What is the present condition of this church's junior high group?

2. What does this information tell me about each person?

3. What interests do the kids share?

4. What feelings do they have about themselves? the church? their world?

5. What activities are they involved in at school? in the community?

6. What problems do they have relating to friends? parents? school? church?

7. What other needs do the kids have?

8. How can the church respond to these needs?

9. What activities have the kids most enjoyed?

10. What experiences are needed in the future?

11. What support is needed for these experiences to succeed?

Once this analytical data is gathered, compile a group profile—a clear, concise statement describing the young people. For example, "Our junior highers are typical young people who experience joys, as well as frustrations, as they grow and mature. They enjoy active, fun, creative fellowship as well as deep, meaningful discussion on relevant topics. Our church can support them through caring, loving sponsors and programs that meet their needs."

STEP #3 Set goals.

Ernest Hemingway once said, "Never mistake motion for action." In other words, "If you don't know where you're going, you'll probably end up somewhere else." Adults and junior highers become frustrated when they feel the time they spend together is wasted. Setting some long-range goals can eliminate such feelings.

Goals answer the question: "What is it we want to do as a group?" Goals serve as targets group members hope to hit as they work together in Christ. Setting goals does away with needless activities. This may mean some past youth group "traditions" will not be included in the upcoming calendar of events. If certain activities won't help the group achieve its goals, discard them. For example, sponsoring a traditional Easter breakfast may not be an appropriate activity if the group's goals are to build community within the group, help needy people, or learn more about the Bible.

Goals provide a sense of purpose and direction. Together, the kids and leaders need to determine goals by examining programs within their grasp and deciding upon reasonable limits to set.

The one essential ingredient in the goal-setting process is membership involvement. Kids are more committed to a group when they help decide what will happen within that group. Being involved in the planning process provides a sense of ownership. This sense of ownership will result in increased group participation.

STEP #4 Establish objectives.

While goals are general statements that reveal what we hope to achieve over a period of time, objectives are specific, clear statements that help us avoid confusion and aim ourselves in the right direction. Objectives help us reach our goals by giving us realistic guidelines to follow.

Everyone and everything has limitations, including junior highers and the church. These limitations need to be determined before objectives can be established. For example, junior highers only have a certain amount of time to devote to youth group activities. The kids, as well as the church, have financial limitations to consider.

Following are examples of objectives that a junior high group might list to attain their established goals:

Goal

To build community within our group.

Objectives

●We will plan one fun fellowship night each month.
●We will play games that increase interaction and discussion.
●We will implement a "buddy system" and assign each new person to an existing member. The member will be responsible for introductions and for making the new person feel welcome.

Goal

To help our group experience servanthood.

Objectives

●We will plan one service project every two months.
●We will help others through local service projects, we will sing at nursing homes, we will serve at church functions.
●At the end of each service project we will discuss the experience and how we felt about being servants.

STEP #5 Plan to meet your goals and objectives.

After determining group needs, goals and objectives, move on to the planning process. This process involves three steps.

1. Brainstorming. Gather interested kids and leaders and consider activities and ideas that will meet the established needs, goals and objectives. This is a time for brainstorming and dreaming, so list any and all ideas.

Consider holidays, seasons, and the church and school calendars. Avoid conflicts with important events such as prom or homecoming; try to capitalize on school vacations and holidays. During vacation time, when the group isn't locked into a weekly time slot, scheduling can be more flexible. For example: Plan a morning event one day, an afternoon event the next, an all-day trip the next, a lock-in the next, and so on.

So often, when school stops, youth programs stop. For junior highers, this means lots of time on their hands since many are still too young to work. Utilize these special times; brainstorm for all kinds of programming possibilities.

2. Prioritizing and finalizing. Because brainstorming generates more ideas than a group can possibly use in a year, prioritize all ideas. For example, if a group plans to meet twice a month to discuss serious issues, those issues need to be listed in order of importance. This prioritizing process should take into consideration questions such as:

●Is this idea suitable for junior highers?
●Is there enough time to develop the idea into a meaningful experience for the group?
●Are the leaders enthusiastic about the idea?
●Are the kids enthusiastic about the idea?
●Who could lead the activity?

●How will the idea contribute to the group's cohesiveness and spiritual growth?

●How could the event be publicized?

3. Make detailed plans and create a calendar of events. Effective planning for junior high ministry is similar to going on a journey: As we travel toward our destination (goal), we experience growth opportunities (objectives) along a predetermined route (plans).

Planning involves firming up details for each activity such as title or topic, date, beginning and ending times, location, possible registration fee, ideas for publicity and dates to begin promotion for major events. (See Chapter 11 for tips on publicity.) Planning also involves establishing alternatives (or backup activities) in case of emergencies.

Leaders need to select the best method to accomplish each objective. An objective for an activity might be "to help the kids learn each other's names." Achieve that objective by having the kids make name tags. After participants have worn the tags throughout an activity, gather all the name tags and mix them in a pile. Ask for a couple of volunteers to redistribute the tags to their owners. Award prizes to the volunteers who complete their task proficiently. How about letting them be the first ones in line for refreshments?

After all details are complete, create a calendar of events—include all pertinent information. Give calendars to the junior highers, parents and volunteers.

STEP #6 Evaluate constantly.

A master plan for junior high ministry would not be complete without evaluations. Evaluations are ways to check the group's pulse. Did the kids understand the purpose of an activity? Did they find the event exciting? more than they could handle, therefore frustrating?

Evaluations should be conducted as soon after an event as possible. They help leaders examine what has happened, make note of highlights and disappointments, keep the activities focused on goals, and help determine the future direction of the ministry. Evaluations can be conducted in several ways:

● *Informal*—Observe all events and listen. Make notes of comments and share them with the other leaders and volunteers.

● *Written*—Distribute paper or 3x5 cards and pencils to the participants. Have them answer questions such as:

What did you like best about the event? What would you like to see done differently next time? What did you learn?

Keep a file of completed evaluations. They serve as important records of the past, and they help in planning for the future.

● *Small groups*—Divide into groups of six or eight. Ask the kids to discuss positive and not-so-positive aspects of the event. Mingle in the groups and listen to the discussions, or ask one person in each group to record answers and summarize them for you.

● *Comprehensive*—Comprehensive evaluations are thorough appraisals of the leadership, event, participants, organization and results. Questions on a comprehensive evaluation could include:

Leadership

●Did the leaders enjoy their particular responsibility? Why or why not?

●What changes in the leadership team would result in it functioning better?

●What resources were used?

●How well did the leaders do their job?

●Were they adequately prepared? Explain.

●How could they improve upon the way they related to the group? to each other?

●Were responsibilities divided in a manner that promoted teamwork? Explain.

The Event

●How did everyone feel about the event?

●How did the setting contribute to the effectiveness of the activity?

●What type of publicity was used? Was it effective? Explain.

●Was the response to the event expected? Why or why not?

●How did the date, time and location contribute to the activity's success or failure?

The Participants

- What attracted young people to this event?
- Did they know what to expect? Explain.
- Was cost a factor in determining participation? Why or why not?
- What factors affected attendance?
- What did the participants learn from the activity?

Organization

- Did the event run smoothly?
- Did this event trigger any ideas for future programs?
- What was good about the planning?
- What could be improved?

Results

- Did the event accomplish the objectives? Explain.
- Were there any unexpected benefits? If so, describe them.
- What would you do or plan differently next time?

CHAPTER 9

EXPERIENTIAL LEARNING AND MINISTRY OPPORTUNITIES

There are so many dimensions, methods and theories of learning, that at times it's difficult to define. At the risk of over-simplification, we could define learning as the process that integrates experiences and insights into a person's lifestyle. Learning is inherent in a person's decisions, values and actions. In his book *A Learning Process for Religious Education*, Richard Reichert states the learning process has four stages:

- starting point
- significant experiences
- reflection
- assimilation

Basically, the *starting point* in the learning process is a person's present state: the total of his or her past experiences, value system, decision-making methods, behavior, readiness, environment, needs and abilities. When junior high leaders are unaware of a group's starting point, an activity they have prepared may fail.

The second stage, *significant experiences*, are events that influence the way a person thinks about his or her lifestyle and future options. Sometimes significant experiences occur unexpectedly and force us to grow; sometimes significant experiences can be planned. Without such experiences we stop developing; with too many or the wrong kind, we fall apart. We need significant experiences to grow, and we grow because we are ready for them. Junior high leaders should plan significant experiences where the kids learn more about the Christian faith. Significant experiences can happen in all of our programming: Bible studies, retreats, service projects, worship, etc.

The third stage of the learning process is *reflection*. In this stage, a person searches for an answer to the question, "What is the real meaning of what has happened to me?" Reflection involves analyzing, seeking advice, gathering facts and praying. Reflection can take place during a significant experience or over a long period of time. It can be a slow, painful realization or a spontaneous "Aha!" of sudden insight. Reflection leads to a decision that determines if behavior is confirmed or changed. Reflection involves solitude as well as dialogue. Junior high leaders should provide plenty of opportunities for the kids to ponder activities by themselves as well as to interact with others. One-on-one conversations, small group discussions, debates and role plays are all effective settings where kids can gain perspective on significant experiences.

Assimilation, the final, trial-and-error stage of the learning process, often is filled with doubt, confusion, hesitation or uncertainty about a new pattern of behavior. It is the initial attempt to "try out" what has been learned.

Assimilation is learning by doing. "In a single sentence, assimilation is implementing a decision based on reflection prompted by a significant experience."[1] Assimilation can be scary, especially for a junior higher, who is convinced he or she should act differently but does not know how to begin. Many times, assimilation demands a change in behavior that means less time for the pursuit of personal pleasure—no easy task for any age. Leaders need to support and provide opportunities for kids to put into practice the results of their reflection. It means providing situations for young people to apply their faith to decision-making, and to express Christian values of self-worth, concern for others, servanthood and a relationship with God.

The premise for experiential learning is: The more people are involved in the learning process, the more the kids will understand. Because junior highers are action-oriented, experiences that allow them to become totally absorbed are very appealing. Experiential learning fosters sharper insights, refined speaking and listening skills, and more precise decision-making and problem-solving skills. Experiential learning fosters friendship-building because the learning process is relational. Laughter is just as much a part of experiential learning as serious concentration.

At first, leaders may be uncomfortable with experiential learning. It requires careful planning, a reliance on the group to get involved, and a willingness not to tell the kids what they "ought" to learn from the activity. Experiential learning requires leaders to serve as helpers, enablers, facilitators, commentators and timekeepers. As the group becomes more comfortable with this type of learning, the leaders may be able to participate more. There are several elements to any experiential learning activity:

●Carefully define your objectives. What will the group learn? Are the objectives realistic and within the group's reach?

●How much time do you have? What type of setting is available to meet the objectives?

●What kind of experiences do you envision? How do you picture learning taking place?

●How many people will be involved? What is the most effective way to ensure maximum participation? Does size dictate the use of small groups?

●Define the role and tasks of participants in each group. Are they to work as a team or as individuals?

●What resources will each group need? Make certain the group understands how the resources are to be used.

●What is to happen as a result of the group working together? How do you plan to use what the kids learned?

●Make certain everyone understands the directions, including behavior limits and time restrictions.

●Create the scene, set the stage, instruct the participants. Provide plenty of time for reflection.[2]

Feel free to vary the following examples of experiential learning. The ideas are not listed in order of effectiveness; the needs and abilities of your group will determine what is appropriate. (The resource section in the back of this book lists books, magazines, movies and tapes that offer more activities and guidelines in many of these areas.)

1. Simulation games. Simulation games are activities designed to help participants experience real-life situations such as the effects of a nuclear war, hunger, prejudice, rumors, lying, cheating, stealing, beginning a new job, beginning high school, etc. Simulation games force participants to decide how they would act in a given situation. Some guidelines for implementing these games are:

●Allow ample time for discussion.

●Don't use a simulation game if the real thing is available; for example, take kids to fix up a poverty-stricken neighborhood rather than describing it.

●Hold a simulation game in a location away from the group's normal meeting room. This adds an element of surprise and newness.

●Respect the emotional capacity of participants. Don't create more frustration or feelings than they can handle.

●Avoid asking the kids to do something the leaders would feel uncomfortable doing.

Following is an example of a simulation game that deals with nuclear war.[3]

The Survivor
by Larry Keefauver

Before the game—Gather newsprint, a marker, 3x5 cards, and a paper and pencil for each person.

The opening—Ask the young people to sit comfortably, but somewhat spaced apart, around the meeting room.
Read to them the following about a possible world situation:

The date is July 1, 1999.
Due to a poor harvest, low crop production and the failure of the world

economy, the Third World nations in Africa and Asia have developed nuclear weapons to blackmail the superpowers.

One of the small Third World nations decided to launch missles to force a response. This terrorist country warned that more retaliation would come if the country wasn't given food. When the two superpowers failed to reach an agreement on what to do, the Third World nation launched a full attack on the United States and Russia.

One of the areas heavily hit is your city. All food and water supplies are contaminated and the "dirty" nature of the nuclear bomb has forced severe shortages in housing, food and water.

You are in a civil defense shelter with enough uncontaminated food and water to keep half of the people in your group alive.

The game—Give everyone a blank sheet of paper and instruct each member to list 10 qualities that he or she possesses (for example: loving, caring, compassionate, efficient, etc.).

Next, ask group members to work together and list on newsprint the qualities and skills they feel are necessary to survive in a post-nuclear-war society. Remind them they are planning for a future society; they might want to first list farming skills, medical knowledge, carpentry skills, etc. Have them rank the items on the newsprint from most to least important.

Assign each person one of the following professions: business executive, doctor, professor, politician, psychologist, social worker, priest, homemaker, nurse, building contractor, farmer, mechanic, day laborer, water treatment specialist, computer programmer, dentist.

Tell the participants, "On the paper you used to list your personal qualities, write a paragraph giving reasons why you should be chosen to live ... help rebuild society. Why is your profession important? On your paper, rate the chance of the group deciding that you will be one of the few chosen to live: good, poor, almost none, none."

Have each person read to the group his or her paragraph saying why he or she should be chosen to survive.

The entire group should vote for the people they feel should survive. (If there are 10 group members, five will be chosen to survive.) Use 3x5 cards for a secret ballot. Tally the ballots and list on newsprint the people who were selected and their skill/society title.

Debriefing—Discuss these questions with your group:

● How did your secret survival possibility rating compare with the group's selection? Were you surprised? angry? pleased?

● What kind of society did the group construct? Do the people selected have both the skills and values needed to construct a viable society? Would the society you created have a realistic chance of survival in a post-nuclear-attack situation? Explain. How did prejudice affect your selections?

● How did your faith affect your voting? Select one of the following and explain:

"My faith was the primary criterion for selecting."
"My faith played an important role in selection."
"My faith had some influence in my selection."
"My faith did not enter into the selection process."

●Have each group member complete this sentence: The most important thing I learned in this game was ...

Discussions should not be hurried since the kids need to express their feelings before they can rationally look at what happened. Only as the group members discuss what they learned are they able to apply new ideas, new concepts, or changed behavior to their lives.

2. No-loser recreational activities. No one likes to lose, especially junior highers. Early adolescents are trying to find their identity and suffer enough from a poor self-image. We shouldn't add to this by playing games that stress competition and choosing sides. The church should provide a setting where all people feel they are winners and that they are needed.

All games and activities need to be carefully chosen. Just because they look clever or fun does not guarantee they are suitable for the group. Leaders should consider several matters when selecting appropriate games:

●Will the group enjoy the activity?

●Will the activity embarrass members or isolate others who will be laughed at?

●How does the game meet the program's purpose and objectives?

●Would you consider participating in this activity yourself?

The objective of no-loser recreation is to build up others, not to tear them down. When the emphasis of a recreational activity is on mutual support and encouragement, the need for keeping score or declaring a winner loses its importance. Recreation, without winning at all costs, gives kids a chance to test their friendship skills and practice sharing and caring. Following is an example of a no-loser recreational activity that stresses affirmation—everybody wins!

Ten

Form a circle, then distribute a paper and pencil to each person. Allow five minutes for the kids to write 10 things they like about themselves.

Have an individual read his or her list of 10 items. Allow three different people to share specific examples of how they have seen one of those 10 qualities in that person. For example, "I saw Karen show how much she cares for others when she volunteered to help Karla with her confirmation assignment." Give each person a chance to read his or her qualities and be affirmed.[4]

3. Role plays. Role plays are a variation of simulation games. Participants are presented with a real-life situation, assigned roles, and asked to act it out. Afterward the group discusses feelings and observations.

Some role plays demand that actors make character judgments and ethical decisions. Leaders can initiate interesting results by asking kids to assume the role of someone very different from themselves; for example, a parent, an alcoholic, a starving child, a disabled person, etc.

When presenting a real-life situation, it's best to be brief. Too much talking may reveal a solution before kids have a chance to get involved. Following are examples of role plays:

Role Play #1

Characters: Mom, Dad, Teenager
Situation: Mom and Dad have decided to divorce. They've struggled with an unhappy marriage for years, and feel it's time for some happiness. They explain their decision to the teenager.

Role Play #2

Characters: Believer, non-believer
Situation: Believer tries to witness; non-believer resists.

Role Play #3

Characters: Three friends
Situation: One friend overhears the other two gossiping about a classmate. They say the person is pregnant. The friend knows this isn't true.

4. Mime. A challenging, creative way of involving young people in learning is through the medium of mime. Mime is extremely effective because it requires silence—the use of actions rather than words. Since junior highers live in a world that constantly bombards them with audio-messages, they respond to highly visual stimuli.

In *The Basic Encyclopedia for Youth Ministry*, Dennis Benson and Bill Wolfe say that mime is relatively easy to learn and do:

> *All of us use mime in varying amounts in our daily routine. We signal to other persons using our faces and bodies. We wave our hands, point our thumbs down to tell our disapproval, point to our watch when we want others to be aware of time. Thus, it is natural to expand this to develop an elaborate system of conveying our feelings.*
>
> *... Expenses for materials are minimal. Props are not necessary since they are constructed in the imagination. Little makeup or costuming is required. The scripting is done either through personal creation or by using passages from the Bible. On occasion, music can be helpful, though not necessary.[5]*

Mime relies on the audience to participate in an exchange of ideas and emotions. The mime becomes the message since body movement and facial expression are the prime communicators. Mime is more directed at telling a story rather than playing a game. Mimes can depict a Bible story, parable, proverb, historical narrative, psalm, religious poem or hymn. Humor is often part of mime since it accentuates movement in the creation of characters.

Junior highers are capable of relating to how a person might feel, think and act in a given situation; however, background information may need to be given in some cases. For example, before kids can mime the parable of the good Samaritan, they need to learn about the prejudice against the Samaritans.

Junior highers make significant self-discoveries through experiencing the non-verbal portrayal of other personalities and through sharing their inner feelings.

5. Drama. Since the early days of the church, drama has

been used to express people's faith and their encounters with God. Drama is an exciting way to involve kids in the learning process. By assuming characters, the junior highers discover reasons for the characters' feelings and behaviors. Learning comes from the commitment to a project, the discussion of a play's message, the development of the principal parts, and the reaction of the audience.

Drama is an exciting avenue for building community within a junior high group—it takes teamwork to present a play. Kids can use standard plays or skits that are available from Christian bookstores or denominational offices, or they can write their own plays. Junior highers are wonderful at staging Bible stories and creating dialogue between major characters. They can brainstorm for possible Bible stories, characters, props, costumes and script. Some fun stories to reenact are: Moses and the burning bush (Exodus 3:1—4:17), Joseph and his jealous brothers (Genesis 37:5-35), Job and his friends (the book of Job), Jesus at the wedding in Canaan (John 2:1-11).

While some junior highers may enjoy performing, those who are inhibited may prefer working behind the scenes: making costumes, helping with makeup, being a member of the stage crew, collecting tickets, ushering, serving refreshments.

Reader's theater is a simple and practical technique for encouraging teenagers' interest and talent. There are no lines to memorize. Kids can rewrite biblical stories or passages, providing parts for several people.

An example of reader's theater is to have the entire junior high group read 1 Corinthians 13—the love chapter. Have the reader wear white, cover the stage with red carpet, paint the backdrop red, hang red construction paper hearts from the ceiling, play the sound of a beating heart in the background (check the local library for a sound-effects record).

Reader's theater, plays and skits can be performed in worship, at nursing homes, for younger children's Sunday school, etc. Whatever the occasion, dramatic presentations are opportunities for junior highers to share and give of themselves.

6. Puppets. One of the most simple and inexpensive resources available to youth groups are puppets. Junior high groups can begin a puppet ministry by spending as much or as little money as they want. Elaborate puppets and stages can be purchased at many department stores, toy stores or drama supply companies. Or a simple stage can be made by turning a table over on its side, by tacking a sheet across an open doorway, or by cutting a cardboard refrigerator box to size. Puppets can be made from paper plates, paper sacks, socks and other materials found around the house.

Puppetry is more than an opportunity for young people to entertain; it is an opportunity for kids to express their true feelings through another voice and body. At a time when many adolescents feel awkward about their voice and body, they can use a puppet to become whoever they want. They can ask questions, make statements, and even make mistakes, and still feel comfortable because they are not directly in the spotlight.

Puppetry involves kids in a team effort as they select stories, write their own scripts, create scenery, and work with lighting and sound. Puppets appeal to people of all ages.

7. Clowning. This popular ministry makes use of imagination by means of non-verbal communication. The clown is a symbol of the biblical concept of servant. "He who is greatest among you shall be your servant; whoever exalts himself will be humbled, and whoever humbles himself will be exalted" (Matthew 23:11).

The clown also symbolizes Jesus' command for us to be childlike. "Let the children come to me, do not hinder them, for to such belongs the kingdom of God. Truly I say to you, whoever does not receive the kingdom of God like a child shall not enter it" (Mark 10:14-15).

Clowning enables young people to develop caring skills while being a different character. In this way, they can stretch themselves and risk being laughed at. It is important for kids involved in clowning to understand a few basic guidelines:

●Clowns do not force themselves on others.
●Clowns aim to do more than simply entertain.
●Clowns give of themselves to bring joy to others.

One of the best resources on clowning is *Clown Ministry* by Floyd Shaffer and Penne Sewall. It includes everything a group needs to know about starting or enhancing a clown ministry: makeup and costume tips, how to create a clown name, skits and other ideas. The authors discuss the importance of beginning with small activities, such as giving out balloons at a nursing home, before advancing to more elaborate activities, such as interpreting a Gospel message at a church service or planning an entire clown worship service.

Clown ministry helps young people experience servanthood and become like children. Through the junior highers' experiences, these biblical concepts will become cemented in their lives.

8. Liturgical dance. The appreciation of dance varies depending on tradition, history and biblical understanding. We need to respect the attitudes that prevail in our churches and not put young people in the middle of an emotionally loaded issue.

If churches are against dance, it may be that they are unaware of the meaning dance can add to worship. If this is the case, don't give up—change can occur. Before introducing dance to a congregation, tell them your purpose and intent. Read to them various scripture references pertaining to dance such as, "Praise him with timbrel and dance; praise him with strings and pipe!" (Psalm 150:4).

Liturgical dance is a marvelous way of interpreting the faith. It can be used for storytelling, interpreting prayers and accentuating hymns or anthems. For example, three young people could wear choir robes and interpret a choir anthem with simple movements. Forming a circle and moving clockwise could symbolize our oneness in Christ, arms raised could symbolize praise, arms raised and swaying to the right and left could symbolize the Holy Spirit moving in our lives.

Other forms of dance can be used in junior high ministry. Folk dancing offers insight into other cultures and periods of history; circle dances, or those that encourage the exchange of partners, are good community builders.

9. Media. Kids have an affinity to music, art, film, video and other means of communication. Junior high leaders should capitalize on this interest and utilize media in experiential learning. For example, the kids can:

●Produce a play, videotape the performance and then show it to other churches

●Take slides of their summer junior high youth group trip, then add background music and put on a show for parents

●Combine pictures, videotapes, slides and music and create a junior high ministry display for a local shopping mall

●Incorporate music, dance and drama to interpret hymns, Bible passages or to present sermons

One media technique junior highers enjoy is interviewing. Interviewing is an effective means of reaching the kids when they need to hear from a "voice of experience," but the lecture method is inappropriate. This learning experience simply requires a cassette tape recorder, tape and microphone. It provides opportunities for kids to gather information from individuals and then reflect on the information gathered.

Like any other meaningful experience, interviewing needs to be planned carefully. Junior highers should wrestle with the objectives and methods for conducting the interview. Junior highers also need to learn how to listen. People are usually quite eager to share—it's amazing what doors will be opened to them. Good listeners focus on the feelings expressed, or on points of the story that will lead to further disclosure. Open-ended questions, or those that have no right or wrong answers, are the most revealing. Finally, interviewers need to learn how to close an interview and thank the participant for his or her openness. Once the tape recorder has been shut off, the interviewee will remember the experience.

Playing back what has been recorded offers all kinds of learning possibilities. The group can share the answers received to their questions, as well as their own reactions to what was said. Hearing from people who "have been there" helps teenagers test their ideas against real experiences, deepens their sensitivities, and expands their tolerance for other viewpoints.

10. Intergenerational relationships. These can be one of the finest examples of mutual ministry the church has to offer. Intergenerational ministry is more than interacting with the elderly. It also can include junior highers and their parents, or junior highers working with children. Whatever the circumstances, it is an opportunity for both generations to give to each other out of need.

Regrettably, we live in a culture that separates generations rather than brings them closer. Junior highers have very little opportunity to relate to people in their community who are younger or older. Even within the family unit, there is no longer a guarantee that teenagers will be exposed to the needs and contributions of grandparents, aunts, uncles and cousins. Today, the extended family is no longer a reality.

Faith is caught and taught through relationships. It's a lot like the apprenticeship style of learning a skill. Whatever the range of ages involved, there is something to be gained by giving to others and learning to receive. The sensitivity of young people enables them to appreciate that people of all ages have gifts to share.

Take the following points into consideration when involving junior highers in intergenerational activities:

●Both generations should be given an opportunity to contribute to the other.

●Both generations need to understand the abilities and limitations of the other.

●The place and time for being together should allow for a caring relationship.

●There must be planned continuity to the relationship.

●Both generations need time to reflect on what is happening between them.

11. Social activities. We are all social creatures—and junior highers place a high value on having a good time with others. So often it is the social atmosphere that draws young people to an event rather than the purpose or intent of the event.

Teenagers will have no difficulty putting together a list of social events in which they would like to participate. No matter what the group decides (roller skating, New Year's Eve party or hayride), the most important factor is that everyone has fun.

Every successful social event for junior highers has the following ingredients:

●Certain people exhibit a sense of welcome and warmth.

●Activities are designed to involve everyone present (no matter how large the group).

●The setting is appropriate.

●There is plenty of food to enjoy that is served in a dignified manner.

The best social activities are the ones that are carefully planned. This does not mean that a party or social event should be run with military-like precision. It does mean that a lot of thought goes into caring for all the people who attend—making sure all is done to ensure they have a good time.

Having enough people to help is also significant to the success of a social activity. There should be people to greet kids and give them special instructions. Others should be ready to involve them as soon as they walk in the door, introducing them to people already present or engaging them in conversation. When the time comes for the group to interact, play a game or dance, the helpers should jump right in with the kids. All the "little details" help make uneasy junior highers more comfortable in a social situation.

Junior high groups can "add spice" to their social events by choosing unusual places to have activities. A barn is a natural gathering place for mixers and food if you're planning a hayride. Sometimes you can get special rates at skating rinks or bowling alleys if you hold your event during unusual hours (bowling at midnight or skating at 8 a.m.). Not every activity or party has to be in someone's home or in the church basement (although those settings can be used for some pretty creative themes).

Food plays a big part in any successful gathering for young people. Selecting food for an activity means serving appropriate refreshments—hot chocolate or hot cider goes better with ice skating than banana splits. Another approach to food selection relates to the activity. Food can be used effectively to help develop a theme or enhance a learning experience. If you're having a speaker or mission study on Mexico, serve Mexican food such as tacos, burritos, enchiladas and refried beans.

The way food is shared in a group also says something to young people. Junior highers often need advice on simple table manners. They appreciate food being served as if people care. Serving ice cream sundaes in cups or dishes means more to kids than a simple announcement like, "The ice cream packs are on the table. Serve yourself. Good luck!"

12. Exchange programs. These take a lot of work but can be valuable learning experiences for older junior highers.

Hosting activities or visiting with junior highers from different parts of the country or community can be real eye-openers.

There are so many diverse cultural, ethnic and religious groups in this country that the possibilities for learning are unlimited. Junior high groups from rural areas could exchange for weekends, or longer periods of time in the summer, with kids from the inner city. Groups from the Midwest could spend time with people from the Northeast. Young people from Scandinavian backgrounds could host their peers who come from Middle-Eastern families.

The time spent together can lead to exploration of the differences as well as similarities among teenagers. Discussing or doing things that are customary for a particular area of the country, eating foods indigenous to an area, participating in ethnic festivals, worshiping in other traditions, all lead to a greater awareness beyond self.

13. Trips. A first cousin to exchange experiences is planning and taking a group trip. Anything is possible, from an afternoon field trip to spending several weeks exploring cross-country. Any purpose will suffice, from visiting new places, to investigating a problem, to spending time together having fun and building community. (Trips may be scheduled at inconvenient times for some people in the group. Nonetheless, with good advance planning, maximum participation can be guaranteed.)

There is nothing like a common pilgrimage to bring people together who don't know each other very well. The key to making this type of experience valuable to participants is making certain they know why they are taking part in the experience. It can be disastrous if part of the group is participating in a trip for the wrong reasons.

Traveling together presents opportunities for members to assume responsibilities such as cooking, planning recreation, washing vehicles, preparing daily worship, or chronicling the daily events in the group diary. Group members learn what it takes to live together. They learn to give up some personal desires for the sakes of others.

Another aspect of traveling is making certain the pace permits time for relaxation. Long rides, trips or tours can be physically exhausting; time to play is an essential component. Traveling brings out the best and worst in people. Being exposed to such traits makes traveling together a prime experience for learning how to get along with others.

Trips open up a whole new world for junior highers. Not only are they introduced to experiences, people and places that are not familiar to them, trips also provide opportunities for them to share what they've learned with people back home. This is especially important to do for group members who were unable to come. Sharing pictures or slides taken on the trip is one way of reflecting and remembering the experience.

14. Service projects. Reaching out to others embraces both the witness and service dimensions of the Christian life. Junior highers have a great capacity to do both. Some of the best learning opportunities come from trips that combine travel with some sort of service project or mission. Although outreach can and should happen at home, many junior highers seem to feel more comfortable testing what it's like to give of themselves in different environments. There's something about reaching out to others that impacts deep spiritual maturity; learning what it means to be a servant adds a deeper dimension to life.

Junior high leaders may find it difficult at first to initiate service projects and trips with kids. Many community organizations aren't eager to host junior highers because of the misconception that adolescents are irresponsible. Nonetheless, opportunities to reach out and help people are important ingredients in the maturation process. Certainly this is true for Christians—servanthood is part of our legacy.

There's as much to be learned from the actual physical labor involved in a service project as there is from the people being helped. Practicing what we preach strengthens what we believe. Words that become deeds make faith a living reality.

There is no predetermined formula for successful outreach experiences, but there are certain guidelines that are practical to follow:

●What does your group need to learn? What is it capable of doing?

●What possibilities exist for outreach projects? Are they realistic for your group in terms of time? expense? location?

●Is the group ready and interested in participating in a work project?

●What exactly do the hosts of the service project want the group to do?

●Does the project lend itself to group life? What is available through the project that allows the kids to share their faith and their concern for one another?

Some leaders may not feel comfortable organizing a service project for their junior high group. If this is the case, there are many organizations who will plan for leaders. Many times, besides planning the service project, they plan the evening programs as well. Check with organizations such as Group or your denominational offices.

Whenever junior highers are involved in outreach, top off the experience with a presentation for the congregation. Show slides, play taped interviews, have the kids tell their favorite story, etc. Sharing the experience with others cements memories in everyone's mind. The kids and congregation members share in the exciting and meaningful experience.

15. Camping. All kinds of camping experiences are available for kids. For those who like the rugged outdoors, there are survival and adventure camps. For those who prefer less strenuous activities, there are hiking or canoe trips. For those who like modern conveniences, there are residential camps that provide cabins, pool, dining hall and meeting rooms. Other experiences include backpacking, cave exploration, bike hikes, horseback trips or tent camping.

Some survival camping is designed for the junior high level by using creative crisis to force kids to become dependent on others in the group. The physical challenge involved teaches self-reliance; interdependence is developed out of necessity, if they are to endure. Learning to cope with fear is one of the emotional battles fought in this kind of environment.

Biking and hiking make use of solid physical exercise and are excellent learning activities. One biking group set out on a journey knowing only their destination. The learning experience was centered around working and asking for food and lodging. The kids repaid their hosts by doing chores.

Keeping a balanced pace is the secret to making camping

special. Allow time for recreation and for appreciation of nature. Explore the mountains and hills; look at the sky; check out the lakes, rivers or streams; hunt for the little creatures that crawl and live under rocks or in trees.

Hold daily worship in a most scenic spot; two meaningful times are sunrise and sunset. Singing, and talking about the Bible and the surrounding sights and sounds, make for lifetime memories.

Camping is especially suited for providing kids with quiet times. Don't permit them to bring radios or tape players. Daily, give the kids quiet time alone, to walk through the woods, or to find a special spot to call their own. Listening to the wind, the sound of rushing water or feeling the breeze, all help kids ponder God and their place in creation.

16. Hunger. Several avenues of learning can be used to teach about this global concern. Since junior highers have a great compassion for the oppressed, this is a perfect subject for them.

Sometimes massive problems engulf us. Rather than feeling overwhelmed and helpless, early adolescents need to see that their efforts can make a difference. For example, although a program they conduct on hunger won't erase the pain of starvation, it will heighten people's awareness. Teenagers can learn a great deal from conducting research on hunger and other global concerns. From what they discover, they may be motivated to organize service projects or fund raisers. Some groups discover the need to feed people in their own community is as great a concern as feeding the hungry halfway around the world. Following are some experiential learning activities that heighten kids' awareness:

●Collect money, food or clothing for UNICEF or other agencies for world distribution.

●Contact or support politicians who lead social action programs—whose efforts are directed toward meeting the needs of the poor.

●Sponsor a hunger forum for the entire community and extend awareness beyond your group.

17. Prayer. Most teenagers react with uncertainty about prayer because of the limited exposure they've had to its practice. Hardly anybody denies the importance of prayer in a Christian's life, but few people develop effective means for teaching kids how to communicate with God.

Prayer is a deeply personal experience and therefore, loaded with learning possibilities. Kids need to be exposed to the variety of prayer styles, what prayer is and isn't, and the proper use of prayer (it is not magic). Kids need to be encouraged to set aside special times in their life for prayerful meditation. We genuinely shortchange junior highers if we don't provide opportunities for them to explore this vital link in their relationship with God.

Junior highers relate well to experiences with imaginative prayer. This approach asks kids to envision having a conversation with God. The narrator directs kids to sit comfortably in a chair, or lay down on the carpet and close their eyes. The narrator leads the group on a prayer journey, stopping at certain points along the way to let kids silently express their thoughts to God. It is important the leader be careful not to suggest what a person should say, but rather, creates a setting in a teenager's mind that makes talking to God seem natural. For example:

> Imagine that you are sitting on a rock in the mountains. The sky is bright blue; the clouds look soft and feathery; the trees are gently swaying in the breeze; the air smells fresh following an afternoon shower. You sit, quietly enjoying the beauty of God's world. You hear someone approach; you turn and see Jesus. He talks to you and listens to your worries. You tell him everything. What does he say? What does he suggest? Jesus hugs you. He tells you he loves you and promises to strengthen and comfort you throughout your life.

Junior highers are eager to share their feelings and describe their imaginary encounter with God after this type of experience. It is a fascinating experience, and needs to be sensitively directed.

Another meaningful prayer experience is individual meditation. Meditation can be used in any setting, but is most effective during a camp or retreat. Individuals are given a scripture passage to read and questions to answer. They are encouraged to go off by themselves for a private devotion. Following is an example:

"Therefore, if any one is in Christ, he is a new creation; the old has passed away, behold, the new has come" (2 Corinthians 5:17).

● What does this verse mean to you?
● Does this verse mean that all of our past mistakes are forgotten? all of our sins forgiven? Explain.
● How do you feel about Christ forgiving all your sins?
● Complete this sentence: "As a new creation in Christ I will ..."

---

18. Journals. A journal is a very helpful tool that allows kids to reflect on their relationships, activities and emotions. One journal-keeping method is for kids to set aside five minutes each day to record anything at all in their journals: thoughts, feelings, fun activities, strange happenings, worries, goals, etc.

Another method is for kids to imagine they are writing to a special person—either living or dead. The kids can begin the entry with a statement that describes a current situation or emotion, then proceed to write an imagined conversation. It's amazing what insights will be revealed through an imaginary conversation. After writing this type of journal entry, kids are encouraged to read it and make note of the emotions it contains.

Journals also serve as permanent records of group events such as retreats, camps, road trips, etc. Each day a group is together and shares an experience, time should be allotted for journal writing. Have the kids record the day's happenings, insights and ideas, emotions and thoughts. At the end of an event, journals are most useful in helping individuals recall significant experiences they'd like to share as a large group. Such times can be deeply moving.

Many leaders shy away from using journals. No one can guarantee how every experience will turn out. We live in a society that is so success-oriented that putting kids into a situation where they are instructed to use their imaginations can be too threatening. Nevertheless, kids who are affirmed, as well as challenged, almost always exceed expectations. Even if they fail, they can still learn. Moments of sharing after any risky experience are usually quite meaningful.

The list of learning experiences for junior highers could go on and on—anything we do has the potential to teach. The world is waiting at your doorstep to be experienced—and each experience is an opportunity to learn.

CHAPTER 10

DISCUSSIONS

Learning how to talk with people is part of the maturation process and a channel through which individuals gain insight into the Christian faith.

In our society, we love to talk. We talk about personal problems with friends; parents talk about their children; children talk about their parents. In past decades, discussions were held at town meetings or around a cracker-barrel in a country store. Years ago there were stump speakers; now there are talk show hosts.

Discussion is a particular form of talking; it is different from an argument and free conversation. In an argument, someone tries to prove the other person is wrong. In a free conversation, people talk about anything that comes to mind and move from topic to topic without any specific purpose or goal. Discussion is none of these. It is the conversation between two or more people in search of an understanding on an issue of common interest. Each participant talks as well as listens.

Junior highers love to talk. They appreciate opportunities to express feelings and points of view. Such opportunities allow leaders to build a strong relationship with early adolescents.

A discussion can be planned as the focal point of a meeting or can take place on the spur of the moment in response to something that needs attention. General characteristics of good group discussion include:

● The issue must be of interest to those involved.

● The setting should be informal and conducive to learning.

● Questions and responses come, not from the leader but from the group.

● Different opinions are respected and encouraged.

● Individuals are respected for their points of view.

● Participants gain a deeper appreciation for one another when they express what they think.

● Learning is emphasized rather than teaching.

● Participants contribute out of their knowledge and experience.

● Advance preparation makes for a better group experience.

The purposeful exchange of ideas in an informal setting also contributes to the building of community. Just because members of a junior high group attend the same school or live in the same neighborhood doesn't guarantee they know each other. Providing an environment for open discussion and communication contributes to a healthy group spirit. Few places exist where early adolescents can open up and discuss their feelings or thoughts about their lives. A youth group should be one place where teenagers feel comfortable communicating what's on their minds.

Purposes for discussions may vary: to exchange information, to come to a consensus for taking action, to reach agreements about relationships, to release tensions. Discussions help bring junior highers face to face with their ideas and the thoughts of others.

Good discussions are the result of careful planning. Part of that planning is understanding the potential and the process. Good group discussions have the potential to bring people together to gain a better understanding of who they are. Participants should feel affirmed and accepted, no matter what their viewpoint. Affirming the dignity of each person in a discussion leads to greater exploration of an issue.

Discussions help foster junior highers' ability to think for themselves and assume responsibility for their thoughts. The recognition that an individual belongs to a group that values his or her opinions leads to a greater sense of self-worth.

Before successful discussions can occur, members of the group must become acquainted with one another. Simple crowdbreakers help people know more about each other than names. For example, before a discussion, divide kids into trios. Have them answer questions such as:

●Who was your favorite elementary school teacher and why?

●If you could travel anywhere in the world, where would you go?

Helping people learn about each other breaks down barriers that keep them from establishing trust. We cannot assume, just because some members have been together since nursery school, that they know everything about each other, or feel at ease with each other.

Successful discussions call for kids to trust one another. As respect and affirmation are expressed, junior highers begin to realize they are supported. The degree of trust that exists within a group is a key determining factor in what type of conversations will take place. So often in church youth groups, discussions focus on personal issues; members are asked to examine themselves or share ideas. No one should be forced to divulge feelings he or she is uncomfortable discussing in public.

Allowing the kids to participate when they are willing, makes them good listeners and contributors. Careful listening to what others have to say takes concentration. Those who feel comfortable in group discussions pay attention to each other instead of worrying about what they'll say next. Junior highers are just developing these feelings of ease in a group and need to be encouraged.

Individuals within a discussion group play a variety of roles. Astute leaders will recognize the silent member, the dominant discussion member, the joker, the "yes" person, and the diplomat. As junior highers become more comfortable in discussion settings, the types of conversations they have will change. At first, it is normal that young people, working on developing trust, seldom go beyond touching the surface of an issue. Over a period of time, leaders can help members participate at a deeper level of conversation by providing non-threatening experiences to clarify and justify their comments, comparing and contrasting their points of view with others, and helping them evaluate their thoughts and what others have to say.

Successful discussions require an atmosphere of respect. There must be respect for:

●the importance of the issue

●each person in the group and what he or she contributes

●the group leader and the direction he or she offers

Choosing types, or methods, of group discussion will depend a great deal on the issue, objectives, maturity of participants, size of the group, degree of desired formality or informality, and the way members relate to each other. Many methods junior highers seem to enjoy are summarized in *The Basic Encyclopedia for Youth Ministry*, by Dennis C. Benson and Bill Wolfe.[1] I've combined their ideas with others, and created a list of methods for you to choose from.

Discussion Methods

1. Circle seating. For youth groups just getting acquainted with the discussion process, circle seating works best. This arrangement allows the leader to coax the kids to talk. Each person can be seen by the entire group as he or she contributes to the discussion. For the most effective use of time and participation, include no more than 15 to 20 in each group.

This process involves shy people and encourages them to share. It also provides time to practice listening skills and heightens the anticipation of discussion since each person must wait his or her turn as the discussion moves around the circle.

2. Small group conversation. This method divides a large group into small groups of two to eight people. It is a quick way to get a lot of people involved in discussion. The subject is introduced in a 5- to 10-minute presentation, directions are given and assignments are made. One person in each small group is designated "reporter." He or she accepts the responsibility of later reporting to the large group what was discussed.

3. Fish bowl. In this approach, two circles are formed, one inside the other. The outside group observes and evaluates as the inside group discusses the assigned topic. A time limit is set and group members are reminded it is essential they participate. The outside circle focuses on questions such as:

- Is anyone not participating?
- Is anyone talking too much?
- Do people interrupt each other?
- What were the main points of the discussion?
- How could you summarize the discussion?

After a 10- to 15-minute discussion, the inner group gives the outer group members a chance to share their observations. Next, reverse the circles and repeat the process. At the conclusion, both circles react to the entire experience.

4. Modified fish bowl. Observers in the outer circle can exchange places with folks in the inner circle during the discussion if someone is willing to trade.

5. Case history. This technique uses a real situation to stimulate conversation. The circumstances in which a person had to make a decision are explained, short of the decision he or she made. Group members are asked how they would handle the same situation. For example: "One 15-year-old girl discovered that she was two months pregnant. She was very confused. Should she tell her parents? get an abortion? keep the baby? give it up for adoption?" After discussion, leaders may wish to share what the real person decided.

6. Formal debate. Two groups are formed to debate an issue. Both sides are determined to prove their position is correct, based on the evidence they present. Opinions have no place in debates since all statements must be based on facts, statistics or quotes. This approach prevents participants from wandering off the subject and challenges them to think and question. Debates force one to think fast, reason and listen. They are highly structured; you win by following the rules.

7. Audience-involvement debate. This form of debate gives the audience an active role. One side of the room is labeled "for"; the other "against." The subject is announced, and people sit on the side of the room that corresponds with their opinion. While representatives of each group debate the issue, members of the audience may interrupt with questions or express their own points of view. At the end, persons who have been persuaded to change their thinking may move to the other side of the room. The side with the most new recruits, wins. The primary focus of this method is to stimulate thought and to encourage expression of viewpoints; winning is secondary.

8. Mini-congress. Issues are presented as a resolution, much like elected officials present their stand for or against a matter to be voted upon. Speakers are limited to three minutes; they may speak no more than five times; and they may be interrupted by another person wishing to ask a question or amend the resolution. *Robert's Rules of Order* provides the parliamentary procedures to follow.[2] This approach permits individuals to address provocative present-day issues. If you wish, voting can take place after all the speakers have had their turn.

9. Dialogues. This form of discussion is not a debate, but rather two people discussing what they know about a given subject from reading about it, experience or their own research. Use dialogues with junior highers when participants have time to assemble information so that the experience will be meaningful. Before the dialogue takes place, individuals should do their homework and have notes to use when it comes time to speak; leaders should set a time limit on the dialogues and not allow the conversation to become an argument. Use the dialogue technique to explore topics such as the compatibility of science and religion, or whether the Bible should be interpreted literally.

10. The Lafayette Square spot. In Washington, D.C., across from the White House, there is a park where people gather to present causes and speak freely about problems, peeves or points of view. They are people who take seriously their right to exercise free speech.

Designate a spot in the meeting room where members can go to express their feelings about an activity. Designate a second spot for those who wish to offer a differing opinion. The ground rule is that complete freedom of speech is assured. Both speakers and listeners are expected to practice courtesy and good taste. Although the spot may not be used often, junior highers will know there is a place in the church where they are free to express their feelings.

11. Press conference (or interview method). This discussion technique is great for people who don't feel comfortable speaking in front of a group.

One way to use this method is to have junior highers interview parents. Kids can turn the tables on their mothers and fathers who seem to always be asking questions. At least a week prior to the interview, have the group members discuss some elements of a good interview and what questions they'd like to ask parents. Compile their questions.

Carefully plan the interview. Give teams of kids cassette recorders, microphones, tapes and the list of questions. Have them report back to the group.

In addition to parents, interview people from the community such as a member of Alcoholics Anonymous or Mothers Against Drunk Drivers. A person who has "been there" and lived through hard times, may not feel at ease giving speeches, but might willingly answer questions.

12. The open forum. No matter what the size of the group, a forum provides a setting in which any number of kids are given an equal opportunity to speak freely. A presenter introduces a topic, then asks for reactions or questions. Perhaps reactions might first be offered by a panel, then members of the group can comment. Likewise, the panel also can be included in answering questions that arise. This is not a debate, but an opportunity to exchange points of view.

13. Panel discussions. A panel discussion is not a free conversation because participants know their subject in advance, have met and discussed the points they want to cover, and have had time to research their particular area of input. Panels usually include three to six people who sit in a semi-circle and exchange ideas informally. A moderator presides.

In a panel discussion, simple guidelines should prevail in order to hold the interest of the audience. Panelists should talk no more than one minute at a time, stay on the subject, respect all opinions, keep arguments at a minimum, and be as prepared as possible.

The moderator often determines the success of a panel discussion. Before the meeting, he or she should meet with the participants to outline the presentation to be made. A series of questions is drawn up to stimulate discussion after each panelist has spoken. The moderator sits in the center of the panel and introduces each speaker with a bit of biographical or background information. The discussion should flow smoothly; the moderator interrupts speakers only when it is appropriate and to make certain all have a chance to speak. He or she keeps the discussion on track and does not offer personal opinions. The moderator calls on the audience for questions. At the end of the discussion, the moderator summarizes what has taken place.

Effective Discussion Leaders

Whether it is a panel or small group, good discussions need leaders. Junior highers need guidance as they explore the many different ways of exchanging their thoughts and feelings. Discussion leaders not only plan and guide conversations, they also encourage everyone present to participate.

A leader needs to have an open mind, a sense of humor, and a genuine interest in what people have to say. He or she should know how to create a friendly atmosphere where people are free to express themselves. The leader needs to respect all opinions, be impartial and generous enough to accept ideas he or she disagrees with. He or she also should be a good listener and draw out the group's thoughts rather than express his or her own.

It is the responsibility of the discussion leader to see that all participants have an opportunity to express themselves. The leader also must learn when to allow digression. Occasional "tangents" are natural and help clarify an issue. Nonetheless, a leader must keep people on track, encourage them to say what they mean, and restate comments when necessary, to verify their intended meaning. A leader also must help participants understand opposite points of view and use simple language to keep the conversation flowing.

A leader needs to be aware of those who are timid and lead them into the conversation. This is a good way to keep one person from dominating a discussion. Questions should be followed by a period of silence, to give people in the group time to think. If there is no response within a reasonable amount of time, the leader may call on someone to comment, or make sure the question was understood.

From time to time, it is helpful for a discussion leader to briefly summarize. This helps the group stay on track, prevent repetition, see how the discussion has progressed, and keep the discussion moving. A discussion leader must keep in mind that his or her comments should be brief and, when questions are asked, he or she should not answer them, but redirect them to group members. The discussion leader is not there to assume the role of "resident expert."

It is the duty of a discussion leader to observe time limits and recognize when a conversation needs to end. The leader should summarize the points, recap how far the group progressed in considering the subject, and affirm the participants.

Although informal discussions seem to proceed with minimal organization, good discussion leaders know otherwise. Adults who want to promote worthwhile discussions for their junior highers use an outline to help guide a conversation. The outline should be flexible enough so that adjustments can be made as the session unfolds, and should function as a target or focal point for the discussion.

Good leaders know how to use questions to stimulate discussions. The opening question for discussion should be carefully thought out. Some leaders pose a provocative or dramatic question, aimed at getting an immediate response and often based on an emotional reaction. Others prefer to gradually lead into a topic by starting with non-threatening questions that everyone in the group can answer. Some possible starter questions include:

- How do you feel about ... ?
- What would you like to see happen ... ?
- What bothers you when you see ... ?
- In what ways might a person ... ?
- What are your feelings when ... ?
- What do you say to a person when ... ?
- Describe what it was that caused you to ... ?

Questions can be repeated from time to time to keep the group focused on the discussion topic.

Discussion leaders should not be upset with periods of silence. Not every question can be answered immediately; the kids may need time to think. Quiet time often means the wheels are churning inside. Likewise, some group members might need several days, a week or even months to formulate their answers.

Good leaders help create a healthy, caring, affirming atmosphere. In creating such an atmosphere for discussion, leaders need to remember the following:

1. Don't argue with expressed points of view. Teenagers need to feel that what they say is important, even if it is wrong. Proving a point may make us sound knowledgeable, but it also may breed resentment. All we can do is offer an alternative way of looking at an issue and respect the teenager's right to disagree.

2. Refrain from offering advice. Unless a junior higher specifically asks for it, most discussions are not the place to give advice. In helping an early adolescent reach a decision, an effective leader asks questions that lead the young person to make up his or her own mind.

3. Help kids feel comfortable. At first, a lot of junior highers are afraid of group discussion. They are not sure how to express their feelings or fear criticism from others. No one likes being thought of as foolish. Far too many times, junior highers are made fun of by authority figures so they hide behind silence. Adolescents need to feel at ease in a group in order to contribute.

4. Don't force kids to answer. A comfortable environment is one in which junior highers do not feel forced to answer. However, there are times when a leader should raise questions which he or she is certain the kids are silently asking themselves.

5. Remain neutral. Leaders should not take sides since the purpose of good discussion is to help group members develop their own understanding or response to an issue. Taking a stand may prevent a junior higher from deciding how he or she feels about a particular matter.

6. Listen rather than talk. There is no question that, in many areas, adult leaders know more than junior highers. However, the focus is not on what the adults know, but rather, on what the young people need to discover. Learning is much more effective if it comes from one's own experience. We grow and develop through our own efforts. A sound rule for adult leaders might be: Try to talk less so the group can learn more.

7. Allow kids to work through problems. It takes a lot of patience for a leader to stand by and watch a group of junior highers find their way, but the most meaningful discussions are the ones the kids work through themselves.

8. Help kids feel secure. Leaders, concerned about creating an atmosphere of security, are sensitive to why some members do not participate. In any group, some will not contribute as much as others. While total participation is a goal for good discussion, leaders need to remember why some junior highers hesitate to speak up. Some kids withdraw because they are intimidated, are afraid to express themselves, or are avoiding challenges. Once these kids feel secure, they will participate.

9. Sort through feelings. Try to grasp what each speaker is saying and sort out feelings that may influence the way a junior higher thinks. Encourage participants by responding, "I can tell you feel strongly about ..."

10. Show appreciation. Junior highers who feel respected by group members and leaders, even when their opinions differ, want to be part of that group. Feeling accepted leads to an acceptance of others.

11. Evaluate. For discussions to be effective, leaders should constantly evaluate. Evaluate your discussions by answering these questions:

●Do members of the group feel at ease with one another when it comes to discussion? Why or why not?

●How do individuals interact verbally and nonverbally with one another?

●Do discussion times lead to a cohesive, caring group? Explain. Are members developing an awareness of one another? Explain.

●How do the discussion methods used strengthen trust between members of the group?

●Do individuals feel threatened by any of the discussion methods? Why or why not?

●What evidence is there to indicate junior highers feel comfortable sharing their ideas and feelings?

●Do members of the group participate freely? If not, why?

●Do members of the group feel their contributions to the discussion are respected by the group? If not, why?

●Does the group respect the directions given by discussion leaders? If not, why?

●What factors get in the way of good listening?

●What did group members learn about themselves in the course of the discussion?

●What evidence is there that the topic discussed made an impact on individual daily life?

Discussions are a major part of junior high ministry; discussions help kids grow intellectually, emotionally, socially and spiritually. When leaders help kids state their opinions and listen to others, they help kids become concerned about others; they help kids mature into responsible young people.

CHAPTER 11

BUILDING ATTENDANCE

A perennial question asked by adult leaders is "How can we get more kids to come?" There may be many reasons why some activities receive a poor turnout. The purpose of this chapter is to explore ways to involve young people in order to increase attendance.

It is usually helpful to ask why some kids don't participate. It may not be a matter of desire; it may be a matter of ability:

- I don't have a ride.
- Everyone has money to give and I don't.
- I have to babysit on those evenings.
- That's the only night my family has together!
- With all my other activities, I just don't have time.
- I have too much homework.

There may be as many reasons for not attending as there are young people.

For many junior high groups, another reason for poor attendance is apathy or indifference. This lack of interest in what's going on can be expressed in several ways: absence, late arrival and early departure, unwillingness to volunteer or participate in what the group is doing, or emotional withdrawal. Apathy generally comes from kids feeling they are unimportant to the group, that they have no control over what is going on, or that what they contribute will not make any difference. Some teenagers remain withdrawn because they do not know anyone in the group or they fear being rejected. Apathy sets in when junior highers feel they play no part in the decision-making process of the group. There is no sense of community or togetherness.

Leaders need to recognize kids' reasons for not attending, try to get them excited about junior high ministry, and encourage them to regularly attend activities. Following are some ideas.

Involve Kids in Leadership

Before programs and activities are scheduled, sensitive adult leaders should talk with kids to learn what needs to be done to make the junior high program more appealing. Brainstorming sessions or personal interviews may provide answers to concerns such as:

- How can we get along better with each other?
- Why are only certain people allowed to lead the group?
- Why do we need so many rules?
- Do we always have to meet on Sunday evenings?
- Are the adults the only people allowed to plan our activities?

Asking junior highers to share and help solve the concerns and problems involves them in their group's life.

All young people like to know they are valued by their group. Junior highers especially need a positive feeling about themselves as they function with their peers and with adults. For this reason, junior high youth groups need adult leaders who care. These adults need to care enough to allow:

- Time for careful, organized planning and follow-through
- Opportunities for young people to participate in group decisions

●Extra effort to extend a personal touch to all

When young people experience this care and concern from all members of the group, apathy, indifference and missed meetings are less of a problem.

Publicize Activities

Attendance is also greatly affected by how well the junior highers are informed about activities. Publicity and promotion have a lot to do with an event's turnout. Good publicity depends on leaders being organized, creative and aware of the basics of advertising.

There are all kinds of ways to reach junior highers to let them know what's happening:

1. Bright-colored posters. Place these at strategic locations in the church, community or at schools. Include all necessary information, yet keep them simple—uncluttered. Bright colors, large letters, and fun pictures attract kids' attention.

2. Attractive bulletin boards. Designate one area in the church for a bulletin board announcing junior high activities. Allow it to become a focal point for youth announcements, news and information of upcoming events and activities. Keep it current!

3. Telephone calls. Contact people personally by calling them. Some youth groups are small enough that phone calls are an effective way to keep people informed and reminded. Phone trees can be organized by the leaders or by the young people themselves. It is usually manageable for a person to make four or five calls in an evening. The key to this publicity method is to make certain each caller has accurate information and presents it consistently. This style of communication also depends on people making phone calls by a certain date and successfully reaching those whom they are assigned to. With careful training, young people may use the phone effectively to reach out to one another, to speak enthusiastically about a planned activity or to personally invite or encourage attendance.

4. Mail. The most effective, and often neglected, avenue of publicity is the mail. Junior highers love to get mail, especially if it is addressed to them personally. Although cost may be a factor, the expense of a monthly mailing to promote the youth program is well worth the investment. The advantages of a special mailing become evident right away:

●Publicizing junior high events by mail guarantees everyone gets the same information at the same time. (Mailing lists should be kept accurate and include all eligible recipients. Two hundred identical pieces of mail qualify for a bulk rate at the post office. Depending on the size of the group, this may mean combining junior high mail with senior high publicity, or adding a few names like youth leaders, parents and church officials to the list in order to reach the required number.)

●Putting news about activities and programs in the mail provides a teenager with a visible reminder to post at home.

While it may not be possible to reach everyone by phone, mail gains entry into everyone's home.

Depending on the activity and what the kids need to do in order to participate, announcements should be mailed 10 days to one month or more prior to the event. For example, trips may require at least a month's notice in order to meet a registration and deposit deadline. However, two weeks may be ample notice for a skating party if a telephone reservation is all that is necessary.

Monthly mailings can include more than just a list of what's happening the next four weeks. There also can be a separate sheet or section announcing coming attractions or events for the kids to mark on their calendars, even though additional details will be provided later. This kind of advance notice encourages junior highers to reserve a special date in advance and confirms the fact that things are happening for young people at the church.

With the availability of instant-printing services in most communities, it is possible to put together economical eye-catching notices. Newsletters, fliers, folders, post cards, etc., should be attractive and easy to read. Look at magazine or junk mail advertising to get ideas. Advertisers rely on getting the reader's attention quickly. They successfully communicate their message in a few words, using attractive graphics. Youth group mailings can be produced the same way. Leaders should keep an idea file of graphics, clippings from magazines and newspapers that will add a special touch to announcements. Most cities also have art or office supply stores that carry lettering and printing aids to add a special touch to promotional materials. Also, the use of humor, clever cliches, even mystery and intrigue, can make a mailing piece attractive. We don't have to tell everything in a piece of mail, just enough to whet the appetite and provide basic information such as who, what, where and when.

Leaders can promote attendance by mailing personal notes from time to time. It's amazing what a post card will do. One youth worker I knew made it a point to write several post cards a day to kids in her group. She took the roster of junior highers, divided the names on her calendar, and listed one or two kids to contact each day during the year. Even when she was traveling, she sent a card just to say, "I'm thinking of you. Hope to see you at next week's meeting. I've missed talking to you." Or she used the card to recall a special memory the two of them shared.

When someone is absent or unable to attend, a card saying, "You were missed!" makes a big difference. It matters to kids that someone cares when they are sick, or when something special happens to them. Sending a get well card or a note about the part they had in the school play, is more important than we may realize. Such contacts do make a difference when it comes to a young person feeling cared for. And don't forget, kids want to be places where they feel they count!

5. Word-of-mouth. Youth leaders should take every opportunity to enthusiastically promote all activities and invite kids to participate. This means expressing sincere interest to group members we see while we're out shopping, "I'll see you Saturday night at the hayride!" Or stopping kids after a church service and reminding them, "We're having a special meeting this afternoon. I really hope you'll be there!"

The most important factor in publicity is making sure arrangements have been made in advance to prevent last-minute surprises. In other words, wait to announce an activity until all details are taken care of: the location has been reserved, the date is suitable and the cost is exact. Counting on one thing, then having to make adjustments, creates confusion for junior highers and their parents. Leaders lose credibility when dates and times are changed after an event has been announced.

Many times attendance isn't what we'd like because junior highers develop the attitude that not much is happening at church. These young people do notice if adults keep their word and follow through on what they promise. Changing plans at the last minute or cancelling an event can kill a junior high program. Frequently, leaders become frustrated because once an event is announced, few people indicate an interest or make reservations. However, if only five kids show up for a pizza party, at least those five can say they had a pizza party! To cancel because only five people signed up affects the five who wanted to participate. To say no to the five may cause them to doubt their value within the group. "No one cares about what we want to do!" It may take awhile for kids to realize that there are things going on and taking place as announced. Leadership that establishes credibility with kids usually gets a response.

Publicity has a way of infecting a junior high group with enthusiasm. Its purpose is not only to inform, but to spark an interest in what's going to happen and to build anticipation. Remember, publicity reflects the image we want to project about our junior high program. If it is dull or plain, that's exactly what young people will expect the events to be.

Visit Kids' Homes

Another way to promote attendance and show an interest in the kids is to visit them in their homes. Adults gain valuable insights about group members when they can spend some time with them where they live. Often we learn things about young people in their home environment that otherwise would remain unknown. Meeting parents and siblings, and seeing where they live, expands our understanding of that individual. We can learn a lot just by looking at the pictures on the walls or the items tacked to the bulletin board in a junior higher's room.

Visits should always be prearranged. People appreciate being notified that someone is coming to visit. When making arrangements, simply state the reason you would like to drop by. It is also important to ask if it's convenient. This gives each person a chance to decline, which is his or her right. Not every teenager feels comfortable having the youth leader come into his or her home. There may be some things at home the teenager isn't ready to make public. If a junior higher seems uncomfortable or refuses a home visit, perhaps we could suggest meeting at a neutral place, like a local food establishment. This arrangement still gives us a chance to talk. Remember to make notes after such conversations. Often these one-on-one conversations are times when heart-to-heart sharing takes place. Trust also is established that leads to greater opportunities for ministry.

Adult leaders may wish to involve other members of the group, especially if inactive teenagers or newcomers are to be visited. Visiting skills can be taught to a small group who may thoroughly enjoy this activity.

Visit at Schools

As revealing as a home visit can be, so can a visit with junior highers at their school. Youth leaders need to be in tune with the current school environment and be aware what it's like where kids spend five days of the week.

School systems have policies regarding outside visitors that need to be respected. Perhaps there is someone in the congregation involved in education who can provide such information. Obviously, visiting cannot take place while a student is in class, but it may be possible for a leader to visit at lunch time and eat with a group of students in the cafeteria. Some kids really enjoy having their youth leaders come to school, and it provides an opportunity for them to introduce us to some of their friends.

Although some schools are sensitive about the separation of church and state, there are several possibilities for establishing a relationship with administrative personnel or teachers. Each fall it might be helpful to visit the schools, introduce yourself as the youth leader and provide the appropriate staff with a list of names of the young people in the youth group who attend that particular school. Offer to assist school personnel in any way the student should need help. A visit with the principal simply to become acquainted serves a purpose, but it's much better to contact staff members directly involved with the students.

Leaders might want to approach guidance counselors, coaches, club advisors or the school nurse. These people have a different relationship with students than administrators and classroom teachers do. Students often confide personal matters to these people. School professionals are also more open to supporting leaders. Leaders may have insights into home situations that school personnel don't. Sometimes youth leaders can work as a team with school staff in dealing with a problem. The youth leader may have a better relationship with the parents while the guidance counselor can work more effectively with the student. The school nurse may welcome an outside resource in dealing with certain problems. Likewise, the guidance counselor may be especially grateful for input in understanding a crisis situation. These opportunities for cooperative ministry make a youth leader's presence on school grounds welcome.

When junior highers see their church youth leaders respected as part of a team by school officials, it makes a difference in how junior highers perceive us and the youth group. Leaders may be able to reach a teenager through a school contact easier and more effectively than anyplace else. Attending volleyball games or other athletic events, reading the school newspaper, and showing up at concerts are all ways of keeping ourselves informed and visible.

There can be problem areas that youth leaders need to respect. Many schools are leery of church workers who appear on the scene to recruit or proselytize. This is generally why school officials feel they must close the door to youth leaders. Nevertheless, if visits are made solely for the purpose of helping to expand the network of support for the young people already involved in the church, school personnel are more receptive. Our own attitude will often determine the reception we receive, whether school administrators feel they can trust us and if others in the system consider us a worthy resource. The proof of the kind of relationship we have with the school will come when they turn to us for help with a specific concern.

One way to affirm the school principal or other staff is to invite them to a church activity and present them with some special honor or recognition for their dedication to youth.

Seldom are school personnel recognized outside the educational community. This token of mutual respect affects not only those persons who are being honored, but also the young people who have experienced the leadership and concern of both groups.

Welcome Visitors

For almost two decades I have been involved with junior highers. Only once during that period have I ever walked into a youth ministry office that had a welcome mat at the door. While the fact remains that churches who want an active junior high program will not find the key to success in the purchase of a welcome mat, they will find success if kids feel welcomed and loved—especially kids who are visiting or are new members.

Even subtle factors, like a welcome mat, help create lasting first impressions. When junior highers feel a warm welcome, a sense of rapport, and a genuine expression of interest, they are more likely to return.

Leaders who have a genuine concern for welcoming a new person, regularly examine the kind of impression the group makes. Leaders can involve the group in a sort of self-analysis. Some hard questions can be asked:

●Is the group dominated by certain individuals or a subgroup?

●Do all who attend feel they can contribute to activities and discussions?

●Do people feel free, or inhibited, in expressing their point of view?

●When a newcomer arrives, do members of the group appear to be phony? honest? authentic?

●How do the kids welcome new people?

Leaders should have a predetermined pattern for introducing visitors or new members. The new teenagers, dropped off at the church by an anxious parent, may feel frightened when suddenly surrounded by a group of strangers, not knowing names, wondering if he or she will be accepted. Following are some ideas for welcoming visitors and new members:

1. Model a welcoming attitude. When new people arrive,

it is important that someone greets them immediately. We can model an enthusiastic welcome by meeting new people at the door and introducing ourselves. When group members see leaders welcoming guests, they'll take note of how it's done and be more likely to do the same.

2. Assign a host or hostess. Immediately introduce the guest to a group member who serves as a host or hostess. The host or hostess stays with the guest the entire activity and introduces him or her to the other members. Adults will have to judge how many times the new person will need to be paired with a host or hostess before he or she feels comfortable. It might take several meetings before new people are ready to venture out on their own.

3. Determine common ground. Discover mutual interests or topics on which a conversation can be built. Ask questions such as, "How does it feel being new to our state?" "What hobbies do you enjoy?" "What are your favorite television shows?" Practice good listening skills and look at the person while he or she is responding.

New people can sense our genuine interest if we follow up what they've said with a comment or an additional question. It also helps if we share information about ourselves without the other person having to ask. If new people make a comment about members of their family, we can respond in kind about our family.

Closed questions—ones that can be answered with a yes or no—make it difficult to carry on a conversation and should be avoided. Likewise, it is important to smile while talking to a new person, but laughing at a comment can lead to a misunderstanding. We should be genuine and sincere, yet not probe into areas that people aren't willing to talk about. Some matters may be too personal for them to share at the beginning.

The manner and attitude in which people approach one another does more for creating a spirit of community than all clever crowdbreakers combined. A junior high group should be more than just a gathering of friendly people. Warm acceptance is the foundation on which the Christian experience is built.

4. Introduce the new person to others. Once leaders, hosts or hostesses learn new things about a guest, they can introduce him or her to others with similar interests. For example, "Oh, you're from Nebraska? John and Alan recently moved here from Lincoln." "You enjoy biking? Susan and Steve recently competed in a local bike race." Common courtesy and good manners dictate that leaders introduce new members and give some brief background information such as where they live; school; grade; and if they are new to the community, where they lived prior to moving.

Perhaps the group can create a cheer or exercise to express a warm welcome. For example, have everybody form a line and hold hands. Have the new member stand at the end of the line. Slowly begin wrapping the line around the person, cinnamon roll style. On the count of three—give a massive squeeze.

5. Offer a snack time. Provide time at each gathering for people to get to know one another. An attitude of acceptance is nurtured when people have time to relax and informally discover things about each other. All too often we fail to recognize the value in letting kids alone for 15 minutes just to talk. Snack time is an excellent way to create a hospitable setting where people can take a break from what they're doing and just sit and talk.

6. Follow-up.   Whenever a visitor attends a group function, a follow-up contact should be made. A simple phone call or post card can express, "Glad you joined us, hope you'll come again. Our next get-together is scheduled for ..." Ask group members to follow up at school or in some other way. Whatever methods are used, help group members see the important part they play in making new people feel at home.

7. Conduct an informal question-and-answer time. One of the benefits of having newcomers is the opportunity they provide a group to practice friendship skills. After a few weeks, when the new people begin to feel at home, take five or 10 minutes from a meeting and conduct a question-and-answer time. Ask more details about places they have lived, size of their family, places they've traveled, special interests or talents, what their impressions are of the community, what are their first impressions of the group. This last question can serve as a basis for evaluating how the group welcomes strangers.

This interview needs to be conducted in a positive, affirming way. Getting a person to talk about what it's like to be a newcomer can be an emotional moment. Leaders can use the opportunity to guide the discussion on the importance of acceptance in the community of faith, and accent the things we share in common.

8. Visit their homes. In preparing to visit new members' or visitors' homes, it's helpful to remember a few guidelines:

●Ask how they've enjoyed their previous visits to the junior high group.

●Be enthusiastic and positive. How can we expect someone to become interested in future involvement if our activity descriptions are dull?

●When offering invitations to future events, make them specific. Explain what will happen, where the event will take place, and when it will occur. Offer to give the person a ride. It may make a difference knowing he or she will not have to go alone.

●If the young person is unable to attend the activity you suggest, plan to extend a follow-up invitation for the next activity. People who are inactive or new will need constant encouragement.

●There is a difference between encouraging someone to attend an activity and nagging. If the person we are visiting doesn't want to come, there may be reasons. Nagging may result in resistance that will make future efforts less likely to succeed.

●If people have visited for a while, then stop coming, don't put them on the spot by asking the reasons for their inactivity.

●It's difficult to talk to someone who is extremely negative or resists efforts on our part to be friendly. Nonetheless, close the conversation with a positive note and an expression of interest in the person. Plan a follow-up contact.

●Before ending the visit, leave something with the person: a gift from the group, a schedule of events for the month, a special brochure with lots of pictures of happy faces, a copy of the group's directory. Whatever the gesture, it is a tangible expression of our concern and leaves a reminder of our genuine interest.

9. Discuss with the entire group the elements for welcoming

new people. Focus on what would make a new person want to return. Share with the group members their responsibility in welcoming new people. Discuss the fear we all have of rejection, what it means to be rejected by a group, how the kids might make people feel they are on the outside (telling "in" jokes, etc.), and teaching simple conversation skills.

Talk to junior highers about their role in helping new kids feel they are part of the group. Ask questions such as:

●What are ways people make you feel welcome?

●What does it mean to belong?

●Describe some experiences where you've felt accepted.

●How do you feel when you belong?

●What are special ways you can show you care for someone?

●What places do you feel welcome?

●What group would you like to join?

●What does it mean to belong to God?

●Why does God need people to touch the lives of others?

10. Encourage kids to bring their friends. More people attend church functions because of invitations from people they know than on their own initiative. This poses a question for junior high leaders: Do we want to encourage junior highers to invite their friends?

My feeling is that junior highers appreciate the opportunity to bring friends to church functions. Certain guidelines may need to be followed for this age group, but a more positive attitude exists among adolescents when they feel their friends are welcome. For example, if someone wants to invite a friend, it should be with the understanding that the friend comes to participate as if he or she were a regular member of the group. Visitors should understand that we want them to have a good time like everyone else, and that implies getting involved and abiding by the group rules.

Another guideline regarding friends could be that only a limited number visit at a time. One or two is a manageable limit, especially if the leaders or group members don't know them. It takes time and a lot of attention to assimilate new people into a group. Too many visitors at one time can be disruptive and overload the leader.

There may be times when leaders need to exercise common

sense about the attendance of friends. If their attendance causes problems within the group, that issue needs to be addressed. At the same time, friends can contribute to community building. Sometimes a lot depends on the attitude of the kids who've been invited. Whatever the situation, adult leaders should make the effort to get to know friends. Show a genuine concern for them. If they express an interest in returning, consider the possibilities of their becoming regular members of the group.

Group members and their friends need to avoid giving the impression that the group is exclusive, that only certain people are accepted and that leaders have favorites. Leaders need to be courageous enough to address this matter if there is any concern at all. Groups are much stronger when they are comprised of a mixture of individuals. Differences within a group help junior highers grow and learn, and put into practice the Christian principle of acceptance.

Other Ideas to Build Attendance

The following methods of contact will reinforce our goal to involve young people and let them know their presence makes a difference.

1. Select one person each week to be called by various members of the group. Someone may call on Monday to offer an invitation, another person can call on Tuesday, and so on until Saturday, when the caller asks if the person needs a ride.

2. Send a Polaroid post card of the youth group with a message on the back, "Who's missing in this picture?"

3. Put secret messages in students' school lockers each day for a week announcing the next junior high youth group meeting.

4. Send young people a series of post cards, one each day for a week. Include a message, continued from day-to-day. For example: Monday, "Hope you'll be at our next junior high meeting." Tuesday, "The meeting will be Sunday at 7:00 p.m." Wednesday, "The theme is on building friendships," and so on.

5. Sponsor a hobby night and invite people to come and share what they like to do in their spare time. The more we know of others' interests, the more they feel a part of the group.

6. Have each active member adopt one inactive member and invite him or her home for dinner. Make it a point to spend one-on-one time to establish a good friendship. Remember, follow-up outside the youth group is important.

7. Send or give a key to those who are missing. Tell them it will open a whole new world if they come to the next meeting. They are the key to the group's success—they are needed!

8. Appoint someone from the group, or ask one of the adult leaders, to visit inactives and have a heart-to-heart talk on why they don't attend. We may discover problem areas we are unaware of or things that could make our meetings more appealing.

9. The next time your group goes on a retreat or trip, call the members who were unable to attend and let everyone take turns saying hello.

10. Develop a peer ministry. The role of the adult in peer ministry is to train and help junior highers learn how to care for one another, how to listen, be sensitive to needs, and know when and where to turn for help. The emphasis is to help teenagers reach out to their friends who are lonely or feel alienated. This is not an attempt to make junior highers into counselors. There are some excellent guides for training young people to care for one another. I highly recommend *Friend to Friend* by J. David Stone and Larry Keefauver.[1] It includes a practical, easy-to-follow approach for young people as well as adults.

11. Publish a junior high group directory at the beginning of the school year. The directory serves several purposes:

●Provides everyone a listing of the people in the junior high program.

●Addresses, phone numbers, birthdays, parents' names, and the school each person attends, can be listed beside each name.

●Kids like to keep in touch with each other—having a phone number handy helps.

●Leaders can encourage members to remember others' birthdays.

●Going over the roster is one way for leaders to stay alert to attendance—who is attending and who isn't.

●If you want to get real fancy, include kids' photographs.

12. Start a secret pal program. Assign group members a secret friend who is to pray for them, remember their birthday, and do whatever "extras" are needed. Give kids free post cards or birthday cards to encourage the secret pal process. This helps junior highers overcome feeling awkward contacting people they don't know, and at the same time, communicates a message to others that the special days in their life do not go unnoticed. The secret pal program can be used for promoting special activities. "See you at the picnic ... your secret pal."

13. Write messages on 8½x11 pieces of paper such as, "Our youth group can't take off without you." Fold into paper airplanes. During Sunday school, or at the school cafeteria, toss them to those who missed a meeting.

14. Go to a costume shop and rent a mask of the president of the United States. Prepare a funny announcement on "official" stationery indicating the president will be visiting the missing person on a particular date. Have other members go along as the press: taking pictures, interviewing the president, etc. You could even videotape the visit and play it back later.

15. Declare a night when you'll try to set a world's record on how many people you can stuff into your meeting room. Have a local newspaper photographer capture the event. Award a prize for the person who brings the most friends. Once the group contest is over, take time to share the other exciting ideas your group is doing. Invite friends to return.

16. Ask parents or young adults in the church to set up a youth group taxi service—providing free rides to junior high events. Prepare a list of names and phone numbers of drivers; send a copy to every junior higher in the church. Be sure kids give reasonable notice before requiring the taxi drivers' services!

17. Put together a junior high group coupon book offering "one free sundae," "half-price discount on next special event," "free hug," or "free back rub" when kids bring the coupon along with a friend.

18. Sponsor a "Tool Box Night." Decorate fliers and posters like a Sears ad page. Feature all kinds of common tools such as hammers, saws and screwdrivers. Ask each person to bring a tool from home. During the meeting, have each person compare the tool to the junior high group. For example, "This hammer reminds me of our group because we 'hit' upon some great discussion topics.''

Tell the kids that together you can build a great youth group; each person is needed. Have them draw an outline of their tool on an 8½x11 piece of paper and print their name inside the outline. Make a collage of tools on the youth room wall. Label it, ''Youth Group Under Construction—Building a Community That Cares.''

Find ways to employ the tool theme throughout the year; for example, plan a ''Hammer and Nail Night.'' Discuss the cross, why it was constructed, what it must have been like for the people who made it, etc.

19. Use Con-Tact paper and markers to make bumper stickers advertising your junior high group. Ask members to put the bumper stickers on the family car or on their school locker.

20. In the springtime, send each of the junior highers a packet of vegetable seeds. Tell the kids that they are needed for the youth group to ''grow.'' Ask the young people to bring the seeds on a certain date to a designated place. Plant a garden and give the home-grown food to a local soup kitchen. This helps kids get to know one another; it communicates the young people are needed; and it provides a way for them to help others.

CHAPTER 12

MEETINGS

Junior highers are exciting people to spend time with; they are eager to know so much about life. This can be a leader's greatest challenge and joy. Each time a group is together, the potential for growth awaits stimulation. This chapter offers meeting designs intended to lead junior highers to grow as individuals and as a group. What makes certain meetings effective and others not?

●Effective meetings use games that build kids up rather than tear kids down. Nobody likes to be humiliated. Back away from competition and play games that require total group effort; play games where everyone wins; play games where skill, speed and grace aren't prerequisites. For example, tell junior highers they have 60 seconds to build a pyramid. Once in position they have to shout the theme of the meeting. Or, ask the group members not to peek or talk and form a line from the person with the longest hair, to the person with the shortest hair.

●Effective meetings are experiential (see Chapter 9). Experiential learning involves kids *actively* in the learning process through the use of simulation games, puppets, drama, service projects, games, etc. Experiential learning allows kids to learn for themselves rather than telling them what they "ought" to have learned. Experiential learning means giving kids hands-on experiences. For example, learn about servanthood by going to a home for the disabled and talking with the residents. Learn about stewardship and tithing by asking each junior higher to look at his or her time and talent and decide how he or she can give more to the church.

●Effective meetings generally last from 60 to 90 minutes. Within that time period, programming is varied and fast-paced. For example, crowdbreakers and get-to-know-you games (10 minutes), songs (10 minutes), main topic/discussion questions (15 minutes), experiential activities (10 to 15 minutes), refreshments (10 minutes). Since junior highers' attention span is short, meetings work best mixed with discussion and experiential learning, rather than straight lecture.

●Effective meetings employ at least one adult per eight students. This keeps the groups small enough to allow for interaction, discussion and friendship building.

●Effective meetings have a purpose, and specific objectives to meet that purpose.

One purpose is getting together for Bible study. Many young people often give the impression that they have no interest in studying the Bible, that it is dull and not applicable to their world. Such an attitude may be a reflection of what adults have communicated to them. If leaders are not biblically knowledgeable or lack a willingness to try innovative ways to discuss Bible passages, the result will be groups who miss opportunities for spiritual growth.

There are all kinds of ways to make the Bible come alive. GROUP Magazine and Group's JR. HIGH MINISTRY Magazine are two of the best sources for fresh ideas.[1] Every issue includes creative approaches to teaching the scriptures and insightful tips for working with young people.

Junior highers, like the rest of us, get much more out of a

participatory Bible study. Any number of procedures can be used.

●Ask someone to read a passage aloud while others write down key words and ideas. Compare thoughts.

●Ask group members to read a passage and then rewrite it in their own words. Sharing their own rewritten versions gives kids a chance to talk about the insights they gained into the meaning of the text.

●Have the kids express a Bible passage in a different form such as a poem, song, letter or historical account.

●Employ art forms. Have the kids interpret a Bible verse by creating a collage, clay sculpture or finger painting.

●Role play the feelings and circumstances of a Bible passage.

●Create commercials. This is one way of getting kids to condense the text into a simple message.

Those who lead Bible studies need to do their homework. There is nothing sadder than the blind leading the blind through pages of the Old and New Testaments. Leaders should not only know a passage, but also should have some understanding of the culture and historical setting of the biblical characters. There are excellent resources available that can save a lot of time in background investigation. Leaders can rely on commentaries, Bible dictionaries, maps, even expository sermons. The better prepared the leader, the better the knowledge to be shared.

Another purpose for meetings is to study and discuss current interests such as friendship, dating, drugs, gossip, how to deal with parents, etc. These meetings are especially effective when the kids generate the topics they want to discuss. Invite other adults to help lead these discussions. For example, ask a rehabilitation counselor to talk about drugs, then answer questions. Ask a panel of parents to attend the meeting, then let the kids ask any questions they'd like.

Bible studies, discussions and other types of meetings can be formatted in various ways. Some people prefer to meet once a week on Sundays, others prefer once a week on weekdays, still others prefer once every two weeks, or once a month. My preference is to schedule a meeting once a week. This allows for continuity and advance planning. When we meet on a weekly basis, kids can depend on something happening. When groups gather every other week or once a month, kids miss huge gaps of time if they miss one meeting, they are more apt to feel "out of it" and not a part of the group. Following are two ways to format a weekly meeting—on Sundays or on weekdays.

1. The Sunday format. This type of approach varies activities from Sunday to Sunday and usually looks like this:

> 1st Sunday — Discussion/Bible study
> 2nd Sunday — Service project
> 3rd Sunday — Guest speaker/film
> 4th Sunday — Social activity
> 5th Sunday — Special event

This pattern works well with groups made up of kids who cannot attend regularly or who have a wide range of interests.

Many times, Sundays can be expanded to include more activities such as a supper hour, recreation period and worship. The schedule could look like this:

> **Sunday**
> 6:00 - 6:30 p.m. Recreation
> 6:30 - 7:30 p.m. Discussion/Bible study
> 7:30 - 8:00 p.m. Snack
> 8:00 - 8:30 p.m. Worship

Parents can prepare meals and snacks on a rotating basis. Depending on the size of the group, hold meetings in homes rather than at the church. If the schedule is to include more than study, the church facilities are probably better suited to meet the program's needs.

Meeting at the church firmly identifies the activity with the church and its concern for young people. It provides a consistency and eliminates confusion as to where the group is to meet and when. It also facilitates transportation needs by making it possible for parents to form car pools.

On the other hand, meeting in homes provides a comfortable, warm, relaxing environment that helps build community. Young people get to meet their friends' parents, and parents feel they are contributing to the program. When meetings are held at various homes, it is absolutely essential everyone have correct information: time, address and directions.

2. The weekday format. There are some definite advantages to meeting during the week after school. Usually the weekday program is multipurpose. It allows for choir rehearsals, study, recreation, supper, and worship within a three- to three-and-one-half hour period. Parents appreciate weekday meeting times because all junior high activities are then scheduled for one day of the week—not various times throughout the week. Weekday meetings help parents who rely on car pools for transportation. If four or five students attend from the same school, parents can set up a driving schedule where each takes a turn driving once a month. This works especially well in areas where participants attend several different schools or have to travel some distance to the church. Some school systems will allow students to travel to the church on a different bus one day a week if that particular bus route goes by the church. Sometimes churches that have their own bus or van will set up an after-school pick up route to help kids get to the activities.

The weekday format is a natural for community building with junior highers. It can begin with an informal recreation period when the kids arrive, giving them some time to relax after school. A snack table can be set up, stereo music can be played, table games or a study corner arranged, and places for clusters of kids to gather informally. If the kids attend more than one school, this will be a time they look forward to visiting and catching up with church friends.

Community building can happen through sharing a meal together family-style. Six or seven young people seated at a table with a host can create an atmosphere of togetherness. Table leaders can generate conversation to help the members get to know one another. Kids can share table responsibilities such as being a runner for food, helping to serve and helping to clean up. The table with the best attendance record each month could get special recognition, for example, give each member extra dessert or a candy bar. Every two months, table assignments could be switched in order to mix the group and help kids get to know more people. Another activity that helps build community after supper is to have each "table family" be a team. Plan contests to see who can memorize the most Bible verses, or who knows the most Bible trivia.

Worship also lends itself to community building. Whether

different adults or groups are responsible for leading it, worship can be planned according to a specific theme, including singing, scripture, a short talk and prayer. Prior to going home, worship underscores the purpose for the weekly meeting and generates a feeling of togetherness.

The weekly format usually follows the school calendar, meaning the group does not meet on holidays, during vacation periods or exam time. The calendar of the church year, for the most part, is compatible with this kind of arrangement.

Meeting after school also lends itself to kids bringing their unchurched friends. In many cases, friends become regular participants and, if your weekday program includes confirmation or membership instruction, they may decide to become a part of your fellowship. A schedule could look something like this:

Weekday
3:30 - 4:00 p.m. Recreation and snack
4:00 - 5:00 p.m. Activities such as choir rehearsal
5:00 - 6:00 p.m. Bible study/discussion
6:00 - 7:00 p.m. Supper
7:00 - 7:30 p.m. Worship

A more extended weekday schedule can be utilized if the group meets on Saturday. Saturday sessions seem to work best on a once-a-month basis. They can run from 9 a.m. to 3 p.m., include lunch, and allow several periods for instruction. The advantage of this format is that it allows for in-depth study of a topic along with breaks for recreation. The disadvantages are when a junior higher misses one meeting, there is a two-month interval until the group meets again.

No matter how you decide to format your junior high meeting, creative ideas are always needed for Bible studies and discussions. Following are 10 meeting designs to use or adapt for your junior high group.

The Body of Christ = Variety

■ Objectives
Participants will:
●Become reacquainted with one another after the summer months.

●Gain an appreciation for each individual and how he or she contributes to the group.

●Develop an understanding of what it means to be a part of the body of Christ—the Christian community.

■ **Biblical Focus**

1 Corinthians 12:4-27

■ **Materials Needed**

Kids' invitations; 10 large sheets of newsprint; clothesline or rope; a Bible, piece of paper and marker for each person.

■ **Before the Meeting**

To ensure the best possible attendance for the first big fall event, make certain all group members and their friends, especially those coming for the first time, get an invitation. Invitations can be extended by phone, mail or in person.

Make the room look festive by decorating with a few welcome signs. Address some of the signs specifically to group members' guests.

Hang large sheets of newsprint on the wall. At the top of each sheet, write one of the following questions:

●How tall are you?

●What color is your hair?

●What color are your eyes?

●How much do you weigh?

●What size shoe do you wear?

●What is your favorite color?

●What is your favorite ice cream flavor?

●When is your birthday?

●How many bathrooms are in your house?

●Is your bellybutton an "innie" or an "outie"?

■ **As the Kids Arrive**

Involve people as soon as they enter the room. Give the kids each a marker and invite them to walk around the room and answer all the questions listed on the newsprint.

Once everyone has answered all the questions on the newsprint, have a volunteer tally the answers; the data will be used later in the meeting.

■ Activity One

Have everyone sit in a circle and remove his or her shoes. All shoes should be placed in the center of the circle. Talk about the features all shoes have in common. Each person then picks out a pair of shoes, not his or her own, and attempts to put them on. Talk about how difficult it is to wear someone else's shoes.

Pile all the shoes at the end of the room and mix them up. Divide the group into even teams for a relay. After yelling "Go!" the first person in each team must turn to the next person in line and describe his or her shoes. That person must then run to the pile of shoes, hunt for the pair described, bring them back and put them on the person who described them. If they are the wrong shoes, the runner must go back again and try to find the right ones. The game continues until the last person in line describes his or her shoes to the first person in line. The team with all their shoes on first, wins.

Bring the group together and talk about feet for a few minutes. Comments might include: "We all need our feet," "Feet are all different shapes and sizes," or "We need to take care of our feet." Read 1 Corinthians 12:4-27. Talk about how all parts of the body are essential, how important it is we take care of our bodies, and how all parts work together to create one unique body.

Discuss how people are unique, each having special talents. Although none of us are exactly alike, we do share common needs and feelings.

Next, review the results of the newsprint survey. What is the total weight of the group? total height? What are the favorite ice cream flavors? What is the most common hair color? eye color? etc. Note that the totals are more impressive when all of the statistics are added together; just as when everyone's talents are added together, the group is more impressive.

■ Activity Two

Have everyone stand in a circle. Any size group up to 30 will do; if more than 30, divide into smaller groups. Take a long piece of clothesline or rope and loop it around each person's waist. Be sure there is no slack between people. Without explaining why, have each person take one step backward, one at a time. Go all the way around the circle. When everyone has stepped back, have the group drop the rope and sit down. Ask:

●What happened to you and those around you when you stepped back?

●What happened when the person next to you stepped back?

●What part did the rope play in this experiment?

●How does the rope represent Christ?

●How does this activity illustrate 1 Corinthians 12:4-27?

■ Conclusion

Say to the group, "The body of Christ is held together by his love. Each of us is different, yet he loves us equally. Each of us has our own contributions to make. Some of us can sing, some can play football, some can draw, etc. We need one another. Like the human body, each of us represents an essential part to the life of the group."

Talk about how boring it would be if all of us were the same; if we all had the same hair color, wore the same clothes, etc. Say, "This group needs the special qualities each of you, individually, bring to it."

Continue by sharing the exciting plans you have for the coming year. Ask participants to make a commitment to attending.

Distribute a piece of paper to each of the kids; have them draw an outline of their hand on it. Inside the hand print, have them write their name, address and phone number. Also have them list their hopes for the group in the upcoming year. Each person then exchanges his or her hand print with someone who will take it home and put it in his or her room as a visual reminder of the way hands are linked, one with another, to make the group special. Say, "Remember, you can always turn to this group member in the upcoming year and ask him or her to lend you a 'helping hand.'"

End with a circle prayer, first pray silently for the person to the right, then to the left, then for the entire group.

Bring Your Pet Night

■ **Objectives**

Participants will:

●Help each person understand how animals fit into God's creation plans.

●Create an awareness of our responsibility to care for animals as part of God's world.

●Discover the important role animals play in our lives and what they can teach us.

■ **Biblical Focus**

Genesis 1—2

■ **Materials Needed**

A large room with a tile floor. It is best to hold this event indoors to eliminate the possibility of distractions that might startle the animals. Optional: markers, construction paper, tempera paint.

■ **Before the Meeting**

Publicize the event well in advance to ensure as many pets as possible are brought to the meeting. The greater the variety, the better.

■ **Activity**

Have each participant introduce his or her pet, explain how the pet got its name, lead the pet to perform any special tricks, and tell interesting or funny stories about the pet.

■ **Discussion**

Read or summarize Genesis 1—2, then ask:

●What do these two chapters say about animals in relation to God's creation?

●How does God feel about animals?

●Why is it important to name things?

●When you give something a name, do you establish a special relationship to it?

●Why is it necessary for special groups to protect the rights of animals?

- Why are some people cruel to animals?
- How do you feel about the fact Americans spend millions of dollars each year on pet food when so many people are starving?
- What value is there in a child having a pet?
- What value is there in an elderly person having a pet? Why do so many nursing homes have pets?

■ Conclusion

End the meeting with a special litany or prayer blessing the animals, emphasizing each owner's responsibility for his or her pet, and thanking God for creating such a world.

Ask the kids to decide on a way they can recognize people in the community who devote their time and talents to the benefit of animals (animal shelter personnel, veterinarians, pet store operators, etc.). For example, use construction paper, tempera paint and markers to create a thank-you note for the personnel of a local animal shelter. Place the bottom of a pet's paw in the tempera paint and make prints on the construction paper. (Wash off the paint quickly before it dries on the paw!) Ask each young person to write a word of thanks for the shelter employees' love and care of the animals.

The Great American Museum of Me

■ Objectives
Participants will:
●Gain an understanding of self as a unique child of God.
●Develop an appreciation for the special qualities other people possess.
●Understand that life is a gift from God; it is each person's privilege to use that life responsibly.

■ Biblical Focus
Psalm 8

■ Materials Needed
Family photographs of grandparents and pictures of historical figures taken from magazines, newspapers, etc.; old-time film or video from public library; projector or VCR; large sheet of newsprint, markers and Bible for each person.

■ Before the Meeting
Display photographs of everyone's grandparents and pictures of famous historical people. Number each exhibit.

■ As the Kids Arrive
Give the participants 10 minutes to try to guess who's who in the picture exhibits. Afterward, see who was the best guesser.

■ Activity One
Assemble the group and show a short, old-time movie like a Charlie Chaplin or Laurel and Hardy film. (Many of these films can be borrowed at no charge from the public library. Some are also available on videocassettes.)
Ask group members these questions about the movie:
●What did you like best about the movie?
●What did you notice in the film that dated it? (You may have to replay part of the film to refresh their memories.)
●Can you describe the clothing, buildings, cars, or anything else that gives clues about its historical setting?
Then focus the kids' attention on the exercise matching names

with photographs. Ask:

●What do you know about these historical figures? When did they live? Why are they remembered?

●Can you tell from their pictures what they did for a living?

●What interesting information, humorous stories or special events can you share about your grandparents?

●How do you suppose they will be remembered in history?

●What are the differences between famous people and our grandparents? similarities?

■ Activity Two

Discuss museum exhibits by asking:

●Have any of you visited a museum and looked at the exhibits? If so, describe what you remember.

●What is the purpose of historical exhibits?

●How do you want your life to be remembered?

●If your life could be portrayed in a museum exhibit, what would be on display?

Give the participants each a large sheet of newsprint and a marker. Ask them to draw a floor plan of a museum room where, years from now, the story of their life will be told. Have the kids list items, displays and write brief descriptions of what they would put in the room.

After their floor plans are completed, share them. Help the group affirm each person on what he or she included in the exhibit; how it is unique to that person.

■ Conclusion

Read Psalm 8. Allow time to discuss what God wants us to do with our lives. Say to the group: "We are part of God's creation and we have a responsibility to that creation—including to one another. Each of us is unique and has a contribution to make. We leave our mark in history by the way in which we live." Let the kids take their museum floor plans home to hang in their rooms as reminders of their responsibility.

The Greatest Love of All

■ Objectives
Participants will:
- ●Consider the meaning of the parable of the Good Samaritan.
- ●Evaluate the way we respond to people around us.
- ●Become aware that the way we think about ourselves influences our attitude toward others.

■ Biblical Focus
Luke 10:25-37

■ Materials Needed
Bible for each person, recording of Whitney Houston's "The Greatest Love of All," record player or tape player.

Load a bag with old shower caps, baggy jeans, holey T-shirts and socks, etc.

■ As the Kids Arrive
Gather the young people for a fun activity called Musical Clothes Grab.[2] Form a circle and play music. While the music plays, pass a bag of clothes around the circle. Whenever the music stops, the person holding the bag must immediately reach into it, pull out a piece of clothing and wear it for the rest of the session!

■ Activity One
Most likely, the young people can recall many Bible stories they've heard since childhood. Have them tell about Bible stories that they remember and why they remember those particular stories. Next, have the kids list their favorite Bible stories and the ones they believe are the best known. At some point in this exercise, the Good Samaritan story will be mentioned. Turn to the passage in Luke and read it. If the kids have different Bible versions, they also could be read from.

Focus on verse 27—love of self is the basis of our love for others—and ask, "What does it mean to love yourself as much as you love someone else? What prevents us from loving ourselves?''

Explain that if we are to truly love ourselves, we need a healthy self-image. Our self-esteem stems in part from the way others see us and relate to us. Ask:

●Who are the people in your life who affect the way you feel about yourself?

●Do they make you feel good or bad about yourself? Explain.

●What type of influence do the following people have on your self-image: mother, father, brother or sister, best friend, pastor or youth leader, other.

Say, ''Jesus wants us to love our neighbors as much as we love ourselves. Yet, in reality, there is a limit to how many people, such as the Good Samaritan, we can care for.'' Ask:

●Who are the people who need your help the most?

●How can you respond to them?

●Are there any people we, as a group, can help?

■ Activity Two

Play Whitney Houston's ''The Greatest Love of All'' and talk about the lyrics. Ask the kids how they think Jesus might tell the story of the Good Samaritan, using present-day examples. Divide into small groups and prepare modern-day skit versions of the parable; use the clothes from Musical Clothes Grab as costumes.

■ Conclusion

Present the skits to the entire group. Arrange to present the skits to the children's Sunday school or to residents of a local nursing home.

May I Have the Envelope, Please?

■ Objectives

Participants will:

●Help each person understand what it means to live his or her faith.

●Provide an opportunity to affirm the faith of another person.

●Develop an awareness that actions speak louder than words.

■ Biblical Focus
2 Corinthians 10:11

■ Materials Needed
Bulletin board, tape, letters or posters. Every group member will need a pen, paper, envelope, stamp, Bible, and recent newspaper or news magazine.

■ Before the Meeting
On the bulletin board, display letters you have received from people about your youth group, or make posters quoting comments you have received about the group.

■ As the Kids Arrive
Encourage the young people to read the comments on the bulletin board and add ones of their own.

■ Activity
Distribute one copy of a newspaper or magazine to each person. Ask the kids to describe what their magazine contains. Ask:
●What is the purpose of a newspaper or magazine?
●What kinds of articles are included?
●What parts of the publication look interesting to you?
●What parts would you take out or ignore?
●What types of news does your publication report?
●What makes a newspaper or magazine article interesting?

Point out that newspapers and news magazines exist to inform us and keep us current on world events. Many stories report on peoples' actions and words. News publications also include editorials. An editorial is an opinion of a writer on a particular issue. The editorial page may be one the kids overlook. Next ask:
●How many of you read the 'Letters to the Editor' section?
●Why are these letters included in the magazine?
●What do they contain?
●Why do people write them?

●Which letter to the editor do you think is interesting in the publication you picked?

There are many types of letters: personal letters, business letters, sales letters, letters of introduction, letters of recommendation, etc. Share some samples with the group. Point out that some letters are very special to us because they communicate a message that greatly affects us; they will be saved, studied and treasured.

Ask where in the Bible letters are found. Talk about the purpose of letters in biblical times. Explain that letters were the only means of communication at that time, besides traveling some distance to deliver a message in person. There were no telephones, radios, television, computers, etc. Much of the New Testament is composed of letters written by the apostles to the early church offering instructions, advice and greetings.

■ Conclusion

Explain that the Apostle Paul thought of his life as a letter. Read 2 Corinthians 10:11. Ask:

●What did Paul mean when he said, "... what we say by letter when absent, we do when present"?

●Think of someone in your family, in the community or a national figure whom you admire and respect. How has that person influenced your life?

●If you had a chance to tell that person what he or she means to you, what would you say?

Distribute paper and pen to the group members and ask them to write a letter to the person they most admire, thanking him or her for the example he or she has set. Have them cite the reasons for their admiration. When everyone is finished, have them seal, address and mail the letters. (Later, if anyone receives a reply, have him or her share it with the group.)

Ask the group, "What kind of letter do you think someone would write about you? What kind of example do you think you set as a Christian?" Close with a prayer asking God to help us be living examples of Jesus' love.

Secret Service Agent

■ Objectives
Participants will:
- Evaluate how people express their beliefs.
- Participate in an expression of Christian kindness, without receiving acknowledgment.
- Reach an understanding that true giving seeks not reward or praise.

■ Biblical Focus
Matthew 6:1-4

■ Materials Needed
Pencils, two 3x5 cards, a balloon and piece of string for each person. You also will need a hat or basket.

■ As the Kids Arrive
Gather the junior highers for a fun mixer such as Balloon Stompers.[3] Divide the group into two teams. Line up each team from shortest to tallest. Then count off. Each member blows up a balloon and ties it around his or her ankle with a piece of string.

Call out a number. The two players with that number come to the center of the room and try to stomp each other's balloon. The person who succeeds in stomping a balloon wins a point for his or her team. Repeat this process until all have played. The team with the greatest number of points wins.

■ Activity One
Distribute a pencil and 3x5 card to each person. Ask the kids to write down on the card four facts about themselves. These facts should include as many "unknown" bits of information about themselves as they wish to share with the group; the more unknown details, the better. Collect the cards, read them aloud and try to guess whom the card belongs to.

Decide who was the most difficult person to guess and why. Discuss what new things the kids learned about each other as a result of revealing little-known facts. Read Matthew 6:1-4. Ask the following questions:

●Who are the people you feel you know the best? What makes you feel you know them well?

●Do best friends know *everything* about each other?

●What do you know about other people's beliefs?

●In what ways do people share their faith that appeal to you? don't appeal to you? Can you cite specific examples?

●Why do you suppose Jesus encouraged his followers to do acts of kindness secretly, as in Matthew 6:1-4?

●Have you ever been around someone who brags or seeks attention for what he or she does? What do you suppose motivates that person to act that way? How does it make you feel?

●Do you think true giving demands a reward or acknowledgment? Why?

●How do you feel about God being the only one who knows the good deeds you've done?

■ Activity Two

Pass out new 3x5 cards. Have each person write his or her name, address and phone number on the card. Ask the kids to fold their cards. Collect them in a hat or basket. Redistribute the cards; tell the members not to reveal the information on the card to anyone.

The card holds the name of that person's "secret friend." The group members should set a time limit (before the next meeting) in which they are to do secret kindnesses for their secret friend. No one is to know who is doing what for whom. Whatever and whenever the opportunity presents itself to do something nice, they should do so anonymously.

■ Conclusion

At the next meeting, reconvene the group and talk about the experience. Ask:

●How did you feel about being on the receiving end and not knowing whom to thank?

●Did everyone keep his or her identity secret? Why or why not?

●What types of kindnesses were expressed?

●How did you feel about doing something for someone without being thanked or recognized?

Tell the kids never to reveal the identities of their secret friends. Part of the learning experience comes from doing something nice without being acknowledged for it.

Shake It!

■ **Objectives**

Participants will:

●Understand Jesus' description of what it means to be like salt.

●Explore the various ways they can respond to situations around them.

●Recognize those in the community who act as agents of change.

■ **Biblical Focus**

Matthew 5:13

■ **Materials Needed**

Each participant will need a Bible, construction paper, pen, scissors, stapler or glue, and a small packet of salt (get from a fast food restaurant). You will also need one bowl of salted popcorn and one bowl of unsalted popcorn.

■ **Activity**

Gather the kids in a circle and pass around the unsalted popcorn; ask everyone to taste some. Ask the participants what food is like without salt. Pass around the bowl of salted popcorn; ask the kids to taste some. Talk about how salt is used for adding taste to food, as a preservative and as a healing agent. Ask the kids to name other ways salt is used and the purpose it serves in our daily lives.

■ **Discussion**

Read Matthew 5:13; build a discussion on the following

questions:
- In what ways are Christians to act like salt in the world?
- Who are people called "old salt"?
- What is seasoned salt?
- What is the purpose of smelling salts?

Check the dictionary description of salt, then ask:
- How does the definition apply to the way Christians are to live their lives?
- What do we mean when we describe someone as the "salt of the earth"?
- What situations or people in your community could use a little salt right now?
- How can you "shake" things up as an individual? as a group?

■ Conclusion

It only takes a little salt to make food tastier. Decide who the people are in your community or church who make life "tastier"—people who are healers, who preserve things of value, who are full of zest. Make special "You Are the Salt of the Earth" awards to present to the people who the kids select. Staple or glue salt packs to construction paper, write up a citation and, as a group, present your "salt award" to people who are the salt of the earth in town.

To Live Is to Fly

■ Objectives

Participants will:
- Participate in an experience that demonstrates how the Holy Spirit works in our lives.
- Understand the importance of balance in our lives.
- Compare our lives as children of God with the flight of a kite.

■ Biblical Focus

John 3:8

■ Materials Needed

Kite, string, pencil and 3x5 card for each person.

■ Before the Meeting

Ask each person to bring a kite to the meeting or go as a group to the store to purchase kites. (Some stores offer group discounts.) Each participant should assemble his or her kite and have it ready for flying when he or she arrives at the meeting.

■ Activity

Take the group to a park or open space to fly their kites. Observe how the kites dance and move in the wind; discuss what it takes to get the kites aloft; design fun contests such as kite gymnastics, kite dancing to music, etc.

■ Discussion

After kite flying, gather the young people and ask the following questions:
- What does a kite need in order to fly?
- What do we need in order to live?
- What purpose does a tail serve on a kite?
- Why do we need a balance in our lives?
- What purpose does the string serve?
- Why do we need some kind of focal point in our lives? What is that focal point?
- How did the kites respond to the elements around them? to the other kites?
- How do we respond to what is going on around us?
- What part did the wind play in flying the kites?
- How can the wind be compared to the work of the Holy Spirit?
- What parallels can you draw between your life and the flight of a kite?

■ Conclusion

Distribute 3x5 cards and pencils. Have the kids write John 3:8 on their card: "The wind blows where it wills, and you hear the sound of it, but you do not know whence it comes or whither it goes; so it is with every one who is born of the Spirit." Attach a card to each kite as a reminder that the Holy Spirit guides each of our lives.

World News Tonight

■ **Objectives**
Participants will:
- Gain an understanding of the words evangelical and Gospel.
- Become aware of the need to keep the Gospel relevant.
- Develop skills in communicating the Good News.

■ **Biblical Focus**
Matthew 13:43

■ **Materials Needed**
Bibles (various translations, if available), pencils and paper for each person; videocassette or audio recording of a news program; newspapers; one orange for every two people.

■ **As the Kids Arrive**
Play a fun mixer such as Peel Out.[4] Form two groups of boy/girl couples. Each couple receives an orange to peel and eat. However, couples may not use hands or feet. To begin, each male wedges the orange in his mouth. At ''go'' the female rips off the peel with her teeth. Couples may pass the orange from mouth to mouth to remove the peel. If the orange falls to the floor, it must be picked up by the teeth. Once peeled, the couples must eat the orange without using hands or feet. The first group to peel and eat the orange is the winner.

■ **Activity One**
Take a quick survey of the group members as to: what is their favorite source of news; what radio station do they listen to; what TV station, newspaper, or people do they rely on for news? Ask:
- What kind of news normally gets our attention?
- Why are certain issues quick to get our attention?
- How do you feel young people are reported on or portrayed

in the news?

Proceed to play the videocassette or audiocassette of a local newscast. Ask the group to check on the "mood of the news": Is the news more positive or negative—good or bad news? Do the same exercise with the newspaper. Have them try to determine how much of the paper contains encouraging, hopeful, good news. Ask group members to determine which news they consider the best news and which they consider the worst news, and share why they feel that way.

Discuss how news was reported in biblical times (by word of mouth) and ask the group members what they think might have been newsworthy in that era. Express to the kids that people then had many of the same concerns about their own needs and events in the world that we have today. Explain the meaning of the words evangelical and Gospel to the group. Talk about what makes the news in the Bible the Good News for the world. Ask the group what it means to them to live with the promise of forgiveness, hope, assurance, etc.

■ Activity Two

Using the Bibles, discuss the different kinds of stories found in the New Testament such as historical narratives, miracles and Gospels. Have the kids divide into teams of three or four, select a story passage and create a modern news report of the event. Skits should contain the facts of the story, plus any creative elements the kids want to include. Give the groups time to prepare and then have them present their "TV News."

■ Conclusion

Summarize the basic message of each story: The world needs to hear good news. Consider the part each of us plays, living as a Christian, in telling the Good News. Each person needs to realize the importance of his or her role as a shining storyteller of the Good News. Close by having everyone read in unison Matthew 13:43, "Then the righteous will shine like the sun in the kingdom of their Father."

You Are What You Eat, Aren't You?

■ **Objectives**
Participants will:
- Develop a healthy sense of self-esteem.
- Learn to appreciate his or her own individual makeup.
- Develop a sensitivity to the special characteristics of others.

■ **Biblical Focus**
John 4:1-42

■ **Materials Needed**
A variety of candy bars, one for each person; an X-ray; brown lunch bags; scissors; glue; magazines; Bible for each person; newsprint; markers; lamp.

■ **Before the Meeting**
Set up an area for making shadow pictures—you'll need a large sheet of newsprint taped to the wall, a lamp and marker.

■ **As the Kids Arrive**
Ask each of the participants to come to the shadow area. Have them stand facing to the newsprint. Shine the lamp from behind them; then use a marker to trace their outline. Put each person's name on the bottom of his or her sheet and hang it in the room.

■ **Activity One**
Gather the group and pass out candy bars for a snack. Let the members select the candy they want and ask them to save the wrapper. After they've eaten, ask the group members to describe the candy they ate, what it looked like, how it tasted, why they selected it, etc. Next, ask them to look at the wrapper, describe it, and tell what the wrapper's function is. When someone mentions that the wrapper lists the ingredients, stop at that point and have each person look at the ingredients on his candy bar wrapper. Ask:
- What ingredients did you know were in your candy when you tasted it?

●What ingredients were you surprised to find?
●What ingredients had you never heard of?
●What ingredients were you unable to taste or see?

Have everyone look at the shadow pictures. In a way, the pictures are like the candy wrappers—an outline of each person's "wrapping." Divide into groups of four. Ask the kids to look at each shadow picture and decide on a candy bar name for each person in their group. Discuss why they selected the names they did. Then show them an X-ray and describe its purpose: to see inside what cannot be seen from the outside.

■ Activity Two

Distribute brown lunch bags, magazines, scissors and glue to each group. Tell the kids the paper bags represent who they are; there is an outside and an inside. They are to find words or symbols in the magazines to paste on the outside of the bag that represent how they think other people perceive them. Next they are to select and place inside the bag, pictures that describe what they are really like.

Once the bags are finished, ask members to share with one another the outside characteristics and inside ingredients. The remaining group members respond by telling one thing they would have selected to paste on the inside and outside of the bag for that person; one thing on the outside and inside that surprised them; and one thing they learned about the person they didn't know.

■ Conclusion

Read John 4:1-42. Help the group members understand that who we are isn't always who we appear to be. Just as there is more to a candy bar than its wrapper, so it is with people. We all have inner, hidden ingredients that make us who we are. Affirm one another by praying in a circle and then having a massive group hug. Let the participants take home their shadow pictures and paper bags.

CHAPTER 13

RETREATS

Retreats offer an uninterrupted period of time for a group to "get away from it all," to study, play, worship and get acquainted. I have found that more spiritual growth and community building result from retreats than from any other form of youth ministry.

While "getting away from it all" is an appealing feature of a retreat, it takes more than that to make a retreat experience worthwhile. Successful retreats require a lot of careful planning: selecting a location; lining up transportation; making food arrangements; checking out lodging facilities and cost factors; enlisting staff; planning a purpose, objectives, theme, study time, recreation time, worship experiences, etc. Yet, anyone who knows the joy of a mountaintop experience with a group of kids will tell you it is worth every ounce of energy.

Retreat planning should involve as many kids and volunteers as possible and begin several months in advance. (In some areas, facilities need to be reserved a year ahead of time.) Planning begins by asking certain questions to determine how the group's time together best can be used:

- Who will be participating?
- What are their interests and needs?
- How well do the group members relate to each other?
- Where is the group in terms of spiritual maturation?
- How can a retreat help the individuals grow in their faith?

Besides answering these questions, planning effective, fun, successful retreats depends on several other elements:

1. Checklist. In the beginning stages of retreat planning, it is helpful if the leader prepares a checklist of all retreat details. As the date of the retreat approaches, the checklist is useful in determining if everything is on schedule, what remains to be done, and if anything has been overlooked. A checklist could include:

_____ Select planning committee and set first meeting date.

_____ Planning committee meets to determine retreat purpose, theme, activities and schedule.

_____ Select retreat site.

_____ Decide on the method of transportation.

_____ Determine the cost per person.

_____ Line up staff.

_____ Develop publicity schedule and set registration deadline.

_____ Meet with staff and delegate responsibilities.

_____ Establish and communicate to participants the behavioral guidelines to be observed.

_____ Determine supplies that will be needed.

_____ Plan the menus for meals and snacks.

_____ Provide for first-aid needs.

_____ Develop a plan for evaluating the event.

_____ Make alternate plans for activities that could be affected by weather conditions.

_____ Meet with parents to give them the retreat details.

2. Planning committee and staff. Never plan a retreat by yourself; always involve interested junior highers and adult leaders. Fully utilize their ideas, talents and energy. Ask for their commitment to attend meetings regularly and to help plan the retreat. Involving other people ensures a successful, creative retreat. And, it's more fun!

The planning committee can recruit adults to serve as staff on a retreat. Successful retreats are dependent on leaders who are committed to young people, who are willing to set aside the time to fulfill their role, and who understand their responsibilities. Some adults may be needed to provide transportation. Others may be needed to prepare food and do the necessary shopping. Still others may be responsible for leading discussions or presenting topics. Leaders can team up with kids and be in charge of menus, recreation, worship, etc. If you go to a retreat site that has cabins, each adult leader can be assigned to a cabin as a counselor. The adults will be in charge of the group of kids in their cabin for the entire retreat.

To determine the number of staff needed for a retreat, consider the following:

●The number of junior highers participating (one staff member per six to eight kids seems to be the best ratio).

●The delineation of responsibilities (how many will be needed to do all the tasks).

Adults should be recruited well in advance to allow time for a staff meeting in which the purpose, theme and staff responsibilities are explained. It is essential that leaders see themselves working as a team, and clearly understand how they will function together.

The staff should be oriented to the material being studied, given special insights into the kids who will participate, informed of behavioral expectations, and helped to prepare for their tasks. During the retreat, it is important to meet regularly with the staff to offer support and to discuss specific concerns.

If possible, staff should not have to pay their expenses. This is one way of telling them they are important and showing appreciation for their willingness to make a time commitment. It means a lot to adult leaders if they are personally introduced to the group at the retreat orientation, given the opportunity to tell why they want to be with the kids, and publicly thanked at the conclusion of the retreat.

Other ways to express appreciation for staff participation are to ask for their evaluation of the event, and send them written thank-you letters—from you, as well as from the junior highers. Thank-you notes are tangible keepsakes of memories made with the group.

3. Purpose and objectives. Ask the planning committee, "What's the purpose for the retreat? Why should we spend so much time with one another?" Purposes can be: to build friendships; to conduct an in-depth study on a topic; to plan the year's activities; to prepare a music program, youth Sunday or trip.

Once the retreat purpose is set, have the planning committee list objectives—how they will accomplish that purpose; for example:

●**Purpose:** To learn more about handicaps.
●**Objectives:** Each participant will experience a physical disability for the entire weekend; the group will discuss their experiences on a regular basis.

All participants need to clearly understand the purpose, and know that each one of them is needed to achieve it.

4. Theme and schedule. A theme ties the retreat together. A theme can be based on the purpose and objectives; for example, a theme for a retreat focusing on friendship could be "Friends in Christ." The theme and participants' abilities must be kept in mind while planning the schedule. With junior highers, a structured format is probably best, although leaders need to determine what best meets the needs of their group. One schedule possibility is:

Friday

6:00 p.m.	Depart from the church.
7:30 p.m.	Arrive at retreat center. Make cabin assignments and advise group when and where to report for first session.
8:00 p.m.	Assemble group for orientation to the facility, review behavioral guidelines, introduce the staff.
8:20 p.m.	Mixers and games.
9:30 p.m.	Snack time.
10:00 p.m.	First session on theme. Introduce the purpose of the weekend, what will be accomplished, and make first presentation.
10:45 p.m.	Break.
11:00 p.m.	Worship/group singing.
11:30 p.m.	Cabin time.
Midnight	Lights out.

Saturday

8:00 a.m.	Breakfast. Assign small groups or cabins to set tables, say meal-time prayers, help with cleanup.
9:00 a.m.	Second session on theme.
10:30 a.m.	Break.
10:45 a.m.	Third session on theme.
Noon	Lunch. After the meal, take time to play table games, sing or announce the afternoon recreation choices.
1:00 p.m.	Recreation. Hiking, organized games, roller skating, quiet time, time for showers or cleanup before dinner.
5:30 p.m.	Dinner. Make this a special meal: tablecloths, candlelight, soft music in background, etc.
6:30 p.m.	Fourth session on theme.
7:45 p.m.	Break.
8:00 p.m.	Special event: games, stunts, contests.
9:00 p.m.	Film, musical group, or other special entertainment.
10:30 p.m.	Snack.
10:50 p.m.	Worship by candlelight/flashlight.
11:30 p.m.	Cabin time.
Midnight	Lights out.

Sunday

8:30 a.m.	Breakfast.
9:15 a.m.	Fifth session on theme.
10:15 a.m.	Break.
10:30 a.m.	Closing worship.
11:30 a.m.	Evaluation. Allow participants and leaders to share what the retreat has meant to them.
Noon	Lunch.
12:45 p.m.	Clean up retreat site and pack for return trip.
1:30 p.m.	Depart from retreat center.

There are many ways to design a retreat. You'll notice the sample schedule does not allow for much free time. I question the value of scheduling a lot of unstructured time into a junior high weekend retreat. If junior highers have too much free time, they become bored. Most adolescents will spend free time just walking around on their own, "looking for things to do." This leads to kids forming cliques, casting a shadow on group spirit. Retreats are more successful when a variety of activities are offered. In fact, have more activities planned than you think you'll have time for, rather than have kids return from a retreat reporting, "We really didn't do much."

5. Location. Choosing an appropriate location for a retreat is dependent on two factors: the purpose of the retreat and the available facilities. If a retreat's purpose is to emphasize urban ministry, meeting at a rustic mountain camp wouldn't be suitable. A more appropriate facility would be a church in the inner city where kids could visit and observe community-help programs, staff workers and local residents.

Another consideration when choosing a location is the distance the group will need to travel. Distance affects transportation costs as well as the time schedule. If a retreat center is located three hours away, and you had hoped to begin the retreat on Friday night, this may not be possible—especially if sponsors have jobs and don't get home until early evening.

6. Transportation. The type of transportation used to get to the retreat location can play a part in building community. When kids travel in a bus, group singing or games can initiate a sense of togetherness. Automobiles may be less expensive, but there are additional matters to consider such as lining up drivers, insurance, staying together on the road, and small cliques forming en route.

7. Expenses. With careful planning, leaders can put together a manageable budget and per-person fee. Remember, junior highers are dependent on parents or some other source to pay their way. Occasionally, groups conduct fund-raising activities. Leaders also need to be sensitive to teenagers who might need financial assistance. Some church budgets provide retreat funds to meet individual needs as well as program expenses and leadership costs.

In setting the cost of the retreat, the following expenses need to be included: transportation, food, facility rental fee, retreat T-shirts, film or VCR rental, recreation prizes, honorarium for guest speakers and other resource materials. Effective programming requires quality resources, so be careful not to shortchange the retreat by skimping in this area.

8. Publicity. The best plans and staff will be useless if a retreat isn't properly promoted and publicized; getting the word out is essential. Announcing the dates and theme of a retreat early never hurts, but getting registration details out late can ruin it! Good publicity motivates people to participate.

In the initial announcements, presentation of specific information in the simplest language is most effective. Posters, fliers, post cards, and church newsletter articles should mention who, what, when, where, why and how much. Nothing, however, beats word-of-mouth enthusiasm. Once the planning committee has set further details, they should begin actively encouraging people to sign up. Kids should be told the sign-up deadline and the persons to contact for registration information. (See Chapter 11 for more publicity ideas.)

9. Rules. A lot of groups love to tell about the water balloon fights or all-night cabin raids that took place at the retreat they attended. However, broken windows in the dining hall or personal injuries are seldom reported with laughter. Depending on what behavior the leaders determine acceptable, every retreat needs rules.

Rules need to be outlined in advance and clearly stated to the kids before leaving home. The best way is to have kids and leaders work together to make retreat rules. Leaders may also need to exercise authority and tell the kids what behavior is necessary and expected of them to ensure a successful weekend together. Adults need to remember that they will have to act on the established guidelines. All adults must consistently enforce the rules.

For the most part, rules should remain in the background and not interfere with people having a fun, positive experience. Whatever rules are set, they should be presented in a positive way. For example, "Turn out the lights and turn off the talking by midnight. Give your body plenty of rest so you'll be wide awake for the retreat activities" is better than saying, "If you are not in bed and quiet by midnight, you will be warned once. After that you will be sent home."

A full schedule, well-planned and executed by prepared leadership, often eliminates the need for having to deal with discipline problems.

Successful retreats require a lot of work, yet the outcome is well worth the effort. Following are several retreat outlines on handicap awareness, human sexuality, Bible stories, talent, community services and Jesus' life. Feel free to adapt the outlines to meet your needs.

Lots of Talent!

■ Purpose
To study Matthew 25:14-30—the hidden talent.

■ Objectives
Participants will:
- Be affirmed in their talents
- Put their talents to immediate use

■ Materials Needed
Paper; pencils; markers; tape; lunch bags; peppermint candies; food for snacks, meals and games.

Note: This retreat is more effective if it is held at the church. The cost is minimal since there is no facility rental fee.

■ Retreat Schedule
Friday

8:00 p.m. **Arrive at the church.** Review the retreat purpose and objectives; tell the kids that they will discover and use their hidden talents. Direct kids where to put their sleeping bags. You may want to have kids meet in a room other than where they will sleep; on the other hand, holding all the activities in the same room is fun—the retreat seems like a huge slumber party.

8:20 p.m. **Crowdbreakers.** Gather the kids in a circle and play Smile Resistance.[1] One person is chosen to be "It." He or she selects someone in the circle, sits on his or her lap, and says, "If ya love me, honey, smile." The person who is being sat upon must say, "I love ya, honey, but I just can't smile." If he or she laughs or even smiles, he or she is "It."

9:30 p.m. **Snacks.** Set the stage for the retreat and emphasize the theme by hiding the snacks. Tell the kids to search for hidden candy bars, oranges and apples.

10:00 p.m. **Session #1.** Gather in a circle and focus the group's attention on the people present. Go around the circle and have everybody tell something unique and special about each person.

Give each person a piece of paper and a pencil. Have the participants trace one of their hands. On the inside of the hand print, have them list their special qualities mentioned by others in the group. Tape these outlines on the wall. Let people see who's who and what makes each person special.

Gather in small groups and have each of the members answer these questions:

●Why do your friends perceive you in certain ways?

●Were you surprised by any of the positive comments? Why or why not?

●Which quality or trait mentioned by your friends do you value most?

●What are some specific ways you can use these qualities in your life? For example, if you possess the quality of enthusiasm, you could help promote and publicize the next junior high event.

10:45 p.m.   **Break.**

11:00 p.m.   **Worship.** Ask each person to describe a certain talent in his or her life which has not been given much attention or been well developed. Silently think of ways to develop that talent. Read and compare Matthew 25:14-30 and Luke 19:11-27. Close with a prayer of thanksgiving for the gift of life and the ability to grow as Christians.

11:30 p.m.   **Cabin time.**

Midnight   **Lights out.**

Saturday

7:00 a.m.   **Wake up.**

8:00 a.m.   **Breakfast.**

9:00 a.m.   **Session #2.** Begin the session by reviewing the first session. Say that the hand outlines on the wall visually display our special qualities; our goal is to put these qualities to work.

Again read Matthew 25:14-30. Help the group members see that their special qualities are their talents. Each person has been given certain gifts that are meant to be used, not buried and forgotten. Divide into small groups and discuss these questions:

●Who are some talented or gifted people you know?

●How do they use their talents to benefit others?

●How does God want us to be responsible for the gifts and talents he gives us?

10:30 a.m.   Break. While the kids have free time, prepare a talent bag for each participant. On paper, write a talent you have observed in each young person. Talents could be, "You cook well," "You write beautiful poetry," "You have a lovely singing voice," "You are strong and able," "You are a helpful person." Write each participant's name on a lunch bag and place the matching talent description inside.

11:00 a.m.   Session #3. Gather the group and distribute the bags. Explain that inside their bag is one of their talents that you have observed. They now have an opportunity to experience the joy their talent can bring to others. For example, a person who cooks well could go home and cook supper for his or her family; a person who sings well could sing in the choir for the worship service; a person who is strong and able could help an elderly person clean or do yard work, etc.

Saturday afternoon and evening the group members are on their own to return home and put their individual talents to work. During the Sunday school hour, they will meet and share what they did to develop their talent.

Send the kids off with the commission: "May you be like the good and faithful servants; use your God-given talents as best you can."

Sunday
9:30 a.m.   **Session #4.** When the group members reassemble during the Sunday school hour, or at another designated time and place, review the purpose and objectives for the retreat. Reread the Bible passages, and review each person's special qualities. Then have the participants share their experiences of putting their talents to work. Discuss:

●What was your reaction when you opened your bag?

●How did you decide to use your talent?

●How did people respond when you shared your talent?

Close with an affirmation activity such as Celebration.[2] Give 10 pieces of peppermint candy to each person in the group. Instruct the members to mingle with the group and give a piece of candy to different individuals, telling them what they specifically appreciate about them. Tell the students to continue until all their candy is gone. (As a leader, plan ahead and make a point of affirming individuals who may get neglected.)

The Missing Years

■ Purpose
To discover Jesus' life as a teenager.

■ Objectives
Participants will:
●Become acquainted with life in Bible times
●Develop an understanding of Jesus' humanity
●Compare and contrast Jesus' teenage years to their own

■ Materials Needed
Bibles; paper; pencils; several pictures of Jesus; yellow crepe paper streamers; water balloons; game equipment; Bible diction-

aries and commentaries; food for snacks, meals and games; toothpicks; Sunday school curriculum and a filmstrip, or journal article, describing village life in Jesus' time.

■ Retreat Schedule

Friday

6:30 p.m.   **Meet at the church.** Review the purpose of the weekend and conduct a brief orientation for the retreat.

7:00 p.m.   **Departure.**

8:00 p.m.   **Arrival.** Assign cabins.

8:20 p.m.   **Crowdbreakers.** Play games such as Porky-Mallow.[3] Divide the kids into two or more teams. Give each person a toothpick and each team a marshmallow. The first player puts the marshmallow on his or her toothpick and then holds the toothpick between his or her teeth. Instruct the kids to pass the marshmallow from player to player by sticking the toothpick into the marshmallow and leaving it in as it is passed. No hands allowed. As the marshmallow is passed, it accumulates one toothpick from each player. The first team to finish is the winner. The end product is a marshmallow that looks like a porcupine—thus the name, Porky-Mallow!

9:20 p.m.   **Snack.** Roast marshmallows, then fix S'mores by placing the marshmallows and a chocolate candy bar between two graham crackers.

9:45 p.m.   **Session #1.** Explain that you'll be exploring a topic that few—if any—people know anything about. Participants' opinions are not subject to judgment; all ideas and thoughts are to be respected.

Begin by reading Luke 2:15-52; 3:21-23. This is a description of Jesus' life—an historical account. Ask the group members to look for missing information. Don't tell them!

Sooner or later the group members should realize that nothing is recorded about Jesus' childhood except his birth, his presentation at the temple when he was a baby, and the incident at the temple when he was 12 years old.

Shift the attention to the group members; ask their ages. How many are 12? 13? 14? Remind them that Jesus was once their age.

Focus on childhood memories. Ask the kids to share memories of their "growing up" years: something funny, a crisis, a special family experience. What does the memory mean to them? Why is it special to them? Ask the kids to use their imaginations to think about experiences Jesus might have had when he was 6 to 11 years of age. Ask speculative questions like:

● What chores did he have to do at home?

● What were his friends like?

● What games did he play?

● Where would he go with his friends in Nazareth?

● Did he have a curfew?

11:00 p.m. **Worship.** Sing all sorts of songs that tell of Jesus: "What a Friend We Have in Jesus," "Jesus Loves Me," "Jesus Is the Rock 'n' He Rolls My Blues Away," "Jesus, Name Above All Names," etc.[4] Divide the kids into small groups. Have them think of a description of Jesus and sing it to the tune "Jesus Loves Me." For example, "Jesus loves me all the time, windy weather, rain or shine. He stands by me each weekday. He's my friend in every way."

11:30 p.m. **Cabin time.**

Midnight **Lights out.**

Saturday

7:00 a.m. **Wake up.**

8:00 a.m. **Breakfast.**

9:00 a.m. **Session #2.** Show the filmstrip or read the journal articles describing village life in Jesus' time. Divide into small groups, then distribute paper, pencils, Bible dictionaries, commentaries, Bibles and other materials. Have kids research the following details about village life: lifestyles, occupations, living conditions, types of food, health problems, recreational activities, communication, focus of community life, government, education, religious customs, holidays, what people did if they needed a doctor or dentist, etc.

Have the kids present their information; allow for additional questions. Compare life in Jesus' time to today. What were differences? similarities?

10:15 a.m.   **Break.**

10:30 a.m.   **Session #3.** Combine the information learned in the morning with each person's imagination. We know what life was like in Nazareth; now try to imagine how Jesus spent his teenage years. Ask these questions:

●What kind of things do you think Jesus worried about?

●What qualities did he look for in friends?

●What things do you think he prayed for?

●What type of conflicts do you think he had with Mary and Joseph?

●What did he laugh about? cry about?

11:45 a.m.   **Break.**

Noon   **Lunch.**

1:15 p.m.   **Recreation.** Have a marathon volleyball tournament until dinner time. Allow periodic rest times by rotating in players. End the tournament by dousing each other with water balloons!

5:30 p.m.   **Dinner.**

6:30 p.m.   **Session #4.** Distribute a paper and pencil to each person. Ask the kids to work alone for a while and write a page in "Jesus' Diary." It's to be a journal of sorts, describing what life must have been like for Jesus as a teenager.

After the kids finish, ask them to find a partner and share the pages. What insights did they gain about Jesus as a teenager from the writings?

7:45 p.m.   **Recreation.** Play games such as Pass the Carrot.[5]

Have everyone form a circle. Place a carrot between the knees of the tallest person; he or she must pass the carrot to the knees of the person to the left, without using hands. This continues until the carrot has traveled around the circle. Break off a piece and send it around again. If a person drops the carrot, he or she is out of the game. The last person left is the winner.

10:00 p.m. **Snack.** Have the winner of Pass the Carrot serve the snack to the others. How about fresh carrots? carrot juice? carrot cake?

10:45 p.m. **Worship.** On the wall, hang several different artists' renditions of Jesus. Have the kids gather by the one they can best relate to. Ask why they chose that particular picture. Allow each person to describe how he or she views Jesus. Focus on the Gospels and their descriptions of Jesus' life.

11:30 p.m. **Cabin time.**

Midnight **Lights out.**

Sunday

7:30 a.m. **Wake up.**

8:30 a.m. **Breakfast.**

9:30 a.m. **Session #5 and worship.** Incorporate the final session with the closing worship. The purpose of the session is to share what each participant imagines Jesus' life was like during the "missing years." Ask kids to read their diary pages. Allow the group to respond. Listen carefully to the normal adolescent needs, concerns and characteristics that are expressed. Make notes of these matters, and use them for a final presentation. Focus on Jesus' common experiences and his spiritual growth. Say that as Jesus grew physically, he also grew spiritually. Ask:

●How did Jesus' spiritual life develop?

●What influences were at work in his religious life?

●What things help us mature spiritually?

Explain that Jesus had many of the same needs and experiences most teenagers have today. Temptation is temptation, whether it is drinking at a party, or spending too much time with friends when you should be helping at home. Try to bond the kids with Jesus through their similarities.

Close the worship with a time of thanksgiving and praise. Gather in a circle; give every other person a length of bright yellow crepe paper streamers. Go around the circle and have one person holding a length of crepe paper tell something he or she is thankful for.

After saying that, have that person toss one end of the streamer to someone across the circle who doesn't have a streamer. The receiver then tells something he or she is thankful for. Repeat the action until everyone has shared. In the end, a bright yellow sunburst will fill the circle.

Ask the group to create a slow-moving, circle sunburst-dance while a reader leads an echo cheer. Have fun! Experiment with raising and lowering the streamers in a flowing motion. The reader will read Psalm 150:1-6. He or she will read a line or phrase, then the others will echo.[6]

Noon   **Lunch.**
1:00 p.m. **Pack and clean up.**
1:30 p.m. **Depart for home.**

Have You Heard the One About . . . ?

■ Purpose
To learn more about lesser-known Bible stories and events.

■ Objectives
Participants will:
●Research forgotten Bible stories

●Develop ways of celebrating the truth of these events in worship

●Appreciate and apply the significance of these stories in their personal faith journey

■ Materials Needed

Food for snacks and meals; Bibles; paper; pencils; Bible dictionaries and commentaries; Bible storybooks, filmstrips and movies; newsprint; tape; balloons; markers; bag of props and costumes such as scarves, hats, sweaters, cups, books, etc.

■ Retreat Schedule

Friday

6:30 p.m. **Meet at the church.** Give a brief orientation of the weekend. Give the kids a taste of what is to come by gathering them around you and reading a selection from a Bible storybook.

7:00 p.m. **Departure.**

8:00 p.m. **Arrival.** Assign cabins.

8:20 p.m. **Crowdbreakers.** Play charades; have the kids try to guess their favorite Bible characters or stories. Or play Sock Grab.[7] Tape off a large circle on the floor, large enough to seat the whole group. Ask the players to remove their shoes before sitting in the circle. (They must wear socks to participate.) On a "go" signal, they must try to collect as many socks as they can—anyway they can get them. Kids are out of the game (and the circle) if both their socks are taken or if any part of their body goes outside the circle. The last person in the circle wins.

9:20 p.m. **Snack.** Eat food that Bible characters might have eaten: nuts, grapes, bread, etc.

9:45 p.m. **Session #1.** Announce to the participants that they will be discovering little-known facts about stories in the Bible. Take a survey: Ask the group members to recall the most popular stories in the Bible. What stories do they remember from Sunday school? List the stories on newsprint, then take a vote and rank the top 10 stories.

Ask the group members to explain why they think these are such well-known stories, and why they are important. Break into five small groups and assign each group two of the stories. Distribute Bibles, commentaries, dictionaries, paper and pencils to each group. Ask the kids to study their stories. Ask:

●What is the significance of each story?

●Who are the characters?

●What are interesting, uncommonly known facts about the characters? the story?

Save the findings for Saturday morning. Conclude the session by selecting one or two stories that are the most unfamiliar. These will be read as part of the evening worship.

11:00 p.m.   **Worship.** Read the two Bible stories. Compare them to life today. How are the situations similar? different? How are the people similar? different? Close with a circle prayer. Have the young people think of a favorite biblical person and thank God for his or her influence on their life.

11:30 p.m.   **Cabin time.**

Midnight   **Lights out.**

Saturday

7:00 a.m.   **Wake up.**

8:00 a.m.   **Breakfast.**

9:00 a.m.   **Session #2.** Begin the session by reviewing the Friday night surveys. Explain how the Bible was written, the types of literature it contains, and how these different types of literature impact our faith; for example, poetry, miracle stories, history, prophecy, etc.

Divide into small groups and assign each group a different type of literature to research. For example, assign one group poetry—they can search the Psalms. Give each group a Bible, dictionary, commentary, paper and pencil. Have them look at the historical period, setting, what the event or word meant to the people, the author's purpose, etc. Gather as a large group and discuss the findings.

10:15 a.m. **Free time.**

10:45 a.m. **Session #3.** Divide into small groups and assign each a section of the Bible. Ask each group to find two to three lesser-known stories—ones they may remember from reading the Bible, but don't know all the details, or ones that are completely new to them. Ask each group to select its favorite story and research it.

●Why was it written?

●What did the event or story mean to the people of the time?

●What is the truth contained in the story? (In other words, how did the people relate to God; how did God relate to his people?)

●What does the story mean to us today?

Have the kids save their research papers until the evening session.

Noon **Lunch.**

1:15 p.m. **Recreation.** Depending on the location of your campsite, go rafting, mountain climbing, swimming, hiking along a nature trail, etc.

5:30 p.m. **Dinner.**

6:30 p.m. **Session #4.** Gather the kids into the same small groups. Have them review their research of the lesser-known event or story. Ask the groups how their story could be retold in modern terms. Also have them think of ways the story could be celebrated; for example, the better-known stories and events, such as Jesus' birth, are celebrated as holidays. Have each of the small groups create a presentation telling their story, and explain the significance of having a celebration, festival or holiday for this lesser-known event. Give the kids the bag of props and allow them to use anything they can find—indoors or outdoors—to help with their presentation. Save these presentations for Sunday morning.

7:45 p.m.   Break.

8:00 p.m.   Show time. Show old movies or filmstrips that tell of Bible stories and characters. Serve popcorn and pop.

11:00 p.m.   Worship. Read the story of the Last Supper (Matthew 26:20-29). Discuss what it meant to Jesus and the disciples; then discuss what it means to us today. Close by celebrating communion with one another.

11:30 p.m.   Cabin time.

Midnight   Lights out.

Sunday

7:30 a.m.   Wake up.

8:30 a.m.   Breakfast.

9:15 a.m.   Session #5. Ask each group to give its presentation on lesser-known Bible stories. Discuss how these stories are included in scripture for a purpose and how they apply to our daily life.

Have the participants role play their characters or some other well-known Bible people. Include a question-and-answer period. For example, a person could role play Moses. Kids could ask, "How did you feel when you saw the burning bush?" "Was it easy to work with your brother Aaron? Why or why not?"

10:30 a.m.   Worship. Ask the participants to share the story they discovered this weekend that means the most to them, and why.

Give everyone a small piece of paper, pencil and balloon. Have the kids write a prayer concern on the piece of paper, fold it, place it in the balloon and blow up the balloon. Allow three minutes for the kids to toss the balloons to each other—mix them up well! Call time, and have the kids pop the balloon they are holding. They must pray for the prayer concern on their piece of paper.

Noon	**Lunch.**
1:00 p.m.	**Pack and clean up.**
1:30 p.m.	**Depart for home.**

A 24-Hour Surprise Safari

■ Purpose
To focus on community services and places of employment.

■ Objectives
Participants will:

●Discover how a variety of community needs are met

●Express appreciation to those in the community who serve but are seldom seen

■ Materials Needed
Rented bus or other transportation, schedule and directions to places to be visited (see the retreat schedule).

Note: This retreat is not a "going away" experience, but rather a concentrated 24-hour exposure to your community—without sleep! The element of surprise is one of the features of this experience. The only thing participants will know in advance is that they will be exploring their community; they will not know where they'll go or who they'll meet until the safari begins. Participants don't have to pack since they'll be up all night. The only expenses are bus rental (or other transportation) and food for breakfast, lunch, dinner and snacks.

If you live in a small town, you could plan the program with a youth group from a major city. Visit them one weekend for a 24-hour safari, exploring life in their community. They can make a return visit some weeks later and explore life in your smaller community.

■ Retreat Schedule
Friday

7:00 p.m.   Assemble at the church. Conduct a brief orientation session. Explain to the group members that they will be going on a 24-hour safari in the community. They will hunt out people and places that serve special needs, but often go unnoticed. They will tour several facilities, visit with personnel, and ask questions. They may be going to places they've never seen before, and visit places they never knew existed.

Distribute the schedule for the safari. Allow time for kids to discuss questions they'll ask and anticipate situations they may encounter. Following are Friday evening possibilities. You won't have enough time to visit all of them, so pick and choose ones that are appropriate to your location:

●Visit a bus terminal, train station or airport. Talk to the terminal manager. What type of jobs exist there? What type of emergency problems do staff members deal with? Many airports have a chaplain; arrange a meeting with him or her and talk about the special ministry that's provided.

●Visit a soup kitchen. Talk to the people who prepare the food. Who supplies the food? Who plans the menu? What is done with leftovers? Talk to the director. Who does the soup kitchen serve? Why are they hungry? What problems occur? Talk to volunteers. Have them describe their jobs and tell why they volunteer.

●Visit and tour the emergency room of a busy hospital. Talk to the personnel. What is it like late at night when people need the attention of a doctor? Ask the staff to describe a typical night in the emergency room.

Saturday
Midnight-on   ●Visit a 24-hour radio station. Talk to the disc jockey or talk show host. What situations do they deal with? What services does a 24-hour station provide (especially between the hours of 12 a.m. to 6 a.m.)? How do they deal with emergencies?

●Visit a police station. If you can, tour the radio control room and talk to detectives. Who is on duty during the night? What problems do they encounter?

●Visit a fire station. Who is on duty? What is life like in a fire station? What emergency situations occur most often during the night?

●Visit a local all-night diner. Talk to the manager. Who are the people who come in to eat? What are their occupations? Is there a camaraderie among the regular customers? Do the diner employees help stranded people? If so, why? how? Take time to get something to eat!

●Visit a local television station. Observe how they get the morning news report ready. Who is on duty during the night? What problems do they encounter?

●Visit the local newspaper. Observe how they get the morning edition ready. How are stories selected? Who chooses the editorial subjects? What's the purpose of an editorial? What problems do newspapers have to deal with?

●Other places to visit at night could be: a 24-hour truck stop (some of them have chaplains and chapels); a bakery or factory that has a night shift; an all-night pharmacy; a crisis or hotline center.

●During the daylight hours visit special centers for the elderly; day care centers; jails; clothing distribution centers; and special church ministries such as runaway houses, counseling centers, hospices, etc.

7:00 p.m.   **Debriefing.** Conclude the safari back at the church by asking questions such as:

●What did you observe? In what ways do the people you observed live a life different than yours?

●How does the lifestyle of people who work at night differ from daytime workers'? How might

it affect time with their family? friends? church?
●What special needs exist in your community?
Ask the group members to meet you Sunday
morning during the Sunday school hour.

Sunday
9:30 a.m. **Follow-up.** Select ways of expressing appreciation
to the community workers. For example, design
a certificate of appreciation to send to the places
you visited. Mail the certificates or divide them
among group members who can deliver them personally.

A View From the Other Side

■ **Purpose**
To become aware of disabled people and their needs.

■ **Objectives**
Participants will:
●Experience a physical handicap
●Think of sensitive ways to respond to handicapped people
●Discover similarities between handicapped and able-bodied
people

■ **Materials Needed**
Crutches, wheelchairs, canes, blindfolds, earplugs, sunglasses, tape, Bibles, paper, pencils, food for snacks and meals.
On 3x5 cards, write different handicaps—one for each person.
Place the cards in a hat. Ask three to four handicapped persons
to come to the retreat site on Saturday evening to discuss their
disabilities. For Saturday night, rent a couple of movies on
handicaps such as "A Day in the Life of Bonnie Consuelo" or
"Leo Berman" (contact your denominational publishing office).

■ Retreat Schedule

Friday

6:30 p.m.   **Meet at the church.** Give a brief orientation of the weekend. Pass the hat which contains the 3x5 cards with handicaps written on them. Ask each person to pick a card; that will be his or her handicap for the weekend. Before leaving, each person should assume his or her handicap: wheelchairs for the paralyzed, blindfolds for the blind, earplugs for the deaf, tape for the mute, canes or crutches for the lame, etc. The kids will experience how difficult it is to pack vehicles, board vehicles, ride, etc., with such handicaps. The participants are further instructed that upon arrival at the retreat site, they are to maintain their handicaps and must make their way to assigned cabins and then to the assembly room.

7:00 p.m.   **Departure.**

8:00 p.m.   **Arrival.** Assign cabins.

8:20 p.m.   **Crowdbreakers.** Play active games, like relays. Encourage the kids to do as well as they can, considering their handicap. Allow kids to decide if they wish to sit on the sidelines.

9:20 p.m.   **Snack.** As with all aspects of the retreat, kids will have to figure out how to participate with their handicap. Have them help pop popcorn, mix juice, cut cake, etc.

9:45 p.m.   **Session #1.** Discuss the following:
●How did you feel when you picked your handicap from the hat? Would you have picked a different handicap if you had a choice?
●With your handicap, what was it like to load the vehicles? find your cabin? participate in mixers? eat your snack?
●Did you feel excluded from an activity because of your handicap?
●What do you think it will be like to be handicapped the rest of the weekend? What problems

do you foresee?

●Did being handicapped make you appreciate things you normally take for granted?

11:00 p.m.   Worship. Focus on Bible verses that assure us of God's comfort and strength in all of our afflictions; for example, ''... fear not, for I am with you, be not dismayed, for I am your God; I will strengthen you, I will help you, I will uphold you with my victorious right hand'' (Isaiah 41:10).

11:30 p.m.   Cabin time.

Midnight   Lights out.

Saturday

7:00 a.m.   Wake up.

8:00 a.m.   Breakfast.

9:00 a.m.   Session #2. Ask one of the leaders to read John 9:1-12. As a group, decide how you can communicate this story to those who are deaf. Then discuss:

●Who was responsible for the man being blind?

●Do people want to blame others, or God, for handicaps? Why?

●Jesus was not uncomfortable around handicapped people. Why do some people avoid those with handicaps?

●Why are some people afraid of the handicapped?

●How do you suppose handicapped people feel when they are around those who are not handicapped?

10:15 a.m.   Free time.

10:45 a.m.   Session #3. Divide the kids into four small groups; assign them each one of the following passages to role play: Mark 7:31-37—Jesus heals a man who is deaf and who has a speech impediment; Luke 5:17-26—a paralyzed man is healed; Luke 6:6-11—Jesus restores a man's withered hand; Luke 18:35-43—a blind man receives sight.

Ask each group to present its role play, then discuss:

●How were the handicapped brought to Jesus' attention?

●What miracles are happening today for the handicapped?

●What do you think of faith healing?

●How do you think handicapped people feel about faith healing?

●Consider the handicap you've been assigned. What would you want Jesus to do for you? What would you want others to do for you?

Noon **Lunch.**

1:15 p.m. **Recreation.** Go on a hike, or play volleyball, basketball, Frisbee, etc. (Throughout the recreation period, kids maintain their handicaps.)

5:30 p.m. **Dinner.**

6:30 p.m. **Session #4.** Ask the handicapped people that were invited to the retreat to talk about their disabilities. Ask them each to give a brief history of their life and circumstances, the nature of their handicap, how they cope, what barriers exist in the community that prevent them from living a full life, and the role their faith plays in their day-to-day living. Then, open the session to questions and answers.

7:45 p.m. **Break.**

8:00 p.m. **Movie review.** Show movies; eat popcorn; drink pop! "A Day in the Life of Bonnie Consuelo" and "Leo Berman" are powerful movies—they're sure to elicit emotions from the kids. Allow plenty of time for discussion.

11:00 p.m. **Worship.** Sing songs of supplication as well as thanksgiving; for example, "Open My Eyes That I May See," "Spirit of the Living God," and "My Hope Is Built."[8] Divide into pairs; ask God for sensitivity and awareness of handicapped people.

11:30 p.m. **Cabin time.**

Midnight **Lights out.**

Sunday

7:30 a.m.   **Wake up.**

8:30 a.m.   **Breakfast.**

9:15 a.m.   **Session #5.** Give the kids a pep talk and say that in a little over an hour they can remove their handicaps. Discuss these questions:

●How do we further handicap disabled people?

●In what way does the church need handicapped people?

●In what way does everyone have a handicap?

●What do handicapped and able-bodied people have in common?

●How do people discriminate against the handicapped?

●How does our church and community help handicapped people?

●What is done in schools to assist the handicapped?

●What can members of the group do to help their handicapped peers?

10:30 a.m.   **Worship.** Allow each person to "remove" his or her handicap. Focus meditation and prayers on giving thanks for our gifts, and developing a sensitivity toward those who are handicapped. Distribute paper and pencils. Have the kids make a personal goal of being more aware of handicapped persons. Ask each participant to complete this sentence, "I will show more sensitivity toward handicapped persons by ..." Have the kids take home their papers as reminders of their commitment.

11:30 a.m.   **Evaluation.** Ask all participants to answer these questions:

●What did you think of this experience?

●In what ways have you changed since leaving home on Friday night?

●Did being handicapped change the way you feel about yourself?

●What was the most memorable part of the

weekend?
Noon   **Lunch.**
1:00 p.m. **Pack and clean up.**
1:30 p.m. **Depart for home.**

Whose Body Is It Anyway?

■ Purpose
To learn more about human sexuality.

■ Objectives
Participants will:
- Openly discuss issues related to love and sex
- Assess the things that influence our sexuality
- Learn to appreciate sexuality as a gift from God and understand our responsibility in expressing it

■ Materials Needed
Body-Image Questionnaire and a pencil for each person; newsprint; markers; candles; matches; tablecloths; tape; music; Bibles; food for snacks, meals and games.

■ Retreat Schedule
Friday

6:30 p.m. **Meet at the church.** Review the purpose of the weekend and conduct a brief orientation for the retreat.

7:00 p.m. **Departure.**

8:00 p.m. **Arrival.** Assign cabins.

8:20 p.m. **Crowdbreakers.** Play games such as Farmer's Riddle.[9] Divide into small groups of eight. Designate a place in the room to be a river. In each group, appoint different students to be two chickens, two foxes, two bags of grain and two farmers. Each student must take on the characteristics of his or her new identity; for example, the chickens can only cluck, the bags of grain can only lay around until the farmers move them, etc.

The farmers have to physically carry the chickens, foxes and bags of grain across the river. The farmers must travel together.

The foxes cannot be left unsupervised with the chickens or the foxes will eat them; the chickens cannot be left unattended with the grain or they will eat it. Afterward, discuss these questions:

● What was your biggest frustration in this exercise?

● How did the group eventually solve the problem?

● What else did you learn?

9:20 p.m.   **Snack.** Serve nutritious food such as fruits and juices.

9:45 p.m.   **Session #1.** Since junior highers are very conscious of their image, especially their physical appearance, begin the weekend with a Body-Image Questionnaire. Distribute a pencil and a copy of the following test to each person.

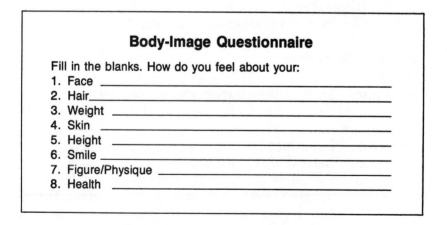

Body-Image Questionnaire

Fill in the blanks. How do you feel about your:
1. Face _____
2. Hair_____
3. Weight _____
4. Skin _____
5. Height _____
6. Smile _____
7. Figure/Physique _____
8. Health _____

Divide into pairs; share the results. Have the kids talk about the things they like and dislike about themselves. What would they like to change about their appearance? Ask each person to describe how he or she feels other people see him or her physically. Ask the kids each to describe how they think God feels about them.

11:00 p.m.   **Worship.** Focus on Bible verses that assure us of God's unconditional love—no matter what we look like or feel like; for example, "But God shows his love for us in that while we were yet sinners Christ died for us" (Romans 5:8). Read other verses that stress how we should love and accept others: "Beloved, let us love one another; for love is of God, and he who loves is born of God and knows God. He who does not love does not know God; for God is love" (1 John 4:7-8).

11:30 p.m.   **Cabin time.**

Midnight   **Lights out.**

Saturday

7:00 a.m.   **Wake up.**

8:00 a.m.   **Breakfast.**

9:00 a.m.   **Session #2.** This session is devoted to the influences at work in our lives that affect our sexuality such as our self-image; trustworthy people; how sex is used in our society; what each person considers attractive about the opposite sex. Divide into small groups and discuss these questions:

●Who are the people you trust to talk to about love, sex, dating?

●What do you think of the sex education classes at school? Why?

●What is the attitude about sex in our society today? Why?

●Have you changed any of your thinking about sex since you started junior high? In what way?

●If someone is considered "sexy," what does that mean?

●How do you feel about discussing love and sex with your parents? What have you discussed with them?

10:15 a.m.   **Break.**

10:30 a.m.   **Session #3.** Divide the group by sex—the boys in one room, the girls in another. Give each group newsprint and a marker. Ask them to discuss the following and write their answers on the newsprint.

●What are the things that interest you most about the opposite sex?

●By group consensus, rank the top seven things you look for in someone of the opposite sex.

●When you think of someone of the opposite sex, what don't you understand? As a group, make a list of the questions you have, ranking them in order of importance.

After 30 to 40 minutes, have the groups exchange lists and questions. Were there any surprises? What were the differences in each list? similarities? Discuss the questions each group has about the other.

11:45 a.m.   **Break.**

Noon   **Lunch.**

1:15 p.m.   **Recreation.** Stage a competition between cabins. Host an all-camp tug of war and an obstacle race. Have the contestants walk a straight line across a fallen log; run around a tree trunk; crawl through an inner tube, etc. The team with the most wins is first in line for dinner!

5:30 p.m.   **Dinner.** Make this a special occasion. Play music in the background; cover the tables with tablecloths; place lighted candles in the center of the tables; dim the lights.

6:30 p.m.   **Session #4.** This session focuses on how our culture influences what we think of love and sex. Discuss:

●What do you think it was like when your parents were your age, and learning of love and sex?

●How do you think music, television, movies, magazines influence the way you think about love and sex?

●What TV shows, movies, music make fun of sex?

●What does the advertising media do with sex?

●What songs do you think of when you think of love and sex?

7:45 p.m.   **Break.**

8:00 p.m.   **Recreation.** Divide into two groups: guys vs. girls. Host all sorts of games and contests; for example, see who can eat the most bananas in three minutes; see who can eat 10 crackers and whistle our national anthem.

10:00 p.m.   **Snack.**

10:30 p.m.   **Candlelight worship.** Focus on our oneness in Christ. In the center of the room, light a large candle to symbolize Christ. Give the participants each a smaller candle and encourage them to light it from the Christ candle. Sing songs such as "They Will Know We Are Christians By Our Love."[10]

11:15 p.m.   **Cabin time.**

Midnight   **Lights out.**

Sunday

7:30 a.m.   **Wake up.**

8:30 a.m.   **Breakfast.**

9:30 a.m.   **Session #5.** Ask the kids what they think of the following, and why: prostitution, the increase of venereal disease/AIDS, homosexuality, abortion, premarital sex, "making out," "dirty jokes," birth control, pornography.

10:30 a.m.   **Break.**

11:00 a.m.   **Worship.** Read several Bible verses that deal with sexuality: Galatians 6:7-9; 1 Thessalonians 4:3-8; and 1 Corinthians 6:19-20, "Do you not know that your body is a temple of the Holy Spirit within you, which you have from God? You are not your own; you were bought with a price. So glorify God in your body." Discuss ways we can keep our bodies a temple for the Holy Spirit. How can we glorify God in our bodies?

Gather in a circle and link arms. As a large group, celebrate God's love and forgiveness by reciting John 3:16, ''For God so loved the world that he gave his only Son, that whoever believes in him should not perish but have eternal life.'' Stay linked and take 10 steps into the center of the circle for a bone-crunching group hug!

Noon   **Lunch.**
1:00 p.m.   **Pack and clean up.**
1:30 p.m.   **Depart for home.**

CHAPTER 14

SPECIAL EVENTS

One thing is certain about junior highers—they love to have a good time. Providing opportunities for associating with friends at a party, taking a trip, or some other fun activity are all parts of true junior high ministry. As adolescents mature socially, they need to learn the value of wholesome fun. Providing fun social times for this age group is as important as providing meaningful Bible study. There are several reasons why.

Early adolescents have a lot of time on their hands. Since they are not old enough to drive or hold a job, time spent outside of school often drags to the point where the kids are bored and frustrated. Frequently, junior highers are immobilized because they are dependent upon parents to provide transportation. There are additional complications if both parents work during the day. Common complaints of these kids are, "I'm stuck at home" or, "I have nothing to do."

Perceptive junior high leaders recognize that weekends,

holidays and summer vacations are prime times to get the kids together. Many churches plan a special activity for junior highers once a month; some offer them more often. Whatever the reason, special events are an integral part of ministries that effectively reach early adolescents. Following are several characteristics of special events:

1. Special events provide kids more opportunities to be together. Weekends, holidays and summertime permit groups to spend anywhere from several hours to several weeks together. Extended time periods allow for a variety of activities, including some that give kids a chance to spend time away from home. These extended special events are great community builders.

2. Special events are opportune times for junior highers to invite their friends to church activities. Unchurched peers may have an unrealistic view of church programs, or feel awkward attending a Bible study, worship or Sunday school class. In most cases, they find fun activities like roller skating or bowling more comfortable, and the environment less threatening.

Special events provide an easy way to introduce unchurched friends to church peers, church activity, and they give un-churched kids a taste of the joy that belongs to the Christian experience.

3. Special events should be exactly what the name indicates—special. One of the distinguishing characteristics of special events is that teenagers choose to come—often because the leaders provide a caring, accepting, encouraging atmosphere. Special events should be unique, a cut above what is offered elsewhere in the community.

4. Special events should be creative. Although that means extra work for the leader, the kids love it when something unusual or unexpected happens. For example, miniature golf can be more than just putt-putting at a local course. Promote the event with tea bags; staple announcements to the tags that read: "This tea is for drinking, but we have a special *tee* party planned for you Friday night at 7 p.m. Bring your friends!" Dress up in wild golfing attire; arrange to transport the group to the course in golf carts. Once there, have some special contests like "hole in one," play one hole blindfolded, or use the putter like a cue stick. Use your imagination. Move on to the next hole—a doughnut shop. Serve doughnut holes for refreshments or have some "golf punch" served in miniature cups.

Often what makes a special event memorable is a creative theme. For example, you could hold a "Banana Night" and use bananas in games, decorations, refreshments, and even in the way you "bunch" the kids together in teams. Kids focus on the theme the entire evening—how can they forget?

5. Special events should be fun. Simply having fun is a valid objective for junior high ministry. Not only is fun essential to kids' development needs, laughter, silly games and ridiculous contests are necessary ingredients in creating a close-knit group. Laughter can have a healthy and healing effect on group spirit; it provides a way to break down barriers. Kids who have a good time relaxing with one another will feel more at ease in serious moments.

Ideas for special events are limited only by your creativity and imagination. The key to special events is keeping them special by not doing the same "fun" activity over and over. Granted, some events may be so popular that they become annual events, but constantly going to amusement parks, bowling or to pizza parlors can become routine and dull. Following are some suggested special events. Some are ideas I dreamed up, some are current national observances.[1] Adapt the activities to fit your group. They are listed in a monthly format, but who said you have to celebrate Christmas in December?

January

●**New Year's Party (January 1)**—dress like babies, play with building blocks and dolls, host a diaper-changing contest and a baby-picture contest—match the baby pictures to the teenagers.

●**Stephen Foster Memorial Day Square Dance (January 13)**—focus the dance around a Southern theme. Serve fried chicken and corn on the cob.

●**Ice Skating Night**—skate on a frozen lake, build a fire, look at the stars, serve hot chocolate out of a "Big Dipper."

●**Snowflake Contest**—have a contest to see who can make

a snowman that most closely resembles the junior high leader, throw snowballs at a target, eat Sno-cones and drink hot cider.

●**Glove Night**—ask all kids to wear gloves, then play games like volleyball, basketball, bowling.

●**Italian Month**—celebrate with a pizza- or spaghetti-eating contest.

February

●**Groundhog Day (February 2)**—have a contest to see who can guess if the groundhog will see his shadow. Award gloves to the winner if there will be six more weeks of winter; award sunglasses if springtime is on the way!

●**Great American Chocolate Festival (February 14)**—freeze some Hershey Kisses. Give one to each participant and see who finishes eating it first. Ask the kids to bring chocolate refreshments: candy, Hershey Kisses, cake, syrup, drinks, etc.

●**Valentine's Day (February 14)**—assign special friends to do fun things for each other during the month; for example, go out for a hamburger, write a thank-you note, surprise them with a lollipop, etc. Top off the month with a Valentine's Party honoring the special friends.

●**Famous Lovers Night**—kids dress as Romeo and Juliet, Adam and Eve, Mickey and Minnie Mouse. Award prizes such as boxes of chocolates, candy hearts or red apples.

●**Hugger and Helper Day**—group performs a loving gesture for a person in need. For example, shovel an elderly person's sidewalks, make a hot meal for a shut-in. Hug each participant for helping.

March

●**St. Patrick's Day Party (March 17)**—serve green food such as lime Jell-O or Popsicles, have a limerick contest and an all-green-item scavenger hunt.

●**Little Orphan Annie Day**—have everyone dress as one of the characters, then act out the story.

●**Pre-Spring Beach Gathering**—turn the youth room into a beach complete with beach towels, beach ball games, Beach Boys music. Ask the kids to wear shorts.

●**Big Feet Bonanza**—play games in bare feet; see whose feet look the most alike; see how many people's big toes are longer than their second toes; on a long piece of newsprint trace each person's foot and label it, "Christians walk the extra mile."

●**Reversible Night**—everything is done in reverse: people wear clothes inside-out; run relays backward; serve dinner, eat dessert first, etc.

April

●**April Fools (April 1)**—see who can create the most hilarious joke. Publish it in the church bulletin.

●**Rainbow Party**—host a water balloon toss, have umbrella relays—run through sprinklers and see who can stay the driest.

●**Easter Events**—organize activities such as an egg hunt, egg-rolling contest, parade with crazy costumes, Easter caroling.

●**Computer Dating Party**—match couples according to questionnaires filled out in advance; relays, races and games should be couple-oriented.

●**"Battle of the Sexes" Night**—design silly, fun contests played boys vs. girls. For example, see who can balance a pingpong ball at the end of their nose, see who can balance on one leg the longest—keeping their eyes closed.

●**Exchange Week**—plan activities with another youth group from out-of-town, host overnight parties in homes, arrange to pay a return visit in the fall.

May

●**National Holstein Observance**—meet at a dairy farm, have a milk-the-cow contest, drink chocolate milk or eat homemade ice cream.

●**Talent Show**—feature acts with parents and children together. Invite the congregation. Judge winners by passing the basket after each act. People vote by putting pennies, nickles or dimes in the basket. The act that collects the most money wins first prize.

●**Horseback Riding**—combine this with an evening campout. Sing songs around a campfire; give certificates for "Most unique riding style" or, "Most likely to survive in the wide open spaces."

●**Squirt Gun Night**—play games with squirt guns, fill them with Kool-Aid and drink the contents for refreshments.

●**Ice Cream Party**—feature sundaes, banana splits and games using various fruit and ice cream toppings. Cover a 10-foot polyvinyl-chloride (PVC) pipe with aluminum foil, then build "the world's largest banana split."

June

●**Bunker Hill Night (June 17)**—host competitive contests and games between the British and Colonial armies. End the evening with a "We Are One in the Spirit" group hug.

●**School's Out Party**—have a "Summer Dreaming" contest. See who can imagine the wildest summer. Award a pillow to the biggest dreamer.

●**Crystal Ball Predictions**—participants get to predict who in the group is most likely to get married first, most likely to become rich and famous, most likely to never grow up, etc.

●**Skateboard Races**—feature special skateboard activities: obstacle course, balance a book on head while riding skateboard, etc.

●**Picnic in the Park**—have some fun in the sun with a potluck picnic. Play softball, volleyball or badminton.

●**Body Building Party**—feature silly stunts that measure strength: have a wheelbarrow race, build a human totem pole, run races piggyback style.

●**Circus Extravaganza**—visit a circus and arrange for a "behind-the-scenes" tour. Ask a performer to come talk with your group about what it's like to be in the circus.

July

- **Fourth of July Pool Party**—swim, sing, watch the fireworks.
- **Loch Ness Monster Day Pool Party**—have a contest to see who can dress up as the scariest monster. Top prize goes to the one whose costume is waterproof!
- **Frisbee Party**—play a variety of Frisbee games, or hold contests demonstrating Frisbee skills. Award Frisbees to the winners.
- **Drive-In Movie Night**—show movies in the church parking lot or on a group member's lawn. Add an authentic touch by serving popcorn and pop.

August

- **National Scuba Diving Week (August 11)**—a beach party with appropriate water activities. Ask a certified scuba diver to demonstrate the sport.
- **County or State Fair Event**—attend the fair as a group.
- **Shampoo Party**—come prepared to wash each other's hair. See who can make the most lather, and who can make the craziest hairstyle out of the shampoo bubbles.
- **Get-Ready-to-Go-Back-to-School Party**—reminisce about summer, make predictions about the school year. Have kids complete these sentences: "The thing I most look forward to is ..." and "The thing I don't look forward to is ..." Discuss the statements.
- **Watermelon Party**—hold a seed-spitting contest and a watermelon-eating contest. Serve watermelon ice cream.

September

- **Grandparents Day Party (September 7)**—honor elderly people, especially those your group may adopt as grandparents. Visit a nursing home.

●**National Hunting and Fishing Day Party (September 27)**—feature treasure or scavenger hunts. Create an indoor pond by filling a tub with water—bob for apples.

●**Field Trip**—visit a local tourist attraction. Dress like tourists and bring cameras!

●**Back-to-School Party**—host the party after the first week of school, discuss what was good and not so good about the week, serve refreshments cafeteria style.

●**Make a Wish Party**—brainstorm ideas for the upcoming year's activities. Encourage the kids to munch while they think; serve nachos, caramel corn, popcorn or trail mix.

●**National Sewing Month Party**—keep the group in stitches. Have a thread-the-needle contest, see who can create the most unbelievable "yarn."

October

●**Explorer Night—Celebrate Columbus Day (October 12)**—dress as sailors, role play the songs "Row, Row, Row Your Boat" and "My Bonnie Lies Over the Ocean."

●**United Nations Day International Party (October 24)**—ask everyone to dress as one of their ancestors and bring a food item from that nationality; for example, dress as a Danish folk dancer and bring Danish pastries.

●**Halloween Party (October 31)**—dress like Saints and play who's who in the Bible. Sponsor a haunted house. Have a "guess the ghost" contest—guess who's hiding under a white sheet. Serve pumpkin pie or roasted and salted pumpkin seeds.

●**National Pretzel Month Party**—eat pretzels for refreshments; play games that have a twist such as Bent Out of Shape.[2] Divide the group into three equal lines facing a caller. The caller begins by saying something like, "All those who didn't take a bath today, grab the knee of the person on your right." The caller continues, "All people who have not read their Bibles today, grab the elbow of the person on your left." "All people who love to eat pretzels, put your right foot on the right foot of the person in front of you." Continue until everyone is tied in knots.

●**Leaf Collector's Party**—focus games and stunts on changing seasons; make collages out of fallen leaves, construction paper and glue. Hang the collages in the youth room; nearby, post a sign that says "Although the seasons change, God's love remains constant."

November

●**Sadie Hawkins Social Event (November 1)**—host a film or video night. Girls invite boys and provide transportation.

●**National Farm-City Week Party (November 21)**—invite folks from rural or urban areas to your place. Compare the similarities and differences of the two lifestyles.

●**Stuffing Party**—see how many people can bunch together in a Hula-Hoop, phone booth, Honda car, pair of long johns, etc. Award boxes of stuffing mix to the winners.

●**Thanksgiving Scavenger Hunt**—award a frozen turkey to the winner. Go door-to-door, collect money and donate it to world hunger.

December

●**World's Largest Pajama Party**—sponsor an overnight party during Christmas vacation at the church. Hold the world's largest pillow fight.

●**Hayride**—load a bus or truck with hay, have kids bundle up with warm jackets and blankets. Come back to the church for hot chocolate, hot cider and a warm fellowship time.

●**Christmas Shopping Spree**—go shopping as a group. Buy items such as mittens, socks, and scarves and donate them to a local children's home.

CHAPTER 15

100 GREAT IDEAS

Here are some new programming ideas to try with junior highers. Keep in mind that no list is exhaustive—and even old, tried-and-true ideas can be modified, expanded or changed by adding a creative twist. Such things happen as the result of *brainstorming* which is simply writing down any and all ideas related to a specific subject—in this case, things to do with your junior high youth group. One idea leads to another, and another. Write yours down whenever they pop into your mind. (They'll even come to you in the middle of the night; keep a note pad by your bed!) Remember, no idea is insignificant.

As you read the following ideas, let them stimulate other possibilities to use in your group. Brainstorm!

1. Plant a flower garden. After the flowers bloom, form colorful bouquets and deliver them to shut-ins and local nursing homes, or decorate your church altar.

2. Visit a nursing home on a day other than Christmas.

3. Listen to rock music and analyze the words.

4. Create your own group T-shirts. Ask kids to submit designs and vote on the favorite. Sell them for a fund raiser.

5. Tape a large piece of newsprint to the meeting room wall, then build a collage of pictures taken at junior high events. Label the collage "Kids in Action!"

6. Produce and create your own musical. Put new words to familiar tunes. Form your own band for accompaniment— ask church members who play the guitar, drums and piano to play for you.

7. Sponsor a dance at the church. Invite a person to be a Christian disc jockey. Have him or her keep the tunes coming throughout the evening.

8. Set up a booth at a mall and distribute literature on world hunger. Collect money, canned goods and clothing to give to the needy.

9. Put together your own slide show about a week at camp, a recent retreat, the junior high choir, etc. Show the slides during Sunday school, worship or at a potluck.

10. Plan a gala New Year's Eve party that includes fun and serious reflection on the use of time. Bring in the new year by focusing on 2 Corinthians 5:17, "Therefore, if any one is in Christ, he is a new creation; the old has passed away, behold, the new has come."

11. Put together a program on careers based on kids' interest. Invite representatives of various vocations to speak.

12. Start a puppet troupe. Buy puppets or make them from material, yarn and buttons. Travel from church to church and present "Profound Puppet Plays."

13. Make your own video. Have the kids act out a parable or miracle—complete with costumes, props and makeup.

14. Have a hobby night. Let group members share their special interests.

15. Design and build a living nativity, complete with animals, on your church lawn or parking lot.

16. Devote a part of each junior high meeting to prayer. Encourage members to pray for important concerns.

17. Make sand candles and have your own candlelight service. Focus on Jesus' words "I am the light of the world"

(John 8:12). Allow members to take their candles home as a reminder of the experience.

18. Visit a local grocery store and learn how food is marketed and how the store disposes of waste. Relate the experience to world hunger. Ask the kids how we can be less wasteful and help the hungry.

19. Rake leaves, shovel snow, cut grass, clean gutters, etc. for the elderly in your church.

20. Visit a church-related college. Ask the admissions counselors to challenge your kids to think about attending such a school.

21. Plan a one-day skill clinic (sewing, carpentry, soccer, etc.) based on members' interests. Invite guests to help your kids sharpen their skills.

22. Play "Name That Tune" with your group using hymns. Award the winners prizes such as kazoos.

23. Design an experience that helps you say goodbye to kids leaving the junior high group and affirms their contributions. For example, plan a pizza party or dessert potluck. Give each junior higher a card that says "We love you"; let everyone sign the cards.

24. Plan a water ski trip to a local lake, beach or resort.

25. Arrange a mock Olympic-type competition. Divide into teams and compete in races such as three-legged, sack, wheelbarrow and relay.

26. Adopt a child in a foreign country. As a group, contribute to his or her support; correspond regularly.

27. Design an experience to simulate what it is like to be handicapped. Invite folks to come talk about their lives. Let the kids experience blindness by wearing a blindfold during the entire meeting; let them experience deafness by wearing earplugs.

28. Write a group creed stating your purpose. Ask an artistic young person to write the creed in big letters on posterboard. Hang it on the wall of your meeting room.

29. Write a personal note to each member once a year just to say, "I'm thinking about you ... I care about you."

30. Bake cookies and send them to college students who have been group camp counselors and group leaders.

31. Write messages on the sidewalks of your church with chalk affirming parents on Mother's Day and Father's Day.

32. Cover a section of wall in the meeting room with newsprint. Use it as a graffiti wall; encourage kids to write thoughts and feelings about their lives. Change the paper monthly.

33. Hang a huge area map on the meeting room wall. Use map pins to designate where each member lives.

34. Keep a group scrapbook of the year's events; include pictures and captions. Review it each spring as a group. You also can put your scrapbook on videotape and edit it for a year-end program. Invite parents!

35. Secure permission from construction companies, then paint billboard messages on the walls of construction sites around town. For example, "Have a wonderful day" or "Smile and hug somebody."

36. Send cards to shut-ins on a regular basis. Add a personal touch by hand-delivering the cards once a month.

37. Volunteer to help with clean-up projects at the church. Name the clean-up crew "Smiling Servants"; adopt as a motto "Service with a smile."

38. Publish a group phone book including members' addresses, school, birthdays, favorite hobbies, talents, etc.

39. Pack a picnic lunch and ride bikes to a favorite spot.

40. Send birthday cards to all the kids in the group. Include a bookmark with a scripture message on it. (You can buy these at any Christian bookstore.)

41. Invite other churches to participate in a volleyball, softball, basketball or kickball tournament.

42. Have the kids bring their favorite magazines to a meeting. Discuss the values the magazines promote. Compare the magazines' values to the kids' values. Which are similar? different?

43. Videotape interviews with people in the church and community. Ask questions such as:
- Do you attend church regularly? Why or why not?
- How can congregations better reach unchurched people?
- What programs would you like the church to offer?

Show the videotape to the junior highers. Discuss how they can help improve the church.

44. Sponsor a workcamp experience. Plan your own or go with programs sponsored by Group or your denominational office.

45. Pray daily for your group. Ask God to guide them as they grow through their adolescent years.

46. Visit a shelter for runaways. Talk to the people who live and work there.

47. Teach your group visiting skills. Reach out to kids in the community who have no church home. Sponsor "Bring-a-Friend" events such as field trips to an amusement park, progressive dinners, roller skating or lock-ins.

48. Make place mats or table favors for a local nursing home. Make them from construction paper, magazines, glue and markers; include trivia questions and Bible verses.

49. Give the kids each a dollar and ask them to use it to help someone in the coming week. Ask group members to share their stories the following week.

50. Go mountain climbing. Stop at the summit and focus a Bible study on God's majestic creation.

51. Wash windows of cars in the church parking lot on Sunday. Leave a note on each windshield "See! God loves you."

52. Read a book and discuss its plot and characters. Act out the story when you finish.

53. Debate on an important issue: abortion, death penalty, drug abuse, etc. Divide into two groups and assign each a position to defend.

54. Arrange to meet with a group of a different race, culture or ethnic background. Explore common questions, similarities and differences about each other.

55. Sponsor a workshop on helping teenagers learn to make decisions and deal with peer pressure.

56. Invite "local heroes" to your meeting (police chief, rescue squad members, etc.). Salute them for their contributions to the community.

57. During Epiphany, go to a planetarium. Ask a local college astronomy professor to talk about the stars and planets.

58. Contact a day-care center. Offer to do a service project such as organize a "play day." The junior highers can lead all kinds of games with the day-care kids.

59. Print cards with a table grace. Use these at church functions or distribute them to local restaurants.

60. Attend a church wedding and follow up with discussion on marriage.

61. Collect stones and discuss how they can be used to build walls or bridges. Have a Bible study about the man who built his house on a rock (Matthew 7:24-27).

62. Invite an elderly person to come to your group at Thanksgiving to tell about Thanksgiving memories. Ask the kids to share some of their favorite memories of this holiday.

63. Make a flag to represent your group. Take it with you wherever you go.

64. Sponsor a skateboard rally on your church parking lot. Set up an obstacle course and contests. Invite spectators and award prizes.

65. Make the world's largest get-well card for someone in your group who is sick. Make it out of a refrigerator box, newsprint, glue and crayons. Have the group members write get-well messages on it, then deliver it.

66. Arrange for your group to visit a community institution such as a hospital, police station, fire station or radio station. Learn what motivates these people to do the work they do.

67. Make a pennant cut of colored felt for each person in your group. Have the kids use liquid embroidery to write their names on their pennants. Hang them in the youth room.

68. Host a party for handicapped children or adults. Use the theme "We Are the Children of God." Sing songs, have a Bible study, show slides and serve refreshments.

69. Kick off a church sports league by attending a pro game together.

70. Make your own songbook including your own songs. (Be sure to secure permission for copyrighted material.)

71. Create a monthly newsletter. Include information about activities. Feature a "Group member of the month" and "Leader of the month."

72. Hold a brainstorming session. Write down all the ideas the junior high group wants to try.

73. Put together a liturgical dance group. Have the dancers wear choir robes as they perform on special occasions.

74. Help the kids write devotional booklets focused on different times of the year. Make copies and sell them to raise money for the group.

75. Rent a video of a popular movie. Discuss its theme, characters, etc., and compare them to our Christian lives.

76. Invite an ex-cult member to talk about his or her experience. Leave time for questions and answers.

77. Go bowling. Award zany prizes: "Most unique style," "Lowest score," "Most likely to wear out the gutter," etc.

78. Attend your kids' school events.

79. Sponsor a series of meetings on sexuality from a Christian perspective. Give kids 3x5 cards and pencils. Encourage them to write questions and drop them in a box. Answer their questions throughout the series.

80. Trick or treat for UNICEF or a local community-help organization on Halloween.

81. Visit churches in your community. Compare the differences and similarities between your church and others. Stress that we all are God's children, even though our religious beliefs may differ.

82. Host a Halloween party where everyone comes dressed as a biblical character. Have everyone act out the Bible story that portrays his or her character.

83. Visit an urban area and learn about the various ministries offered by churches. Offer to assist in some of these ministries: help in a soup kitchen, paint for a service organization, etc.

84. Collect books from the neighborhood and give them to the local prison library.

85. Send school counselors the names of kids in your group. Let the counselors know of your willingness to help if the kids ever have a need or problem.

86. Attend a Christian rock concert or meet with other churches in town and sponsor your own concert.

87. Schedule a workshop on the importance of nutrition and exercise. Discuss such things as anorexia nervosa.

88. Plan an old-fashioned spelling bee using words from the Bible. Invite all church members to compete.

89. Evaluate your group twice a year to determine the effectiveness of the programming.

90. Sponsor a cheerleading squad to support and encourage church athletic teams. Decide on church colors and a mascot.

91. Give your kids a high profile at church. Have them serve as acolytes, greeters and ushers.

92. Sponsor a workshop on money management.

93. Print stickers that include the church phone number and the leader's number. Give these to the kids to stick in their phone books.

94. Attend a church funeral. Follow up with discussion about death and the way it is treated in society. Focus on our promise of eternal life.

95. Have the junior highers help teach vacation Bible school or children's Sunday school. Then, discuss childlike qualities and why we must become like children to enter the kingdom of God.

96. Organize a phone-a-thon so that all kids receive phone calls from every group member on their birthday or other special occasion.

97. Organize a taffy pull; compare it to the pull of sin in our lives. For example, "Some sin is sweet and tempting, but you feel sick if you get too much." "Sin pulls, and pulls, and stretches our spiritual lives out of shape."

98. Sponsor a volleyball game: parents vs. junior highers and their leaders.

99. Make your own bread and grape juice for a group communion service.

100. Design a list of activities for your group to do in a car or bus the next time they travel any distance. For example, switch "seat partners" at each stop. Answer questions such as, "What are you most looking forward to on this trip?" "What is one thing you left behind?"

EPILOGUE

Our youth group was traveling in Florida. We were using our spring vacation to make a dream become a reality.

Months before, someone suggested we take a book we often used for discussion topics and create a musical. One of my staff said, "We could write our own script and lyrics." That idea had blossomed into this memorable week in the South.

Throughout the months of preparation for our trip, we had grown closer. So much so that it felt natural and comfortable to talk openly with each other during our daily Bible studies. One day, our Bible study turned into one of those special times between friends—a heart-to-heart, honest conversation about what was happening in our lives. We reflected on what the traveling together meant to each of us. That's when a young person said, "If I ever stop thinking of you as a pastor, I'll always think of you as a gardener."

I wasn't quite sure what that meant, but the explanation

proved helpful, and left a lasting impression on me. The young person continued, "Pastor David, you are a seed planter. You help us grow."

A junior high leader is like a gardener; he or she has the ability to plant seeds in the lives of impressionable teenagers. Adolescence is a time when the soil is fertile, ready for planting. Kids are receptive to all kinds of ideas. When the ideas take root, they determine the growth of identity, personality and faith. We have an awesome responsibility to influence young people in a positive way.

Now that you've read this book, I hope some seeds have been planted in your mind, too. I hope you have:

●Renewed your interest in junior high young people
●Affirmed your role as an adult leader
●Discovered exciting, fresh activities to use in your ministry
●Read something that sparked creative ideas
●Realized this is the time for you to make things happen in your junior high ministry

I pray that you eagerly take the words from this book and put them to work in your ministry. I am confident that you will touch young people's lives, and together, create joyful memories.

Sometimes junior high leaders get discouraged because they don't see the end result of all their hard work and prayers. Ecclesiastes 11:6 tells us that this is to be expected, "Do your planting in the morning and in the evening, too. You never know whether it will all grow well or whether one planting will do better than the other" (TEV). Not everything we plan as teachers, pastors or leaders goes the way we intend. Sometimes, unexpected changes in the weather or the mood of the kids don't provide a conducive atmosphere for what we want to teach or share. It could be that the most detailed plan, or most organized meeting, can't accomplish what a personal, caring relationship can. Often, it's the little things that keep the seeds—planted long ago—alive:

●Something you said on a walk along the beach or through the woods
●A private moment shared on a retreat
●A conversation on a bus ride to a special event

●A note you wrote that said, "I care—you are important to me."

I'm convinced that long after the days of Sunday school, camps, retreats, trips, and all the other activities are over, it's the *personal relationship* between the leader and teenager that will be remembered. So, venture forth with courage. Know that not *every* seed you throw out will take root, but some will. And that's what makes it all worthwhile.

Don't underestimate God. Even when things seem to fall apart for you and the kids, you can still succeed. Don't quit. Young people pay the price when there is a constant turnover of youth leaders. It takes time to build trust, to discover each other, to learn to communicate. The gardener must remain faithful to his or her task. He or she must go to the garden to weed, cultivate, fertilize and provide the other necessary ingredients for a good harvest. The scriptures promise that those who remain faithful will "receive the crown of life" (Revelation 2:10).

Take heart. The best is yet to come. These young people are special gifts from God—full of energy, waiting to bloom where they are planted. Jesus said it long ago, but it's applicable to junior high ministry today "… A sower went out to sow some seed" (Mark 4:3). He's talking to you, my friend.

—David Shaheen

NOTES

Chapter 1

[1] John Naisbitt, *Megatrends: Ten New Directions Transforming Our Lives* (New York: Warner Books, 1983), p. 14.
[2] Ibid., p. 45.

Chapter 2

[1] *Religion in America*, Gallup Report #222 (Princeton: Princeton Religion Research Center, 1984).
[2] Jerome Kagen, "A Conception of Early Adolescence," in *Twelve to Sixteen: Early Adolescence*, ed. Jerome Kagen, (New York: W.W. Norton and Co., 1973), pp. 93-94.
[3] Ibid., p. 96.
[4] Ibid., p. 6.

Chapter 3

[1] Erik Erikson, *Insight and Responsibility* (New York: Norton,

1964), p. 90.

[2]H. Katchadourian, *Biology of Adolescence* (San Francisco: Freeman, 1977), pp. 27-28.

[3]Denny Rydberg, *Building Community in Youth Groups* (Loveland, CO: Group Books, 1985), p. 81.

[4]Claudia Wallis, "Children Having Children," *Time*, 126 (December 1985):79.

[5]C.H. Robinson and Marilyn R. Lawler, *Normal & Therapeutic Nutrition*, 15th ed. (New York: Macmillan, 1977), pp. 313-314.

[6]James O. Lugo and Gerald L. Hershey, *Human Development*, 2nd ed. (New York: Macmillan, 1979), p. 623.

[7]J.W. Vander Zanden, *Social Psychology* (New York: Random House, 1977), pp. 112-113.

[8]S.G. Sapir and A.C. Nitzberg (eds.), *Children With Learning Problems* (New York: Brunner/Mazel, 1973), p. 70.

[9]William C. Crain, *Theories of Development: Concepts and Applications*, 2nd ed. (Englewood Cliffs, NJ: Prentice-Hall, 1985), p. 106.

[10]David Elkind, *Children and Adolescents* (London: Oxford University, 1974), pp. 101-104.

[11]John W. Santrock, *Life Span Development* (Dubuque, IA: William C. Brown, 1983), p. 415.

[12]Ibid., p. 419.

[13]Ibid., p. 420.

[14]Ibid., p. 422.

[15]Crain, *Theories of Development*, 2nd ed., pp. 120-124.

[16]James W. Fowler, "Stages of Faith: The Structural Development Approach," in *Values and Moral Development*, ed. Thomas C. Hennessy (New York: Paulist Press, 1976), pp. 173-211.

[17]Thomas A. Droege, *Faith Passage and Patterns* (Philadelphia: Fortress Press, 1983), p. 29.

[18]Ibid., p. 56.

Chapter 5

[1]John W. Drakeford, *The Awesome Power of the Listening Heart* (Grand Rapids: Zondervan, 1982), p. 163.

[2]Ibid., pp. 163-164.

[3]Ibid., p. 153.

[4]Ibid., pp. 165-170.

[5]Roland Larson, "Caring Enough to Listen," GROUP 9 (October 1983):68-69.

[6]Merton P. Strommen, *Five Cries of Youth* (New York: Harper and Row, 1974), pp. 12-29.

Chapter 6

[1]Mary R. Schramm, *Gifts of Grace* (Minneapolis: Augsburg, 1982), p. 64.

[2]J. David Stone and RoseMary Miller, *Volunteer Youth Workers* (Loveland, CO: Group Books, 1985), pp. 37-40.

[3]Ibid., p. 51.

Chapter 7

[1]Merton P. Strommen and A. Irene Strommen, *Five Cries of Parents* (San Francisco: Harper and Row, 1985), pp. 16-17.

[2]Ibid., p. 72.

[3]Ibid., pp. 92-94.

[4]Ibid., pp. 130-147.

Chapter 9

[1]Richard Reichert, *A Learning Process for Religious Education* (Dayton, OH: Pflaum Press, 1975), p. 58.

[2]John and Lela Hendrix, *Experiential Education: XED*, (Nashville: Abingdon, 1975), pp. 28-29.

[3]Larry Keefauver, "The Survivor" in *GROUP Magazine's Best Youth Group Programs*, Vol. 1 (Loveland, CO: Group Books, 1986), pp. 146-147.

[4]Denny Rydberg, *Building Community in Youth Groups* (Loveland, CO: Group Books, 1985), p. 89.

[5]Dennis C. Benson and Bill Wolfe, *The Basic Encyclopedia for Youth Ministry* (Loveland, CO: Group Books, 1981), p. 192.

[6]Floyd Shaffer and Penne Sewall, *Clown Ministry* (Loveland, CO: Group Books, 1984).

Chapter 10

[1]Dennis C. Benson and Bill Wolfe, *The Basic Encyclopedia*

for Youth Ministry (Loveland, CO: Group Books, 1981), p. 68.

[2]Henry M. Robert ed., *Robert's Rules of Order* (New York: Jove Pubns., 1982).

Chapter 11

[1]J. David Stone and Larry Keefauver, *Friend to Friend* (Loveland, CO: Group Books, 1983).

Chapter 12

[1]GROUP Magazine and Group's JR. HIGH MINISTRY Magazine, Box 481, Loveland, CO, 80539.

[2]Cindy S. Hansen ed., *Try This One ... Strikes Again* (Loveland, CO: Group Books, 1984), p. 21.

[3]Lee Sparks ed., *Try This One ... Too* (Loveland, CO: Group Books, 1982), p. 39.

[4]Hansen ed., *Try This One ... Strikes Again*, p. 26.

Chapter 13

[1]Thom Schultz ed., *The Best of Try This One* (Loveland, CO: Group Books, 1977), pp. 44-45.

[2]Denny Rydberg, *Building Community in Youth Groups* (Loveland, CO: Group Books, 1985), p. 82.

[3]Lee Sparks ed., *Try This One ... Too* (Loveland, CO: Group Books, 1982), p. 43.

[4]Yohann Anderson ed., *Songs* (San Anselmo, CA: Songs and Creations, Inc.), pp. 146, 33, 82, 62.

[5]Cindy S. Hansen ed., *Try This One ... Strikes Again* (Loveland, CO: Group Books, 1984), p. 25.

[6]"A Praise Party," *GROUP* 11 (June-August 1985):11.

[7]Thom Schultz ed., *More ... Try This One* (Loveland, CO: Group Books, 1980), p. 21.

[8]Anderson ed., *Songs*, pp. 135, 87, 136.

[9]Rydberg, *Building Community*, pp. 38-39.

[10]Anderson ed., *Songs*, p. 6.

Chapter 14

[1]William D. Chase & Helen M. Chase, *Chase's Annual Events: Special Days, Weeks and Months in 1985* (Chicago: Contem-

porary Books, 1985), Index.

[2]Lee Sparks ed., *Try This One ... Too* (Loveland, CO: Group Books, 1982), p. 17.

RESOURCES

BIBLE STUDIES

Dennis Benson's Creative Bible Studies
   by Dennis C. Benson
   Group Books
   Box 481
   Loveland, CO 80539
Offers leaders 401 creative ways to
deepen their students' understanding of
the Bible.

User's Guide to the Bible
   by Chris Wright
   Lion Publishing Corp.
   10885 Textile Rd.
   Belleville, MI 48111
Makes the Bible come alive with photographs, graphics and short, pertinent
text.

Search the Scriptures
   Serendipity
   Box 1012
   Littleton, CO 80160
Good materials for learning biblical prin-
ciples through an experiential group
study format.

CAMPING/RETREATS

The Group Retreat Book
  by Arlo Reichter
  Group Books
  Box 481
  Loveland, CO 80539
Complete book on how to plan and program retreats. Contains dozens of retreat designs.

Junior High Jamboree
  Group Magazine Events
  Box 481
  Loveland, CO 80539
A special annual event specifically designed for junior highers and their leaders. Includes daily workshops and concerts.

Christian Camping International/USA
  Resources
  Box 646
  Wheaton, IL 60189
Provides camping resources for junior high ministry.

CLOWN MINISTRY

Clown Ministry
  by Floyd Shaffer and Penne Sewall
  Group Books
  Box 481
  Loveland, CO 80539
Features the "how-to" aspects of clown ministry and provides many short clowning skits.

The Complete Floyd Shaffer
Clown Ministry Workshop Kit
   Box 12811
   Pittsburgh, PA 15241
A cassette series and leaders guide for
clown ministry.

COUNSELING

Counseling Teenagers
   by Dr. G. Keith Olson
   Group Books
   Box 481
   Loveland, CO 80539
A complete, authoritative reference to
understand and help today's adolescents.

Friend to Friend
   by J. David Stone and Larry Keefauver
   Group Books
   Box 481
   Loveland, CO 80539
A simple and basic guide for helping peo-
ple. Great for peer counseling programs.

CURRICULUM PUBLISHERS

In addition to your denominational curriculum publishers, here's a list of other
publishers of junior high curriculum:

Accent Publications
   Box 15337
   Denver, CO 80215

Gospel Light Publications
   2300 Knoll Dr.
   Ventura, CA 93003

David C. Cook Publishing Co.
   850 N. Grove Ave.
   Elgin, IL 60120

Scripture Press
   Box 1825
   Wheaton, IL 60187

DANCE

A *Time to Dance*
  by Margaret Fisk
  The Sharing Co.
  Box 2224
  Austin, TX 78768

Let's Move and *Let's Move Again*
  by Janet Litherland
  Contemporary Drama Service
  885 Elkton Dr.
  Colorado Springs, CO 80907
Two kits for liturgical dancing.

DRAMA

The Greatest Skits on Earth
  by Wayne Rice and Mike Yaconelli
  Youth Specialties
  1224 Greenfield Dr.
  El Cajon, CA 92021
A collection of funny skits from the
IDEAS Library.

Contemporary Drama Service
  885 Elkton Dr.
  Colorado Springs, CO 80907
Write for a catalog of their drama
resources and products.

GAMES

The Try This One series:
The Best of Try This One (Vol. 1)
More . . . Try This One (Vol. 2)
Try This One . . . Too (Vol. 3)
Try This One Strikes Again (Vol. 4)

The Return of Try This One (Vol. 5)
   Group Books
   Box 481
   Loveland, CO 80539
Each book has a fun collection of games,
crowdbreakers, discussions and fund
raisers from GROUP Magazine's "Try
This One" section.

IDEAS Library
   Youth Specialties
   1224 Greenfield Dr.
   El Cajon, CA 92021
IDEAS books contain skits, games, crowdbreakers and comedy sketches for any
youth group meeting.

The New Games Book and *More New
Games!*
   by Andrew Fluegelman
   Doubleday & Co. (Dolphin Books)
   245 Park Ave.
   New York, NY 10017
Contains unusual and fun games in which
there are no losers.

MIME

The Mime Book
   by Claude Kipnis
   Harper and Row
   10 E. 53rd St.
   New York, NY 10022

Mime: The Technique of Silence
   by Richmond Shepard
   Drama Book Publishers
   821 Broadway
   New York, NY 10003

An *Introduction to Mime*
Contemporary Drama Service
885 Elkton Dr.
Colorado Springs, CO 80907
An introductory filmstrip on the art of mime.

PERIODICALS

Group's JR. HIGH MINISTRY
Box 481
Loveland, CO 80539
Each issue provides practical, theologically sound leadership articles and eight complete meetings for junior high ministry.

Youthworker
Youth Specialties
1224 Greenfield Dr.
El Cajon, CA 92021
A quarterly journal for those in youth ministry.

Common Focus
Center for Early Adolescence
Carr Mill Mall, Suite 223
Carrboro, NC 27510
A newsletter that informs youth workers and educators about developments in the field of early adolescence research.

PROGRAMMING

*GROUP Magazine's Best
Youth Group Programs (Vol. 1)*
Group Books
Box 481
Loveland, CO 80539
Over 200 pages of fast, easy-to-use programming ideas for youth groups.

The Exuberant Years
  by Ginny Ward Holderness
  John Knox Press
  341 Ponce de Leon Ave. N.E.
  Atlanta, GA 30365
Contains lots of programming ideas for
junior high groups.

Junior High Kit
  Lutheran Church - Missouri Synod
  Board for Youth Services
  1333 S. Kirkwood Rd.
  St. Louis, MO 63122-7295
Fifteen pieces provide information about
the junior high experience.

Junior High: Growing
Selves, Emerging Faith
  by Mike Carotta
  Harper and Row
  1700 Montgomery St.
  San Francisco, CA 94111
This unique, student-based program
focuses on the typical events of junior
highers and shows the relevance of the
Gospel to their lives.

How to Plan and Direct
Junior High Super Stars
  by Linda Stafford and Ridge Burns
  Scripture Press (Victor Books)
  Box 1825
  Wheaton, IL 60187
Discusses the place of big events in junior
high ministry and outlines a plan for
Super Stars-style competition.

Explore: Resources for
Junior Highs in Church
  Judson Press
  Box 851
  Valley Forge, PA 19482-0851
A series of books containing programming
ideas for junior high groups on a variety
of subjects.

Junior High Ministry
  by Wayne Rice
  Youth Specialties
  1224 Greenfield Dr.
  El Cajon, CA 92021
A look at junior high ministry. Includes
characteristics of junior highers, programming ideas and survey results of 90
junior high workers.

PUPPETS

Write for a catalog on puppets, scripts
and pre-recorded shows from:

Puppets From One Way Street
  Box 2398
  Littleton, CO 80161

Puppet Productions, Inc.
  P.O. Box 82008
  San Diego, CA 92138

Creative Puppet Ministries
  Box 1603
  Kill Devil Hills, NC 27948

RESEARCH

Early Adolescence and
Religion: A Status Study
　　by Anita M. Farel
　　Center for Early Adolescence
　　Carr Mill Mall, Suite 223
　　Carrboro, NC 27510
Provides information about church and
synagogue youth programs that are re-
sponsive to the needs of young people as
well as information about their religious
development.

Source
　　Search Institute
　　122 W. Franklin Ave.,
　　Suite 525
　　Minneapolis, MN 55404
A four-page bimonthly information
resource on issues facing children, ado-
lescents and families.

Young Adolescents and Their
Parents: A Summary of Findings
　　Search Institute
　　122 W. Franklin Ave.
　　Suite 525
　　Minneapolis, MN 55404
This report presents results of the most
comprehensive study ever done of the
characteristics, beliefs, values, and behaviors of young people in fifth through
ninth grade. The young adolescents' parents were also surveyed.

RESOURCE LISTINGS

Resource Directory for Youth Workers
  Youth Specialties
  1224 Greenfield Dr.
  El Cajon, CA 92021
A "yellow pages" of youth ministry
resources. Contains hundreds of
resources with addresses.

Early Adolescence: A Resource Directory
  Center for Early Adolescence
  Carr Mill Mall, Suite 223
  Carrboro, NC 27510
Includes organizations, periodicals and
bibliographies in key subject areas.

Practical, Effective Youth Ministry Resources From

Building Community in Youth Groups
by Denny Rydberg

Building Community in Youth Groups shows you how to:
- Establish trust within your youth group
- Create an atmosphere conducive to talking and listening
- Develop ways to change "me" attitudes among group members
- Challenge young people to grow
- Create opportunities for members to become more accountable to one another

Over 100 creative activities and discussion ideas help you break down barriers between young people and transform your group into a Christlike, caring group. Your kids will experience a deeper, richer level of Christian maturity as you put these practical ideas to use.

7×10, paperback
illustrated, 180 pages
ISBN 0931-529-06-9, $11.95

The Youth Group Meeting Guide
by Richard W. Bimler

This practical ministry tool offers you 88 complete and effective meeting designs. No longer will you have to worry or wonder, "What will I plan for the next youth meeting?" Dozens of contributors offer their expertise and provide you with meeting designs based on the NEEDS of your young people:
- Self-image
- Careers and vocations
- Death and dying
- Jealousy
- Stress
- Stewardship
- Life at high school
- Friendship

Bimler guides you in designing your own meetings with: step-by-step planning, goal setting, choosing themes, evaluations, and many other youth group meeting strategies.

6×9 sturdy paperback, 254 pages
ISBN 0936-664-17-7, $11.95

Enrich Your Ministry With Group Books

Youth Ministry Cargo
by Joani Schultz and dozens of contributors

Get on board for a journey through the kaleidoscope of creative ideas in **Youth Ministry Cargo. Cargo's** packing list includes a variety of topics for meeting young people's needs. You'll be amazed at how simple, everyday objects will help kids grow in their faith. Each entry is followed by "Variations," or alternatives, to help you adapt the idea to meet your group's specific needs. Your group members will enjoy the clever and unique learning approaches. Use these ideas to teach about poverty, self-image, peace and justice issues, Christlike faith, music, worship, and a host of other subjects. Games, craft activities, service projects and fund raisers are also included. Each idea is quick to read and easy to implement. Who knows where your journey will take you as you mix, match, or come up with your own ideas!

7×10 paperback
illustrated, 400 pages
ISBN 0931-529-14-X, $18.95

Starting a Youth Ministry
by Larry Keefauver

Whether your church is just beginning a youth ministry or revitalizing an existing one, this book will help you "make it happen." Larry Keefauver offers you experienced advice on how to:
- Clarify your motives and goals for youth ministry
- Adopt a Christ-centered purpose for your youth group
- Earn the support of your pastor and other congregational leaders
- Build good relationships with the youth
- Develop and organize effective Bible studies
- Manage time and solve problems
- Coordinate schedules, committees and youth leaders
- Fine-tune your program so that it will endure

Starting a Youth Ministry will help you effectively direct your energy as your start (or restart) working with youth in your church.

5¼×8½ paperback, 80 pages
ISBN 0936-664-19-3, $5.95

Look for these—and other Group Books—in your Christian bookstore. If you can't find them, order directly by sending your check or money order (plus $2 postage and handling for each order) to: Group Books, Box 481, Loveland, CO 80539. For free information on all Group Books and Group Publishing's youth ministry products and services write: Free Info, Group Publishing, Box 481, Loveland, CO 80539.